Waterloo

Marketing Planning

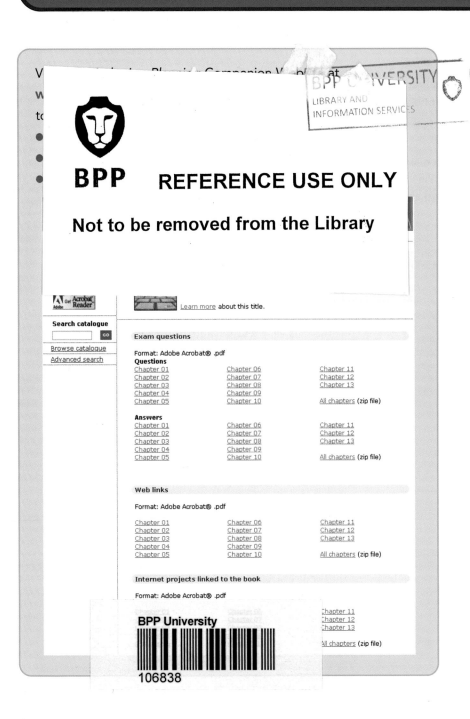

Learn more about this title.

Search catalogue

GO

Browse catalogue

Advanced search

Exam questions

Format: Adobe Acrobat® .pdf

Questions

Chapter 01	Chapter 06	Chapter 11
Chapter 02	Chapter 07	Chapter 12
Chapter 03	Chapter 08	Chapter 13
Chapter 04	Chapter 09	
Chapter 05	Chapter 10	All chapters (zip file)

Answers

Chapter 01	Chapter 06	Chapter 11
Chapter 02	Chapter 07	Chapter 12
Chapter 03	Chapter 08	Chapter 13
Chapter 04	Chapter 09	
Chapter 05	Chapter 10	All chapters (zip file)

Web links

Format: Adobe Acrobat® .pdf

Chapter 01	Chapter 06	Chapter 11
Chapter 02	Chapter 07	Chapter 12
Chapter 03	Chapter 08	Chapter 13
Chapter 04	Chapter 09	
Chapter 05	Chapter 10	All chapters (zip file)

Internet projects linked to the book

Format: Adobe Acrobat® .pdf

Chapter 01	Chapter 06	Chapter 11
Chapter 02	Chapter 07	Chapter 12
		Chapter 13
		All chapters (zip file)

Marketing Planning
Strategy, Environment and Context

Jim Blythe
Visiting Reader, Plymouth Business School, University of Plymouth

Phil Megicks
University of Plymouth

**Financial Times
Prentice Hall
is an imprint of**

Harlow, England • London • New York • Boston • San Francisco • Toronto • Sydney • Singapore • Hong Kong
Tokyo • Seoul • Taipei • New Delhi • Cape Town • Madrid • Mexico City • Amsterdam • Munich • Paris • Milan

Pearson Education Limited
Edinburgh Gate
Harlow
Essex CM20 2JE
England

and Associated Companies throughout the world

Visit us on the World Wide Web at:
www.pearsoned.co.uk

First edition 2010

ISBN: 978-0-273-72471-1

British Library Cataloguing-in-Publication Data
A catalogue record for this book is available from the British Library

Library of Congress Cataloging-in-Publication Data
Blythe, Jim.
  Marketing planning : strategy, environment and context / Jim Blythe, Phil Megicks.
– 1st ed.
    p. cm.
  Includes bibliographical references and index.
  ISBN 978-0-273-72471-1 (pbk.)
1. Marketing–Planning.   2. Marketing–Management.   I. Megicks, Phil.   II. Title.
  HF5415.13.B5655 2010
  658.8'02–dc22

                                                  2010001386

10 9 8 7 6 5 4 3 2 1
14 13 12 11 10

Typeset in 10/14 pt ITC Charter by 35
Printed and bound by Graficas Estella, Spain

The publisher's policy is to use paper manufactured from sustainable forests.

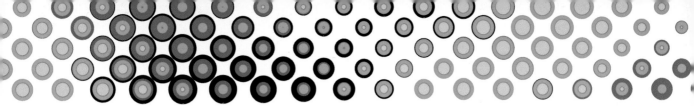

Brief contents

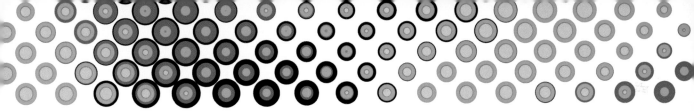

Contents

Supporting resources

Visit **www.pearsoned.co.uk/blythe** to find valuable online resources:

Companion Website for students
- Links to relevant sites on the web
- Sample exam questions with specimen answers
- Internet projects linked to the book

For instructors
- Complete, downloadable Instructor's Manual
- PowerPoint slides that can be downloaded and used for presentations

Also: The Companion Website provides the following features:
- Search tool to help locate specific items of content
- E-mail results and profile tools to send results of quizzes to instructors
- Online help and support to assist with website usage and troubleshooting

For more information please contact your local Pearson Education sales representative or visit **www.pearsoned.co.uk/blythe**

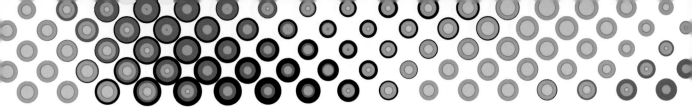

Preface

Planning is never straightforward. All of us can predict the future to an extent, of course, but there are so many factors involved in running a business that accurate predictions are hard to come by: add to this the difficulty of working out exactly what to do for a given set of circumstances, and one can easily see why planning is difficult.

Yet without some kind of plan we have no idea what we should be doing when we go into work on Monday morning. For marketers, planning revolves largely around what we think our customers and consumers will want us to do: we then need to work out how we can profit from meeting their needs. This book is intended to guide the reader through the maze of factors that affect marketing planning, and provide some tools and techniques for cutting through the undergrowth.

The book includes case studies taken from real companies which are out there in the real world, fighting real, competitive battles. These firms take widely differing approaches to planning, because their circumstances and needs are also widely differing. We have included a fictitious case study which follows a company through the entire process of marketing planning, stage by stage and chapter by chapter, finishing with a completed marketing plan. Each chapter contains Talking Points which are intended to make you think rather than just accept the received wisdom, and of course there are review questions to test your understanding of the chapter contents.

The book is written around the syllabus for the Chartered Institute of Marketing (CIM) module, The Marketing Planning Process, but it covers everything the reader will need to study a marketing planning course at both undergraduate and MBA level. The aim has been to produce a straightforward, logically framed, readable text to cover this complex area. In doing so, we have relied on help from our colleagues at the CIM and at Plymouth Business School, and on the support of everybody at Pearson, from David Cox, who helped us turn a basic idea into a coherent plan for a text, through the many people in production who turned our manuscript into the book you now hold in your hand.

In practice, of course, no plan survives first contact with the enemy – it is the planning process that is important, because it focuses the minds of managers and provides a framework which should be sufficiently flexible to allow for the unforeseen. In the words of General Dwight Eisenhower, supreme commander of the Allied forces at the time of the D-Day invasion in 1944: *'Plans are nothing – planning is everything.'*

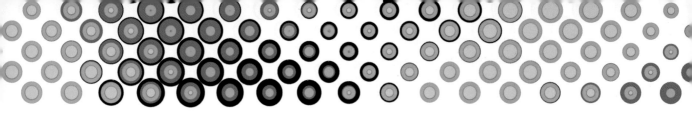

Guided tour

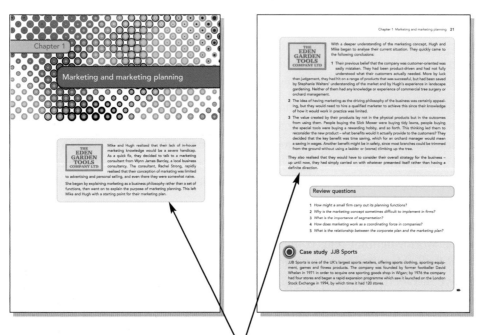

Marketing Planning comes with a unique **Running case study** giving you a great opportunity to examine the marketing planning process step by step.
Each chapter presents a new marketing planning dilemma which needs to be faced by Mike and Hugh. This dilemma is addressed at the end of the chapter.

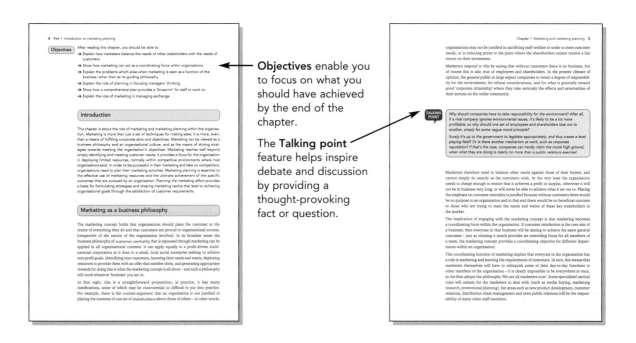

Objectives enable you to focus on what you should have achieved by the end of the chapter.

The **Talking point** feature helps inspire debate and discussion by providing a thought-provoking fact or question.

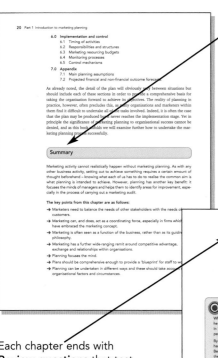

The **Summaries** clinch the important concepts that have just been presented to reinforce the chapter learning.

Each chapter is supported by **References** directing your independent study.

Each chapter ends with **Review questions** that test your understanding and help you track your progress.

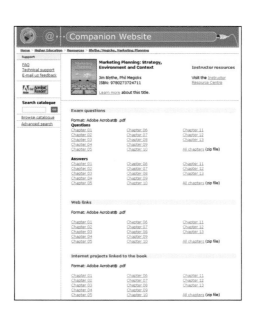

Each chapter concludes with an insightful **Case study** which provides a range of material for seminars and private study by illustrating the real-life applications and implications of the topics covered in the chapter. These come with discussion questions.

Visit the *Marketing Planning* Companion Website at **www.pearsoned.co.uk/blythe** to find valuable student learning material including:

● Links to relevant sites on the web
● Sample exam questions with specimen answers
● Internet projects linked to the book.

Custom Publishing

Custom publishing allows academics to pick and choose content from one or more texts for their course and combine it into a definitive course text. Content choices include:

- Chapters from one or more of our textbooks in the subject areas of your choice
- Your own authored content
- Case studies from any of our partners, including Harvard Business School Publishing, Darden, Ivey and many more
- Third party content from other publishers
- Language glossaries to help students studying in a second language
- Online material tailored to your course needs.

The Pearson Education custom text published for your course is professionally produced and bound – just as you would expect from a normal Pearson Education text. You can even choose your own cover design and add your university logo.

To find out more visit **www.pearsoncustom.co.uk** or contact your local representative at: **www.pearsoned.co.uk/replocator**

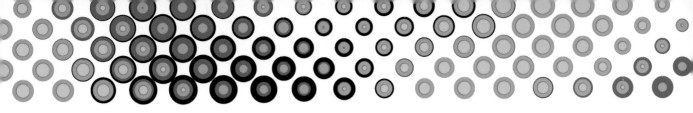

Acknowledgements

We are grateful to the following for permission to reproduce copyright material:

Figures

Figure 13.3 from 'What is Strategy – and Does it Matter?', Richard Whittington, Copyright 2001, Thomson Learning (EMEA) Ltd. Reproduced by permission of Cengage Learning.

Tables

Table 1.1 – this table was published in 'Relationship Marketing', Christopher, M., Ballantyne, D., and Payne, A., Copyright Elsevier (Butterworth-Heinemann 1991); Table 2.4 from 'Strategy: Process, Content, Context', Bob de Wit and Ron Meyer, Copyright 1998, Thomson Learning (EMEA) Ltd. Reproduced by permission of Cengage Learning; Table 4.1 adapted from KOTLER, PHILIP, MARKETING MANAGEMENT, 11th ed., © 2003. Reproduced by permission of Pearson Education Inc., Upper Saddle River, New Jersey; Table on page 243 from The Horticultural Trades Association (HTA) http://www.the-hta.org.uk/page.php?pageid=210, The Horticultural Trades Association's Garden Industry Monitor.

Text

Extract on page 39 from *The Richer Way*, Richer Publishing (2009); Quote on page 239 from The Horticultural Trades Association 'About the HTA' web page http://www.the-hta.org.uk/page.php?pageid=2.

In some instances we have been unable to trace the owners of copyright material, and we would appreciate any information that would enable us to do so.

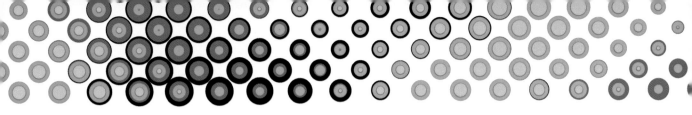

Introducing the running case study:
The Eden Garden Tools Company Ltd

The Eden Garden Tools Company Ltd is a gardening tools manufacturer based in Coventry. The company has a relatively short but highly successful history. It was started in 1994 by two friends, Mike Winton and Hugh Parris, after they graduated from university. Mike left with an engineering degree, gained as a mature student; previously he had worked for his family's agricultural equipment company and thus had a great deal of experience in engineering but no formal qualifications. Hugh was also a mature student, having decided to take a liberal arts degree after having had a somewhat aimless existence in his 20s. Hugh's experience labouring for a landscape gardening company had given him several ideas for improving gardening tools – in particular, lawnmowers had proved to have major drawbacks when used on uneven or odd-shaped lawns.

'The lack of any qualifications or experience for what I was planning to do didn't hold me back in the least,' he once said in a TV interview. 'All I had to do was get Mike to do everything.' Hugh outlined the lawnmower problem to Mike, who worked out a design for a mower that could cut evenly on the type of uneven lawns that many people have. The Slick Mower was the first of several innovative products the company introduced.

The new company found it difficult to get financing, but Mike's family contributed £150,000 in seed capital in exchange for 50 per cent of the firm, which was to be held by the family business. Mike and Hugh kept the remaining shares, holding 25 per cent each.

In 1995, the fledgling company began manufacture and hired Stephanie Walters as marketing manager. Stephanie's background was in marketing for DIY and gardening chain B&Q. She had also worked for Sainsbury's, with responsibility for the Homebase brand, immediately after graduating from Warwick Business School in 1987. Stephanie stayed with the company for almost two years, but left following disagreements about the scope of marketing within the firm. Since then Hugh has taken on responsibility for marketing, which in the case of Eden Garden Tools Company Ltd essentially means selling to major DIY and garden companies such as B&Q, Homebase and large garden centres. This takes up a substantial part of his time.

The company sells more than just lawnmowers, of course. During Stephanie Walters' time at the company, Eden Garden Tools developed a range of hand tools for women, for example spades and forks with handles designed to minimise skin chafing, and ergonomically designed to minimise the muscular strength needed to use them. Tools for the disabled or elderly had also been a success story – special trowels designed to eliminate bending over and a patented planting device that can be used from a standing position or from a wheelchair also proved to be big sellers, even among able-bodied (but lazy) gardeners.

The 2008 recession had a considerable effect on the company, but it was saved because it has a solid export market: the weaker pound made Eden Garden Tool's products more competitive in the eurozone, which helped compensate for lower demand in the UK. In 2009, the company's sales began to recover from the recession, and Hugh and Mike started to consider new products to add to the range.

One product idea that had been around for some time was an electric tree-pruning saw. This would consist of a long pole with an electric reciprocating saw on the end. The pole would need a gripper to hold the saw blade in position in the branch, and the saw blade would move backwards and forwards to cut through. Such a tool would be of more use to a professional gardener, tree surgeon or farmer, since an amateur gardener would not have enough use for such a product to justify the outlay. Amateur gardeners might well want to hire one, though, so it would be an item that many tool hire companies would buy, and even some garden centres might want one. There would be approximately 4,000 people within the UK who would have a use for such a machine, and around 35,000 in the European Union as a whole; world sales could potentially be in the hundreds of thousands.

From the viewpoint of Eden Garden Tools the product presented some problems, however. The electric power packs would be a new venture for the company, as would the small electric motors, but these were engineering problems and could be overcome by outsourcing the components. A more serious problem was a financial one. Following the recession, the company's cash reserves were gone, and although the firm remained liquid, sales were still stagnant and there would be little money to invest in developing and launching a new product. Mike's family were equally unable to help – the agricultural equipment business had been hit hard by the recession, since farmers can always make their machinery last another couple of years, and agricultural prices had fallen during 2009, leaving them short of cash for buying new equipment. But perhaps the most serious problem was that they would be entering a new market. Up until now, they had been selling mainly to amateur gardeners, whereas the new product would be mainly selling in a business-to-business market. Also, it would rely heavily on gaining an export market in order to maximise the economies of scale needed to bring down the costs of manufacture. Global sales were therefore an essential factor for the company, at least regarding this specific product.

Mike and Hugh called a meeting of the shareholders to discuss the way forward. At the meeting were Mike, Hugh, one of Mike's brothers and his father (to represent the family business). They agreed to look for capital outside the company, and to bring in venture capitalists rather than reduce the company's liquidity by borrowing from a bank (even if a bank could be found that would be willing to lend). This would mean diluting the shareholdings of the existing shareholders, but the four agreed that this would be worth it in the long run since the overall value of the company would rise.

Preliminary talks with a venture capital company flagged up a number of issues. First, the venture capitalists wanted to see Eden Garden Tool's business plan, which of course did not exist since Hugh and Mike had always operated on an ad-hoc basis. Second, the venture capitalists were concerned that Hugh was handling all the marketing himself, without any qualifications or experience outside the firm: they saw this as a real weakness. Third, they indicated that they would want around one-third of the company's shares in exchange for funding, and they would want to see an exit strategy in place for five to seven years down the line. Normally this would be a launch on the Alternative Investments Market (AIM), or possibly a full-blown stock market placement. Fourth, they would expect to appoint a non-executive director to the board of Eden Garden Tools to bring some much-needed business discipline to the company.

Mike and Hugh came away from the meeting feeling somewhat daunted. However, they quickly realised that the venture capital company was actually laying out a negotiating position – if they could develop a good enough corporate and marketing plan, they could probably negotiate from a stronger position, perhaps giving away less of the company or removing the need for an extra director (who would, of course, have to be paid).

The pair knew that they would be on a steep learning curve.

Part 1

INTRODUCTION TO MARKETING PLANNING

Marketing planning does not happen in a vacuum. It takes place against a backdrop of corporate plans and objectives, competitive activity, consumer behaviour, and indeed literally hundreds of other factors.

Chapter 1 looks at marketing's role in the greater business function. The relationship of marketing to other business functions and its role in coordinating business activities are discussed, as well as the stages marketers need to go through in developing marketing plans.

Chapter 2 shows how the marketing plan relates to the rest of the company's planning. Corporate plans may need to encompass many more factors than customer satisfaction – and sometimes these factors come into conflict. Chapter 2 helps to explain the conflicts and offers some solutions.

Chapter 3 explains some of the factors that inform marketing planning and which are most influential in directing the way marketing plans are produced. This chapter is crucial in understanding where marketers are coming from when they formulate plans – and where they are sometimes forced to go.

Part 1, as a whole, lays the foundation for understanding the hands-on, practical aspects of marketing planning which follow.

Chapter 1

Marketing and marketing planning

THE EDEN GARDEN TOOLS COMPANY LTD

Mike and Hugh realised that their lack of in-house marketing knowledge would be a severe handicap. As a quick fix, they decided to talk to a marketing consultant from Wynn James Barclay, a local business consultancy. The consultant, Rachel Strong, rapidly realised that their conception of marketing was limited to advertising and personal selling, and even there they were somewhat naive.

She began by explaining marketing as a business philosophy rather than a set of functions, then went on to explain the purpose of marketing planning. This left Mike and Hugh with a starting point for their marketing plan.

Objectives | After reading this chapter, you should be able to:

→ Explain how marketers balance the needs of other stakeholders with the needs of customers.

→ Show how marketing can act as a coordinating force within organisations.

→ Explain the problems which arise when marketing is seen as a function of the business rather than as its guiding philosophy.

→ Explain the role of planning in focusing managers' thinking.

→ Show how a comprehensive plan provides a 'blueprint' for staff to work to.

→ Explain the role of marketing in managing exchange.

Introduction

This chapter is about the role of marketing and marketing planning within the organisation. Marketing is more than just a set of techniques for making sales; it is more, even, than a means of fulfilling corporate aims and objectives. Marketing can be viewed as a business philosophy and an organisational culture, and as the means of driving strategies towards meeting the organisation's objectives. Marketing reaches well beyond simply identifying and meeting customer needs; it provides a focus for the organisation in deploying limited resources, normally within competitive environments where rival organisations exist. In order to be successful in their marketing and take on competitors, organisations need to plan their marketing activities. Marketing planning is essential to the effective use of marketing resources and the ultimate achievement of the specific outcomes that are pursued by an organisation. Planning the marketing effort provides a basis for formulating strategies and shaping marketing tactics that lead to achieving organisational goals through the satisfaction of customer requirements.

Marketing as a business philosophy

The marketing concept holds that organisations should place the customer at the centre of everything they do and that customers are pivotal to organisational success, irrespective of the nature of the organisation involved. In its broadest sense the business philosophy of **customer centrality** that is espoused through marketing can be applied in all organisational contexts: it can apply equally to a profit-driven multinational corporation as it does to a small, local social enterprise seeking to achieve non-profit goals. Identifying your customers, knowing their needs and wants, deploying resources to provide them with an offer that satisfies them, and generating appropriate rewards for doing this is what the marketing concept is all about – and such a philosophy will work whatever 'business' you are in.

At first sight, this is a straightforward proposition; in practice, it has many ramifications, some of which may be controversial or difficult to put into practice. For example, there is the counter-argument that an organisation is not justified in placing the interests of one set of **stakeholders** above those of others – in other words, organisations may not be justified in sacrificing staff welfare in order to meet customer needs, or in reducing prices to the point where the shareholders cannot receive a fair return on their investment.

Marketers respond to this by saying that without customers there is no business, but of course this is also true of employees and shareholders. In the present climate of opinion, the general public at large expect companies to retain a degree of responsibility for the environment, for ethical considerations, and for what is generally termed good 'corporate citizenship' where they take seriously the effects and externalities of their actions on the wider community.

TALKING POINT

Why should companies have to take responsibility for the environment? After all, if a rival company ignores environmental issues, it's likely to be a lot more profitable, so why should one set of employees and shareholders lose out to another, simply for some vague moral principle?

Surely it's up to the government to legislate appropriately, and thus create a level playing field? Or is there another mechanism at work, such as corporate reputation? If that's the case, companies can hardly claim the moral high ground, when what they are doing is clearly no more than a public relations exercise!

Marketers therefore need to balance other needs against those of their buyers, and cannot simply do exactly as the customers wish. At the very least the organisation needs to charge enough to ensure that it achieves a profit or surplus, otherwise it will not be in business very long, or will never be able to achieve what it set out to. Placing the emphasis on customer centrality is justified because without customers there would be no purpose to an organisation and to that end there would be no beneficial outcome to those who are trying to meet the needs and wants of these key stakeholders in the market.

The implication of engaging with the marketing concept is that marketing becomes a coordinating force within the organisation. If customer satisfaction is the core aim of a business, then everyone in that business will be aiming to achieve the same general outcomes – just as winning a match provides an overriding focus for all members of a team, the marketing concept provides a coordinating objective for different departments within an organisation.

This coordinating function of marketing implies that everyone in the organisation has a role in marketing and meeting the requirements of customers. In turn, this means that marketers themselves will have to relinquish some of their day-to-day functions to other members of the organisation – it is clearly impossible to be everywhere at once, so the firm adopts the philosophy 'We are all marketers now'. Some specialised tactical roles will remain for the marketers to deal with (such as media buying, marketing research, promotional planning), but areas such as new product development, customer relations, distribution chain management and even public relations will be the responsibility of many other staff members.

For example, consider two companies in the haulage business. One takes the view that marketing is a discrete and isolated function of the business rather than an overall business philosophy. This company will expect the marketers to bring in business, to liaise with the press and with other publics, to manage the salesforce, to develop interesting brochures and publicity material, and to deal with complaints. Drivers will simply be there to move the lorries from one place to another, load cargo, etc. Dispatchers will control the flow of goods, the accounts department will mail out the invoices, the senior management will control the staff, money and premises to maximise profitability.

The other company in the same industry might take a broader view of marketing, not only putting the customer at the centre but utilising the marketing function as a co-ordinating force that brings together everyone who contributes to customer satisfaction. In a sense this company sees it as a responsibility of the marketing function to act widely within the organisation to establish how everyone contributes to providing value to customers and how each of these can be put together into an integrated marketing effort. This company will therefore empower its drivers to deal with complaints and problems as they arise; the accounts department will be able to offer creative alternatives for customers to pay; senior management will be available for press conferences and publicity opportunities, and will be available to customers when necessary; dispatchers will be empowered to prioritise customers in an emergency, and so forth. The overall success of the firm is likely to be measured in terms of customer satisfaction (although obviously the firm still needs to be profitable, otherwise it cannot stay in the game). The attitude of this company will be that customer satisfaction comes first; profitability will follow. Ensuring that all of this happens within an organisation clearly indicates that there is a key role for planning marketing, which also includes other business functions.

Research shows that market orientation relates positively to business success (Narver and Slater 1990) and that this comes from a culture within an organisation that values its customers and sees them as paramount to fulfilling organisational goals, particularly in competitive environments. Staff tend to be more committed to a market-oriented company, customers are likely to be more loyal and to increase their spending with the company, and the business is likely to survive turbulent economic and fiercely competitive conditions better. Establishing a market orientation is easier when inter-departmental conflict is relatively low, and becomes much more difficult if inter-departmental conflict is high. Market orientation necessarily requires a greater degree of **empowerment** among customer-facing staff, because they need to respond rapidly to customer problems. This in turn implies that staff should be rewarded through market-facing reward systems, for example rewarding them if customer feedback indicates that they have met customer needs especially well. Decentralised decision making is an obvious necessity, which means that autocratic management and inflexible processes are strong barriers to developing a market orientation. Because customer needs change over time, and because the market situation changes over time, people throughout the firm need to learn continually. Market orientation therefore works well when it develops within a learning organisation (O'Driscoll et al. 2001).

In most organisations, in fact, marketing tends to be seen as a function rather than a business philosophy. The function of marketing is viewed in such circumstances as a means of developing the extended marketing mix (the 7Ps – product, price, promotion, place, people, process, physical evidence) in a way that is consistent with the needs and wants of its customers. The reasons why a **functional perspective** is adopted are many: for other professionals, the need to protect their own status provides a personal reason for keeping marketing as a function, for example. Also, creating a true customer orientation is difficult: it means continually trying to think like another person, which most people find hard to do (this may be why most people find Christmas stressful – trying to work out what to give people as gifts means trying to think like them). There are relatively few boards of directors which include marketing professionals – fewer than 5 per cent of the top 100 companies in the UK have a marketer on the board, whereas virtually all of them have a finance director. In fact, boards of directors have a legal responsibility to the shareholders of the company, not to the customers: they can be called to account and made to demonstrate how their decisions were made with share-holders' interests in mind, and this often happens at annual meetings of companies. Directors are well aware that it is the shareholders who appoint them as individuals, even if it is the customers who vote with their feet on whether the company is a good one or not. In non-profit organisations a similar situation exists as, for instance, it is the board of trustees of a charity that is responsible for setting and achieving objectives and they need to fulfil these by attracting and keeping donors, volunteers and other supporters through marketing.

Marketing and other business functions

This issue needs to be addressed in two ways. If marketing is a function of the business, marketers will have a specific relationship with colleagues which will be markedly different from that obtaining in a company where marketing is seen as the primary aim and driving culture of the business. In view of the fact that many (even most) companies regard marketing as a function rather than a primary aim, this set of relationships will be dealt with first.

Marketers will often find themselves in the position of having to persuade colleagues of the necessity for adopting a customer orientation. For example, an accountant is likely to prefer using cost-plus pricing, because this is easy to calculate, ensures that all costs are covered, and appears to guarantee that a given product is profitable. Marketers are likely to prefer pricing according to the market conditions, and will price on the basis of consumer demand as well as taking account of the competition. Even within this very different approach, a marketer might want to pitch the price higher than that of the competitors in order to signal higher quality. This is a concept which is not immediately obvious to many people.

Likewise, production people tend to believe that marketers are there to sell what the company makes, whereas marketers take the view that the company should make what the marketers can sell, i.e. what customers want to buy. These viewpoints are both somewhat extreme, of course. Marketers must accept that the company needs to play to its particular strengths and produce things which it has an expertise in, or a **competitive advantage** which can be exploited. Marketers and designers therefore need to decide together what the company can sell profitably within the constraints of what is feasible in production terms. In some cases, new products might be rejected because they cannot be made for a price which people are prepared to pay, or because a product which is easy and cheap to produce has little or no market. Even in companies where marketing is the overall philosophy of the business this will be true.

In Figure 1.1, marketing is one of the four main functions of the firm. Each function has some relationship with customers, but it is essentially in a one-way, firm-to-customer direction. In effect, the business is doing things to customers in exchange for their money.

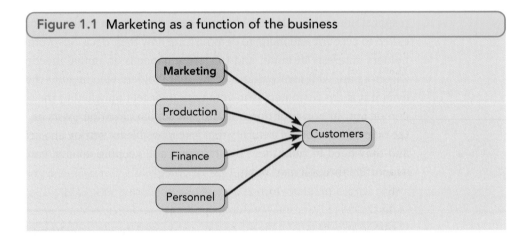

Figure 1.1 Marketing as a function of the business

In Figure 1.2, customers are at the centre of everything the company does, with marketing acting as the mediating function between customers and other functions. This time, the communication is two-way: the business operates by doing things for customers (rather than to customers) in exchange for money. It is the responsibility of marketers to undertake this coordinating role and plan the effort of the organisation across all functions to achieve outcomes that satisfy customers.

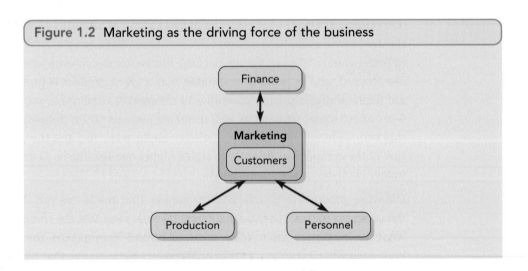

Figure 1.2 Marketing as the driving force of the business

In firms which have a legal department, lawyers may sometimes suggest that the company has fulfilled its obligations in terms of customer service once it has met its contractual obligations. A marketer may want to go beyond the written contract in cases where a good customer has a problem which was not envisaged when the original agreement was drawn up. This can cause conflict, since lawyers operate on precedent and may be reluctant to do something which other customers might then expect as a right.

Budget setting can also cause conflict between professionals. Often, finance directors will set overall budgets and managers will then have to justify their case for having a share of the pot. If times are hard and budgets have to be cut, they are often cut across the board – leading to the paradox that, as business gets worse, the money earmarked for bringing in more business (the marketing budget) is reduced. This is likely to lead to a downward spiral unless the marketers can make a special case for increasing the marketing budget, at the expense of other departments. This is certain to create conflict with colleagues.

Front-line staff such as drivers, receptionists, telephonists, invoice clerks and indeed anyone who has direct contact with customers will obviously have a role in marketing, but may not have job titles which reflect this. Salespeople might be expected to have some understanding of marketing (although this is not always the case), but many other front-line staff do not understand their role in creating a good impression. A delivery driver who simply dumps packages at the customer's premises and demands a signature will obviously create a much worse impression than will a driver who asks where the customer would like the delivery to go and who waits while the customer checks the packages against the delivery note before signing. The same is true of receptionists and telephonists: having a nice smile or a pleasant voice is no substitute for helping a customer who has an appointment but has forgotten the name of the person they are visiting.

Salespeople can present a particular problem, since they have considerable responsibility for dealing with customers, and in fact spend more time with customers than do the marketing managers. Not unnaturally, this fosters a belief that they are more aware of customer needs than are other people within the company, and in many cases this is quite true. However, salespeople may be unable to see the larger picture (Dewsnap and Jobber 1998; Blythe 2000) as they may want to have a new product to sell before it has been fully developed. Their need to have something new to show their customers might overshadow the fact that the new product has glitches which have yet to be overcome. The immediate sale might be more important than the problems which will surface in the longer term. Because salespeople are usually chasing short-term targets rather than long-term business **objectives**, they are very likely to ignore the future. This may be a failing in sales management policy, or in motivational rewards.

From the perspective of planning the marketing effort, it is essential that those responsible for coordinating marketing across all areas of an organisation should be aware of how each function contributes to satisfying customers, and that issues such as those raised here are addressed in the planning process. Planning from the point of view of delivering value to customers is therefore an important factor in determining how the organisation delivers its offer to the market, in a sense being guided by the external factors of the environment, consumers and competitors. Nonetheless many firms tend to adopt a resource-based view of planning, i.e. rather than plan according to the nature of the market (an outside-in perspective), they plan according to the nature of the firm itself (an inside-out perspective). In other words, rather than asking what the needs of the market are and deciding how these can be met, the planners decide what the resources of the firm are and decide what can be achieved within those strengths and constraints. Clearly a balance has to be struck between the two and the process of marketing planning sets out to look at how both external and internal factors can determine what is offered to the market.

Relationships in marketing-oriented firms

In a firm which has adopted marketing as the guiding philosophy of the organisation, relationships with colleagues will be different but not necessarily easier. Understanding the difference between meeting customer needs profitably and giving the customer everything he or she wants is something that many professional marketers struggle with; marketers sometimes need to be reminded that a limited company is not a charity and will have to show a profit or go out of business. Charities and other non-profit organisations such as government agencies also need to be mindful of costs incurred compared with the value created by marketing; they need to ensure that the benefit attained from the limited resources that they have available is maximised.

The conceptual problem for marketing in such a company is this: if everybody in the company has responsibility for marketing, where is the need for a dedicated marketing department? There may be a case for doing away with a marketing department altogether, and breaking down the functional aspects of marketing into an advertising department, a PR department, a sales department, and so forth, coordinated by senior managers who will probably be qualified marketers. The implications are that everyone working for the company will now have to be trained in marketing to a greater or lesser extent. This could be a function of the professional marketers in the firm, or it could be contracted out to consultants.

Even in a customer-oriented or market-oriented firm managers will still have to consider the needs of other stakeholders, including shareholders and employees. This is the function of **internal marketing** – ensuring that everyone is part of the programme and is contributing to the overall aims of the organisation. This cannot be achieved by diktat: people cannot simply be ordered to be customer-oriented. The needs of staff members (promotion, job satisfaction, increased prestige, or even simple appreciation for their contribution) should be addressed if they are to contribute effectively. Sometimes they will need to be persuaded of the importance of being market-oriented.

Competitive advantage and the management of exchange

It is easy to adopt the idea that marketing is solely about meeting customer needs. Indeed, many marketers lose sight of the wider principle under which marketing operates: marketing orientation is about creating a competitive advantage through providing value to customers. In short, we look after our customers' needs because it is the best way we know of persuading them to spend their money with us rather than with our competitors. The same principle applies in non-profit contexts where organisations are seeking to achieve different types of outcome through a similar process of fulfilling the requirements of other stakeholders and audiences. This means that marketing is not an end in itself: it is a means to an end and competitive advantage, which may be achieved in different ways, should enable a firm to fulfil the primary objectives of any organisation. This is true in a range of different contexts where customers have alternative ways of spending their money. It is just as relevant to the public-sector agencies promoting the use of a service such as municipal swimming pools as it is to a privately owned international computer manufacturing business. When undertaking marketing planning there is a critical role in identifying sources of competitive advantage and looking at how these can be built into marketing strategies to fulfil objectives.

Marketing can also be seen as the management of exchange. This definition implies that the marketer is the manager of the exchange process: in fact, in most cases the exchange is managed, or at least negotiated, between the customer and the marketer, so that both are engaged in the co-creation of value and its distribution. The management-of-exchange definition has other conceptual difficulties – not all exchanges can reasonably be considered as marketing. A parent might agree to buy something for a child in exchange for good behaviour, but few people would regard this as marketing. Likewise, an advertising campaign to encourage people to give up smoking would be categorised as not-for-profit marketing, but it is rather difficult to see what the exchange is. These considerations apart, though, the management-of-exchange idea is appealing because it covers a wide range of what marketers do in their day-to-day work, and it also implies that marketing is something that is done 'with' customers rather than something that is done 'to' customers.

Managing the exchange process can either be seen as the management of a set of transactions, or it can be seen as an ongoing process in which individual transactions are subsumed into an overall pattern of **value creation**. In recent years, **relationship marketing** has become a hot topic in marketing. The assumption is that it is better for all parties to establish a long-term relationship with customers because it is easier to keep an existing customer than it is to recruit a new one. Table 1.1 shows the difference between transaction marketing and relationship marketing.

The relationship marketing paradigm has been compared to courtship and marriage (Levitt 1983). This model holds that marketers and customers go through stages in developing the relationship, beginning with a 'first date' in which the customer is wooed, a stage of initial trial when a first purchase is made, a commitment stage equivalent to marriage, a honeymoon stage where the relationship appears rosy, and

Table 1.1 Transaction marketing vs relationship marketing

Transaction marketing	Relationship marketing
Focuses on the single sale	Focuses on customer retention
Quality is the responsibility of the production department	Quality is the responsibility of everyone
Orientation on product features	Orientation on product benefits
Short timescale	Long timescale
Little emphasis on customer service	High emphasis on customer service
Limited customer commitment	High customer commitment
Moderate customer contact	High customer contact

Source: *Relationship Marketing*, Butterworth-Heinemann (Christopher, M., Ballantyne, D., and Payne, A. 1991), This table was published in 'Relationship Marketing', Christopher, M., Ballantyne, D., and Payne, A., Copyright Elsevier (Butterworth-Heinemann 1991).

the marriage stage in which problems and disagreements arise but are overcome by the parties to the relationship. Sometimes the relationship ends in divorce, of course, but often it can continue to be rewarding and to lead to ever-closer bonds between the parties.

However, the courtship and marriage analogy has been criticised (notably by Tynan 1997) on the following grounds:

- Often the power relationships between the partners are far from equal – in fact, some transactions appear to be more like seduction than like a courtship.
- Customers, and especially consumers, have little interest in establishing long-term relationships with firms.
- Most, if not all, companies have to juggle relationships with a great many other 'partners'. This is certainly inadvisable in a marriage.

In practice, relationship marketing has not fulfilled its early promise in consumer markets, although it appears to work well in business-to-business markets. This may be for the following reasons:

1 Business needs change much more slowly than consumer needs. Someone who currently buys baby products will have no need for them as the baby grows up, so will be a customer for only a year or two; a motor manufacturer will have a need for components such as springs and light bulbs for decades or longer.

2 Business-to-business marketing is more likely to provide opportunities to create a relationship of equals. Two firms of about the same general size might form a very effective relationship, whereas firms almost always have much greater resources than the consumers they serve.

3 B2B markets are characterised by personal contacts between buyers and salespeople, whereas many consumer transactions are impersonal, conducted either in self-service retail outlets or online. Relatively few consumer transactions involve salespeople, so the interpersonal element is lost.

4 Businesses (apart from retailers) usually have relatively few customers and fewer suppliers overall than is the case for the average consumer. This means that forming relationships is both easier and more rewarding.

Relationship marketing can be seen as a means to an end, of course: it is there in order to facilitate exchange, and to ensure that exchanges continue into the future, i.e. secure an ongoing stream of business. The marketing planning process has a key role in identifying where relationships are important and how aspects of relationship marketing can be built into marketing plans where appropriate.

Marketing has a further purpose within the firm. Internal marketing (marketing of the marketing philosophy) has become an important area of marketing thought in recent years, especially as organisations have become aware that every employee has an input into the corporate reputation and the success of achieving marketing objectives. Since many employees also have contact with customers, ensuring that they all operate in the same way is of considerable importance, and is more likely to come about if there is a good marketing plan in place. Marketing planning will enable the organisation to see how it can best undertake marketing internally to ensure that the plan is implemented effectively. In a sense internal marketing can be viewed as a means of translating marketing theory into practice through implementation. As we shall see, marketing planning is pretty straightforward in terms of how to do it in principle, but the crux of planning is being able to do it in reality, and this is often down to how marketing managers sell and effectively market the advantages of a market orientation internally within the organisation.

The purpose of marketing planning

In volatile market conditions, where competition is strong and circumstances change rapidly, it may sometimes seem that any kind of planning is pointless. However, forward planning of the marketing effort is essential for all organisations that are in the business of providing customers with value and are aiming to achieve particular outcomes themselves as a consequence. Marketing planning enables the organisation to budget its resources (money, manpower, intellectual property, equipment, premises, etc.) against expected targets, be they sales revenue, charitable donations, or even changed behaviour. Although in principle this may appear to be a somewhat unnecessary and onerous task, for many organisations the benefits of planning can be seen through the focus it provides on the requirements of the market and internally in terms of how each element of the organisation contributes to fulfilling these.

Moreover, because competition has intensified in recent years, planning in general and marketing planning in particular have greatly increased in importance. The increase in competition has come about for a number of reasons, as follows:

- **Globalisation.** As barriers to trade have reduced worldwide, companies face competition from foreign firms, many of which have cost advantages due to lower labour costs, easier access to raw materials, or easier access to markets which formerly belonged to the firm.

- A free-market, entrepreneurial political environment in many economies.
- Rapid technological innovation, creating new competitive drivers.

Marketing planning has been defined as follows (Hollensen 2006):

Marketing planning is the structured process of researching and analysing marketing situations, developing and documenting marketing objectives, strategies and programmes, and implementing, evaluating and controlling activities to achieve the objectives.

Because the proposed process of marketing planning is systematic, it guides management thinking to recognise market opportunities and threats and use these as a basis for formulating strategies and detailed marketing activities to support them in the market. Of course, because markets tend to be more volatile than they were (for the reasons outlined above), the actual plan is likely to need modification in the light of experience. Therefore, regular monitoring of the plan and its implementation will need to take place. Marketing planning is thus an ongoing process, not a one-shot event, otherwise the marketing plan will simply become yet another report which no one ever reads or pays attention to. Indeed, a common criticism of marketing planning and plans is that by the time they have been developed they are out of date, and that all the effort and resources required in compiling them is therefore lost.

Yet it is in the process itself that the real benefit lies as, in undertaking marketing planning, any organisation can review its external markets and what drives them, and examine its internal capabilities, including its particular strengths and any shortcomings that it may have. In so doing it has a basis for setting objectives in the context of what the organisation is trying to achieve, and developing an appropriate offer to the market. What is critical is the iterative nature of the process and an understanding that marketing plans should change as time and forces outside and within the organisation change. However, a plan needs to be produced from the process of planning which provides a basis for taking the organisation forward, and it has real benefits in its own right.

Not least, the marketing plan itself should contain all the information that organisation members (i.e. employees and managers) need in order to know what to do next. The acid test of a good marketing plan is whether people can tell from it what they have to do on Monday morning – vague recommendations which have no concrete instruction in them are not worth writing.

The main benefits of having a plan can be summarised as follows (see Figure 1.3):

1 It should provide a consistent set of instructions which fits with the overall corporate plan as well as with the aims of all the departments involved. This will minimise the risk of having to deal with unforeseen problems, acting on a case-by-case basis which characterises short termism. The plan thus creates overall consistency.

2 The plan should indicate to people exactly what their responsibilities are for carrying out the plan. Ideally, they should be able to monitor their performance against the plan so that they are able to adjust their behaviour if necessary.

3 Apart from knowing what to do, the plan enables people to understand why they are doing things. In other words, people should understand how their role fits into the

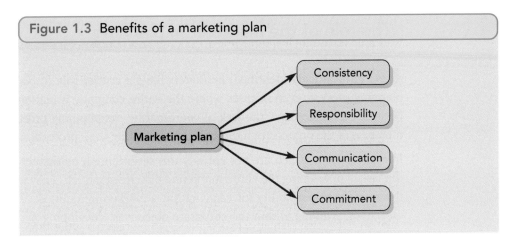

Figure 1.3 Benefits of a marketing plan

larger picture, and should understand what the reasoning is behind their part in the company's success. This is likely to be a strong motivator for staff.

4 A good plan should help to create a group commitment to its implementation.

Marketing planning therefore helps to create sustainable competitive advantage. Even if the plan is not perfect, the process of developing it helps to create a corporate culture which emphasises cooperation, learning and common ownership of outcomes. This is achieved through a focus on customers and competitors in the market, and recognition of what the organisation is good at and can build on, and what it may find more difficult to undertake and how this can be improved.

The plan needs to include the following elements:

1 An assessment of both the internal and the external environment in which the organisation operates. This is the **marketing audit**, and it takes account of all aspects of the company's resources and capabilities, as well as information about customer needs and wants, and the key forces in the markets that they serve.

2 A set of marketing objectives. These may be taken directly from corporate objectives, or they may be specific sub-objectives relating to marketing outcomes which provide a basis for achieving organisational objectives.

3 A set of timescales for the achievement of the objectives. This is likely to vary according to the organisation and the markets that it operates in.

4 A clear indication of individual responsibilities, i.e. a clear statement as to who is responsible for each part of the plan.

5 A system for monitoring the plan in practice, with suitable feedback systems to report back to organisation members. This would include a way of assessing the success (or otherwise) of the plan, and controlling the way that the plan is implemented to ensure that the best use is made of the resources committed.

6 Systems for revising the plan as necessary in the light of new information provided through the monitoring process.

7 A budget of proposed revenues and expenditures associated with marketing.

The role of the marketer in planning

As we have already identified, marketers have a crucial role to play in terms of the planning process, even in cases where the entire company is market-oriented. This is because marketers have the task of coordinating the planning process, leading other members of the organisation through it and eliciting their professional opinions.

In organisations which are not entirely market-oriented, marketers will usually have the task of developing the entire marketing plan from scratch. They will therefore have the primary responsibility for carrying out a marketing audit, developing marketing objectives, working within the corporate objectives, developing marketing strategies aimed at achieving overall objectives, and formulating tactical approaches to achieving the objectives. They will then have responsibility for determining whether objectives have been reached, i.e. whether targets have been hit.

The marketing function therefore has a major task in undertaking planning, and this must not be in isolation but rather should involve all other areas of the organisation that contribute to success in the marketplace. Marketers' contribution can be viewed at a number of levels: *planning* (bringing the resources together to deliver value in the market), *strategy* (determining the most appropriate ways of fulfilling the needs and wants of customers) and *tactics* (implementing an effective mix of activities to meet these customer requirements).

Stages of the marketing planning process

One way of considering the marketing planning process is as a number of stages that are undertaken sequentially, and these are presented below.

1 **Analysis**. The planners need to assess the current situation in which the organisation finds itself. If we don't know where we are, we cannot find a route to get to where we're going. Often regarded as the first stage of the process, it is seen to be the starting point for planning, i.e. identify where we are currently so that we can plan a way forward.

2 **Planning**. This is the crucial stage. Working out what to do in order to achieve the corporate objectives means setting marketing objectives and planning how to achieve them through the most appropriate strategies and tactics. The second step involves putting the plan together and coming up with the detail of how all the different aspects are to be accomplished.

3 **Implementation**. Putting the plan into action means ensuring that everyone is clear about what they should be doing: each member of the organisation needs to know exactly how they are expected to contribute. The penultimate stage involves determining these responsibilities, setting timescales, identifying appropriate structures, systems and processes to enable this, and determining budgets to support the activities involved.

4 Control. Having suitable feedback systems in place enables the planners to adjust activities to bring the firm back on course. Inevitably things will change – no plan survives first implementation, because it is impossible to foresee everything. Flexibility and monitoring are therefore essential. The final stage involves recognising that it will not always be the case – in fact it will be highly unlikely – that the plan will fulfil its original targets. Actions have to be taken to put the plan back on track, or realistically sometimes the specific outcomes in the plan need to be re-evaluated in the light of changing circumstances (this could involve setting or lowering targets depending on performance so far).

A more detailed breakdown of the stages is shown in Table 1.2 (Gilmore et al. 2001; Day, 2002).

Table 1.2 Stages in the process of developing a marketing plan

Stage	Explanation
Mission, corporate goals and objectives	The mission statement is an expression of the purpose of the organisation. It should say what business the company is in, and is likely to include some goals. Goals are general aims the company intends to achieve: they are not usually quantifiable, but they do indicate which direction the organisation is hoping to go, whereas objectives are quite specific outcomes that the organisation sets out to attain.
Assessment of the internal and external environments	The marketing audit is the key tool for assessing where the company is now from both an external and an internal perspective. The audit will include an examination of whether the corporate and marketing goals are appropriate, so it actually overlaps into the previous stage of planning.
SWOT analysis	SWOT identifies strengths and weaknesses within the firm, and opportunities and threats outside the firm. This analysis is commonly used but has the major drawback that it is almost entirely subjective: managers judge what is a strength and what is a weakness, and also what is an opportunity and what is a threat. In practice, they can easily get it wrong. The SWOT analysis provides a platform from which strategies can be developed to achieve organisational objectives.
Segmentation, targeting and positioning	Deciding how the market breaks down is often more difficult than it would appear. Segmenting correctly pays dividends – it can often differentiate one organisation from another. Targeting the most appropriate segments means matching the organisation's capabilities to the customers' needs, and positioning means putting the organisation and its products in the correct place in target customers' perceptions.
Strategic marketing plan	Strategy is about where the organisation is heading and how it is going to get there – effectively which customers are going to be provided with which products. The decisions about which segments to target and where the company wants to position itself are a very important part of this and are at the heart of the planning process.
Tactical marketing plan	The tactical plan is the way in which the company will develop a mix of marketing activities (marketing mix variables) in order to approach the specified segments. This plan should differentiate the firm from its competitors and will provide everyone in the marketing team with a clear set of instructions for what needs to be done.
Marketing budget	With the tactical plan formulated, planners are in a position to determine the budget. This may be determined by senior management (the finance director) or it may be calculated by the planners and then sent to the finance director for approval. The former is more common, of course.
Implementation and performance evaluation	The plan is put into action and the outcomes are evaluated. There should be feedback loops so that the tactics can be adapted as necessary, but in any event the evaluation should be used when formulating the next plan.

Is it really feasible to see the marketing planning process as a systematic, sequential set of stages that should be followed by all organisations? Do all organisations, large and small, local and global, profit and non-profit, have to work through all these stages in the same order if they are going to be successful at marketing?

In reality there must be some variation possible – do all the stages need to be followed, can the order be changed, do you need to start at the beginning and finish at the end? Is planning a finite, straight-line process, or is it something that is cyclical and ongoing?

Surely it can be adapted to the circumstances of the organisation in question, and the various factors that impact on it, in undertaking its marketing effectively!

There are three main approaches to planning, as follows:

1 **Top-down planning.** Senior management set the goals and most of the plans for middle managers. This approach assumes that top management have complete knowledge of what is happening both within and outside the firm, an assumption which is difficult to justify. As an approach, it has the advantage that decisions are made quickly and therefore the plan comes together rapidly. It suffers from the drawback that implementation will take longer as junior managers and employees try to understand the various aspects of the plan. Developing ownership of the plan is also difficult – people usually prefer to join in with the planning process if they can.

2 **Bottom-up planning.** This approach means that the various departments of the company produce their own plans, based on their understanding of the needs of the market and of their own departmental capabilities. These plans are then submitted to senior management for approval and coordination. In these circumstances, a marketing-oriented company will find the process easier because customer needs will act as the coordinating force. This also sometimes means that strategy develops from a consolidation of tactics (Chae and Hill 1996).

3 **Goals-down-plans-up planning.** This approach may be the most common. Senior management set the overall goals, leaving the detail of the planning to the various departments. This enables departments to plan around their own resources, while maintaining an overall direction for the firm.

In the case of top-down planning, marketers may be involved at high level but are more likely to be operating in a marketing department which will have to show how they will bring in the business which the senior managers are planning around. In the case of bottom-up planning, marketers will need to supply the necessary market data on which decisions are made by other departments. In the case of goals-down-plans-up planning, marketers will have responsibility for developing a marketing plan based on the overall corporate objectives.

Whatever the approach adopted, it may well be that the most appropriate means of planning is undertaken for an organisation which takes account of a range of factors that impinges upon the way that it faces up to the task of marketing. In the same vein these factors will determine the way in which marketing planning is structured and implemented: sequentially, iteratively, or as a cyclical process.

Content and structure of a marketing plan

The tangible outcome of the planning process is the marketing plan, which can take different forms in different organisations and circumstances, but broadly includes the following sections:

- Overview of current position and organisational context
- Organisation mission and objectives
- External environmental analysis, including market and industry analysis
- Internal environmental analysis
- Gap analysis and identification of marketing opportunities
- Setting of marketing objectives
- Strategy formulation, including segmentation, targeting and positioning
- Marketing programmes providing a detailed specification of the extended marketing mix
- Implementation, monitoring and control.

A typical structure for a marketing plan is presented below.

1.0 Executive summary
   1.1 Background and context of current position of organisation
   1.2 Identification of key strategic planning issues

2.0 Organisational strategy
   2.1 Organisational mission and objectives
   2.2 Summary of overall position and organisational strategy

3.0 External and internal marketing audit
   3.1 Customer analysis, including identification of environmental drivers
   3.2 Industry competitor and intermediary analysis
   3.3 Market trends and projections
   3.4 Internal analysis of resources and capabilities
   3.5 SWOT analysis

4.0 Marketing objectives
   4.1 Specification of marketing objectives
   4.2 Financial and non-financial objectives

5.0 Marketing strategy
   5.1 Market segmentation analysis
   5.2 Competitive advantage
   5.3 Alternative strategy specification and selection of target markets
   5.4 Marketing programme positioning:
   - Product
   - Price
   - Promotion
   - Place
   - Physical evidence
   - People
   - Process

6.0 Implementation and control
    6.1 Timing of activities
    6.2 Responsibilities and structures
    6.3 Marketing resourcing budgets
    6.4 Monitoring processes
    6.5 Control mechanisms

7.0 Appendix
    7.1 Main planning assumptions
    7.2 Projected financial and non-financial outcome forecasts.

As already noted, the detail of the plan will obviously vary between situations but should include each of these sections in order to provide a comprehensive basis for taking the organisation forward to achieve its objectives. The reality of planning in practice, however, often precludes this, as many organisations and marketers within them find it difficult to undertake all of the tasks involved. Indeed, it is often the case that the plan may be produced but it never reaches the implementation stage. Yet in principle the significance of marketing planning to organisational success cannot be denied, and as this book unfolds we will examine further how to undertake the marketing planning process successfully.

Summary

Marketing activity cannot realistically happen without marketing planning. As with any other business activity, setting out to achieve something requires a certain amount of thought beforehand – knowing what each of us has to do to realise the common aim is what planning is intended to achieve. However, planning has another key benefit: it focuses the minds of managers and helps them to identify areas for improvement, especially in the process of carrying out a marketing audit.

The key points from this chapter are as follows:

→ Marketers need to balance the needs of other stakeholders with the needs of customers.

→ Marketing can, and does, act as a coordinating force, especially in firms which have embraced the marketing concept.

→ Marketing is often seen as a function of the business, rather than as its guiding philosophy.

→ Marketing has a further wide-ranging remit around competitive advantage, exchange and relationships within organisations.

→ Planning focuses the mind.

→ Plans should be comprehensive enough to provide a 'blueprint' for staff to work to.

→ Planning can be undertaken in different ways and these should take account of organisational factors and circumstances.

THE EDEN GARDEN TOOLS COMPANY LTD

With a deeper understanding of the marketing concept, Hugh and Mike began to analyse their current situation. They quickly came to the following conclusions:

1 Their previous belief that the company was customer-oriented was sadly mistaken. They had been product-driven and had not fully understood what their customers actually needed. More by luck than judgement, they had hit on a range of products that was successful, but had been saved by Stephanie Walters' understanding of the market and by Hugh's experience in landscape gardening. Neither of them had any knowledge or experience of commercial tree surgery or orchard management.

2 The idea of having marketing as the driving philosophy of the business was certainly appealing, but they would need to hire a qualified marketer to achieve this since their knowledge of how it would work in practice was limited.

3 The value created by their products lay not in the physical products but in the outcomes from using them. People buying the Slick Mower were buying tidy lawns, people buying the special tools were buying a rewarding hobby, and so forth. This thinking led them to reconsider the new product – what benefits would it actually provide to the customers? They decided that the key benefit was time saving, which for an orchard manager would mean a saving in wages. Another benefit might be in safety, since most branches could be trimmed from the ground without using a ladder or (worse) climbing up the tree.

They also realised that they would have to consider their overall strategy for the business – up until now, they had simply carried on with whatever presented itself rather than having a definite direction.

Review questions

1 *How might a small firm carry out its planning functions?*
2 *Why is the marketing concept sometimes difficult to implement in firms?*
3 *What is the importance of segmentation?*
4 *How does marketing work as a coordinating force in companies?*
5 *What is the relationship between the corporate plan and the marketing plan?*

Case study JJB Sports

JJB Sports is one of the UK's largest sports retailers, offering sports clothing, sporting equipment, games and fitness products. The company was founded by former footballer David Whelan in 1971 in order to acquire one sporting goods shop in Wigan; by 1976 the company had four stores and began a rapid expansion programme which saw it launched on the London Stock Exchange in 1994, by which time it had 120 stores.

In 1998 JJB acquired Sports Division, its biggest competitor, thus becoming the UK's largest sports retailer with more than 250 stores. The company also operates 50 fitness centres around the UK; these have been extremely successful, despite the fact that the retail stores had a somewhat rocky ride during the 2009 recession. In September 2008 the company launched its first MiFit gym in Cardiff. This was billed as the 'cheapest premium gym in the UK', with members paying a one-off membership fee followed by a fee of £9.95 a month. The gym was attached to the local JJB store, and accessed through it, so that members would pass by the goods on display. The company plans to open more of these in-store gyms as finances allow, but MiFit is an entirely separate brand from JJB Health Clubs – there is no cross-selling and no management convergence between the clubs.

JJB Sports has an online retail division which was 99 per cent owned by David Whelan, who subsequently sold his shares. The company sponsors Wigan Athletic Football Club and Wigan Warriors Rugby League Club: in each case the company logo appears on the club's shirts.

The company does face some threats over the next decade. The French retailer Decathlon (a subsidiary of the giant Oxylane company) has entered the UK market and plans to expand from its current six stores. The recession has also taken a toll – at the company's July 2009 shareholders' meeting the board reported that sales were down 40 per cent on the previous year, with gross profit margins also down by 11 per cent due to a sell-off of old stock at cost price. The company was also dogged by reports that executive chairman David Jones had accepted a £1.5 million loan from rival businessman Mike Ashley, who controls Sports Direct, which at the time of writing is the UK's largest sports retailer. The situation was further complicated because Ashley had a personal shareholding in JJB and had accused the company of refusing to buy from Sports Direct (whose company owns the Slazenger, Donnay, Lonsdale and Dunlop brands), allegedly because Sports Direct is a rival in retail markets.

On the positive side, JJB can expect to gain from the increased interest in sport created by the 2012 Olympics, which are to be held in London. As part of the Olympic programme, the UK government plans to get 2 million more people involved in sport between 2008 and 2012 – a very positive factor for any sports retailer or gym operator.

Questions

1 *What needs might JJB's stakeholders have?*
2 *What objectives might be appropriate for JJB over the next five years?*
3 *What barriers to planning might the company encounter?*
4 *How might JJB assess the true competitive threats the company faces?*
5 *What type of planning would be most appropriate for JJB?*

References

Blythe, J. (2000): Intra-departmental conflict between sales and marketing – an exploratory study. *Journal of Selling and Major Account Management*, May.

Chae, M.-S. and Hill, J.S. (1996): The hazards of strategic planning for global markets. *Long Range Planning*, 20 (6) pp 880–91.

Christopher, M., Ballantyne, D. and Payne, A. (1991): *Relationship Marketing* (Oxford: Butterworth-Heinemann).

Day, G.S. (2002): Managing the market learning process. *Journal of Business and Industrial Marketing*, 17 (4) pp 240–52.

Dewsnap, B. and Jobber, D. (1998): The sales and marketing interface: is it working? Proceedings of the Academy of Marketing Conference, Sheffield.

Gilmore, A., Carson, D. and Grant, K. (2001): SME marketing in practice. *Marketing Intelligence and Planning*, 19 (1) pp 6–11.

Hollensen, S. (2006): *Marketing Planning: A Global Perspective* (Maidenhead: McGraw-Hill).

Levitt, T. (1983): After the sale is over. *Harvard Business Review*, September–October.

Narver, J.C. and Slater, S.F. (1990): The effect of a marketing orientation on business profitability. *Journal of Marketing*, 54 (October) pp 20–35.

O'Driscoll, A., Carson, D. and Gilmore, A. (2001): The competence trap: exploring issues in winning and sustaining core competence. *Irish Journal of Management*, 22 (1) pp 73–90.

Tynan, C. (1997): A review of the marriage analogy in relationship marketing. *Journal of Marketing Management*, 13 (7) pp 695–703.

Chapter 2

Marketing plans and objectives

THE EDEN GARDEN TOOLS COMPANY LTD

Because Eden Garden Tools had always been moderately successful, and because Mike and Hugh had always had a 'hands-on' approach to running the business, they had never set any objectives. Now, the venture capitalists were forcing them to set some – at the very least, they needed to set an objective to launch on the AIM within seven years. This in itself would give rise to a number of sub-objectives, some of which would be directly concerned with marketing, and some of which would not.

Mike and Hugh also thought they would need to consider their corporate vision – again, they worked closely together and felt they knew where the business was going – but this would not be adequate for demonstrating direction to other people, notably potential investors.

After reading this chapter, you should be able to:

→ Describe the four main categories of corporate objective, and explain their relationship to marketing objectives.

→ Describe circumstances in which corporate and marketing objectives might be in conflict.

→ Explain where corporate strategy is derived.

→ Explain the difference between vision, mission and strategic intent.

→ Explain the difference between aims and objectives.

→ Describe how complexity affects objective setting.

Introduction

This chapter is about the role of the marketing plan, and its relationship to organisational objectives. Organisations measure their success in many different ways: profit is only one of several measures which might be used, and of course for grass-roots employees profit is not always a relevant factor in their daily work. For senior management in a company, profit is certainly a factor, but it is far from being the only criterion by which success is measured, and other commercial targets such as growth are often important to them. Furthermore, not all organisations have profit or a financial surplus as their primary goal; they may have aspirations to achieve different types of objectives, which may include financial as well as non-financial targets. Non-profit organisations such as charities, government departments and social enterprises will be aiming to achieve a range of outcomes from their operation, and these can equally be fulfilled through marketing planning.

Corporate objectives

There are, in general, four main measures of corporate success (although some firms will have subsidiary measures which may be used). These measures are used as the basis for management targets and are as follows:

1 Profitability.

2 Growth.

3 Shareholder value.

4 Customer satisfaction.

These measures are not necessarily mutually exclusive: marketers obviously argue that customer satisfaction will lead to growth in revenues and profitability and improved shareholder value. However, other professionals within the organisation may have different views, which may not be consistent with what marketers believe.

Profitability

The main reason that profitability ranks highly in terms of objectives is that it is used by investors in the stock market as a key factor in valuing shares. Company directors are under a legal obligation to act in the best interests of shareholders, an injunction which nowadays translates as providing shareholders with a good rate of earnings per share, plus capital growth as the shares rise in value. From the personal viewpoint of directors, a falling share price might result in dissatisfied shareholders or a takeover bid, which could see the directors looking for new jobs.

Profitability suffers from a number of problems as a measure of success. First, it is relatively easy for managers to manipulate the figures (at least in the short term) in order to show a paper profit. For example, profitability rises if growth is funded with borrowed money rather than through **equity**, but the value of shares might fall because the firm is exposed to more risk. Also, managers might massage the figures by not writing off bad debt: the debt remains on the books as an asset, whereas writing it off will depress the company's value. Again, managers can cut investment in the short term, which will reduce outgoings and therefore boost profits, but this will probably lead to longer-term reductions in growth. This often affects marketers because it is easy to cut a promotional budget and improve short-term profitability while damaging the long-term health of the business by not investing in brands.

Profitability, or return on investment, is a flawed measure because it looks at past performance of the firm, not its potential. This inevitably leads to short termism on the part of managers.

Growth

Growth of **sales turnover** or assets is a main objective for 80 per cent of firms (Collins and Porras 1994). The reasons for seeking growth are obscure, but one driver may be that 'being the biggest' equates to being the most secure. Another explanation may be that company founders and directors like the idea of running a large enterprise. Indeed, there is a clear link between the size of a business and the rewards of its senior managers, so growing a business can be a strong motive for its directors in terms of better remuneration packages and the sense of power that running a large business may give them.

In some cases, growth is achieved simply by having a superior product, business plan and managerial ability. For example, the Internet search engine Google grew from nothing to being the world's largest in only eight years (incidentally making its founders the world's fifth richest men). Such rapid growth is extremely rare, however; it is far more common for rapid growth to be achieved through acquisition of complementary or competing firms.

As an objective, growth (like profitability) has a number of drawbacks. First, the current emphasis on sustainability precludes overall growth in the economy, which means that firms can grow only by taking share from competitors. These competitors are unlikely to allow this to happen without a fight. Second, the pursuit of growth is likely to lead to **expansion by acquisition**, which means that managers will have to deal with a constantly changing set of new challenges as companies with different histories, cultures and markets are absorbed into the conglomerate. This is likely to lead to management by formula, where the same targets are set for all firms within the group and where unrealistic objectives are often set.

A study of corporate failures in the late 1980s' recession indicated that the best predictor of corporate failure was a very fast rise in sales (*Financial Times* 1991). The new challenges, unforeseen threats and rapid change involved in dealing with many new customers make for an unmanageable situation for most companies. Expansion by acquisition usually means paying a heavy premium for the firm being bought out – stock markets typically add 50 per cent to the pre-bid share price if a takeover is expected, meaning that the buying company has to be very sure that a suitable set of synergies will be in place after the acquisition has gone through. Often such acquisitions take many years to show a return, so if a company is acquiring other firms at too high a rate the returns will simply not happen sufficiently quickly to deliver a high enough level of profit to remain in business. Added to this is the effect on staff in the company being acquired – change of ownership often means job losses, so those who are best able to find jobs elsewhere are likely to do so before the redundancies start, resulting in a drain of talent to competing firms.

The net result of this is that over-rapid growth often leads to an equally rapid decline. Steady growth targets are therefore probably a good idea: open-ended rewards for very rapid growth are at best risky and at worst fatal.

Shareholder value

Shareholder value depends on three factors: dividends, a rise in the value of the shares, and cash payments in respect of assets sold on. Broadly speaking, shareholders will invest if they believe that the company will provide them with a better return than they would obtain by investing elsewhere. For some, this will mean receiving dividends, while for others the capital gain made as the shares rise in value is of greater interest (usually for tax reasons – capital gains are taxed much lower than income).

Policies aimed at increasing shareholder value are very different from those aimed at profitability or at growth. Stock markets are understandably wary of companies which grow too fast (Copeland et al. 1995) and as we have already seen, the pursuit of short-term profitability damages the firm's long-term prospects because it reduces investment.

Although shareholder value has a strong appeal in conceptual terms, and it fits in well with the directors' legal responsibility to put shareholders' interests first, it can present serious practical difficulties in implementation. First, it is very difficult to tell in advance which of several tactical possibilities would be most likely to increase shareholder value. For example, a price increase might improve profitability, or could equally lead to a shift in the perception of the brand. A PR exercise might well improve the stock market's perception of the company, but the same effort might pay off better if directed at other stakeholders. Second, the bulk of the stock market valuation of a firm lies in its residual value rather than in its dividend stream (Marsh 1990). Second, companies in the UK (and even more so in the US) tend to have short payback expectations on investments – any major capital investment will be expected to pay off within five years at most, whereas German and Japanese companies might be happy to accept a ten-year payback period. This means that some investments are less likely to be made, since the required profit from them might be as much as four times that required by competing companies in other countries. Thus shareholder value is a policy best pursued by mature industries, where capital investment can be low and slow because most of the investment has already been made.

Customer satisfaction

From the viewpoint of a marketer, all three of the above measures of corporate objectives are seriously flawed because, although they may potentially be derived from meeting customer requirements, they are not customer-oriented. The marketing concept tells us that customers have a choice, and if they are dissatisfied they will spend their money elsewhere. Therefore, customer satisfaction is a prerequisite for achieving any other objective. Winning new customers has always been a main objective for firms, but in recent years the emphasis has shifted towards customer retention and, most recently, **customer winback**. Many large companies now survey their major customers regularly in order to determine their satisfaction levels.

Customer satisfaction does not, of course, mean that the company should give the customer everything he or she wants. Everyone would like top-quality products at low prices, but this is a quick way to the bankruptcy court for the company doing the supplying. There will always therefore be a trade-off between the needs of shareholders, employees and managers on the one hand and customers on the other.

Research mainly shows that high customer satisfaction levels are associated with greater loyalty and increased revenues (Anderson et al. 1994; Homburg et al. 2006; Rust et al. 2002). Using customer satisfaction as a measure of success has a great deal of appeal intellectually because it is relatively easy to understand as a concept (Gupta and Zeithaml 2006), but it does need to be put into perspective. It may be difficult to find out whether or not customers are satisfied, for example, and even then there is no guarantee that they will not defect anyway (Lam et al. 2004). In some business-to-business markets buyers might switch to another supplier because their firm has been taken over by another firm and they are given no choice. These buyers will not show much loyalty to the new firm either, of course – given the chance, they are likely to switch back to their former supplier, even if they are equally satisfied with the new supplier. In other cases, buyers might be forced to accept the lowest bid on a contract, even though they know that the existing supplier will do a better job. Therefore, customer satisfaction alone is not always a good predictor of loyalty, even though in most cases it would appear to predict loyalty very well.

Table 2.1 shows the difference between finance-led planning and marketing-led planning.

Of course, focusing on customer need does not, and cannot, ignore profitability. Firms need to be profitable in order to stay in the game – they cannot do otherwise. The marketing approach is regarded simply as the most effective way of getting people to spend their money with us rather than with a competitor.

Table 2.1	Finance-led business plan compared with marketing-led business plan	
	Finance-led business plan	**Marketing-led business plan**
Product strategy	Focuses on turnover, costs and inventory	Focuses on performance, design and choice
Pricing strategy	Focuses on margins, turnover and debt	Focuses on value for money, price promotions and discounts
Place (distribution) strategy	Focuses on turnover, assets and expenses	Focuses on customer convenience, delivery efficiency and credit facilities
Promotion	Focuses on cost, return on outlay and short-term gain	Focuses on communication, brand image and long-term investment in the brand
People	Focuses on productivity, control and salary cost	Focuses on customer-facing skills, empowerment and corporate culture
Process	Focuses on internal efficiency, cost saving and control	Focuses on convenience for customers, added value and customer loyalty
Physical evidence	Focuses on cost, durability and efficiency in use	Focuses on customer loyalty, image and durability

Other objectives

In order to support effective marketing through customer satisfaction, commercial businesses are increasingly looking at other ways of measuring performance, particularly from the point of view of being innovative, so a different set of objectives could include new product introductions, the proportion of sales/profits from new products, number of patents registered, and time-to-market measures.

Yet it is apparent that many organisations do not have commercial corporate targets to meet as they exist for different reasons. Charities and central and local government departments will have non-profit targets, although these could involve achieving financial objectives such as donations in the case of the former, or breaking even or achieving a surplus in the case of the latter. It is also conceivable that some small business owner-managers have alternative objectives as well as profitability and survival, which may relate to their need for autonomy or a particular lifestyle.

An interesting group of organisations is those termed social enterprises that exist to achieve a social mission through trading in goods and services, but with a broader set of goals in mind. They are driven by social and environmental considerations in addition to commercial outcomes – often termed the 'triple bottom line': people, planet, profit (Elkington 1994). It may be that the profits that they achieve are used to address a social or environmental issue, or that such an issue would be the purpose of the business (e.g. supporting local communities, ensuring fair trade or employing disadvantaged people as employees). Some well-known social enterprises include the *Big Issue* magazine, Jamie Oliver's '15' restaurants, and the Eden Project. There will be many thousands of other less well-known enterprises with a social purpose that operate as community cooperatives or trading arms of charities. In the case of these organisations a much broader set of objectives needs to be considered when developing marketing objectives through marketing planning.

Another useful perspective on objectives and how organisations measure performance against them is provided by the **balanced scorecard** (Kaplan and Norton 1992). This approach proposes that managers should view business performance from four perspectives: the customer, the internal, innovation and learning, and financial. The advantage of the balanced scorecard is, as its name indicates, having a more holistic view of organisational performance, beyond simply a financial viewpoint. Taking into account all the different dimensions of an organisation should provide more of a strategic focus and discourage short-term tactics that provide immediate financial return but hinder long-term success.

Marketing plans and corporate plans

If the company is truly marketing oriented, the marketing plan and the corporate plan will be similar if not identical. However, in many cases marketing is seen as a function, and therefore the marketing plan will be seen as subsidiary to the overall corporate plan. The corporate plan is in essence the way in which corporate strategy (overall direction and purpose) is translated into a practical set of actions.

Corporate strategy derives from **mission**, **vision** and **strategic intent** (see Figure 2.1). Two broad definitions of mission are currently in use (Campbell et al. 1990). On the one hand, mission can be regarded as an intellectual discipline and a strategic tool. Under this definition, mission addresses two questions: first, what business are we in, and second, what business should we be in? In some cases the answer to both questions is the same. For example, a cinema chain might say, 'We're in the cinema business' as an answer to both questions. A more market-oriented answer might be, 'We're in the

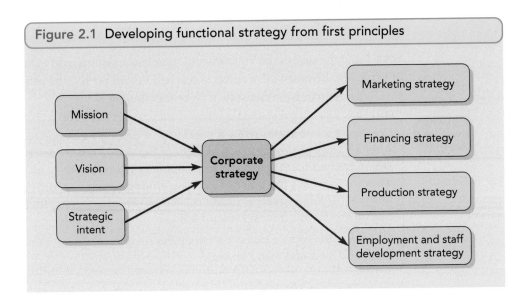

Figure 2.1 Developing functional strategy from first principles

Table 2.2 Elements of the mission

Element	Description
Purpose	This is the reason for the company's existence. This may or may not be profit-related: most companies start out because the founders believe they are doing something which really needs to be done.
Strategy	This is the company's competitive position, as defined by its distinctive competencies. Strategy is a statement of how the company intends to differentiate itself from companies in the same business.
Behaviour standards	These are the norms and rules, sometimes stated as 'the way we do things round here'. Behaviour standards will include the way customers are dealt with and the way staff are treated.
Values	These are the moral principles and beliefs which underpin behavioural standards. Typically, these values have been established by the founders of the company, but sometimes they evolve over time as circumstances change.

cinema business, but we should be in the entertainment business', which redefines the mission in terms of customer need and might lead the company towards offering other entertainment such as restaurants, bars or games areas in its cinemas.

The other definition of mission runs as follows (Campbell et al. 1990):

> *A mission exists when strategy and culture are mutually supportive. An organisation has a mission when its culture fits with its strategy.*

By this definition, the mission is the organisation's character, identity and reason for existence. The mission divides into four parts, as shown in Table 2.2 above.

Vision is the original view taken by the founder of the firm and is often associated with an idea about the future. It concerns the achievement of an ideal, and is sometimes confused with mission. However, vision is about the firm's long-term future, whereas mission is more concerned with the firm's present situation and is usually based on practical issues. For example, Ferdinand Porsche had a vision of bringing motoring within the reach of the working man at a time when cars were unattainable luxuries for all but the wealthy. His vision of a 'people's car' resulted in the design and production of the Volkswagen (literally, people's car).

Although a vision and a mission can be identical, in general visions are associated with goals (as in the case of the Volkswagen), whereas missions tend to be more about ways of behaving. Obviously if a vision is reached, it will need to be reformulated in some way, whereas a mission can stay in place indefinitely.

TALKING POINT

Creating a vision seems to be a good way of getting a company off the ground. After all, visionary leaders such as Richard Branson, Anita Roddick and James Dyson created successful companies, apparently in the face of all the conventional wisdom. So what's the point of studying strategy when a school drop-out (Branson), a former teacher (Roddick) and an art-school graduate (Dyson) have beaten the pants off most Harvard MBAs?

Of course, the picture doesn't show all the people who were visionary, and who tried hard, and who failed anyway!

The third concept underpinning corporate strategy is strategic intent (Hamel and Prahalad 1989). Strategic intent envisions a desired leadership position and establishes the criteria by which the company intends to monitor its progress. Strategic intent is often expressed relative to competitors. Canon, the office equipment manufacturer, had a strategic intent to 'beat Xerox'. The concept of strategic intent implies that there is a general view on where the company should be going rather than a definite statement of an expected outcome, and this means that there should be plenty of flexibility within the statement to allow for staff initiative, team contribution and adaptation in the light of changed circumstances.

Strategic intent suffers from the same problem as vision in that it might eventually be attained and will therefore need to be reformulated. Mission, however, is timeless and can be changed only with some difficulty, since it contains the corporate culture within it. Corporate culture is not only difficult to change, but even attempting change is dangerous: employees resent changes of this nature, understandably, and in many cases equate the corporate culture with their personal values.

Aims and objectives

There is often some confusion about the difference between an aim and an objective. The key difference is that an aim is a general direction, whereas an objective has a measurable outcome attached to it. For example, a company might run a promotional campaign with the aim of raising awareness of its brand. This becomes an objective only if the company says that it wants to raise awareness from a current level of 10 per cent of the population to 30 per cent identifying the brand in a prompted recall test. The objective should also have a timescale attached to it so that there is a clear measure of its achievement (or failure to achieve).

General categories of objective are shown in Table 2.3.

The general objectives in Table 2.3 are usually considered to be at the **organisational level** or **business level** of the firm, i.e. at a relatively high level, and are often termed corporate objectives. At this level they would be incorporated into a corporate plan and associated strategies and operational tactics would be put in place throughout the organisation to achieve the overall objectives. These would relate to each of the business functions (i.e. marketing, production, finance and personnel) for which there would be a separate plan that would feed into the corporate plan. There is in effect a hierarchy of plans and objectives, and it is important that there is a consistency between what is intended at the higher level and each of the functional areas at the level below.

The functional level of marketing will also have its own general classes of objectives. These fall into the following categories:

- **Customers.** These are objectives concerned with segmentation and targeting, and might be assessed by such measures as market-penetration statistics.

Table 2.3 General categories of objective

Objective	Explanation and examples
Business scope	This is about changing the definition of what business we are in. To continue with the example of the cinema chain which decides to expand its range of services to become a leisure complex, the objective could be to have a restaurant and a games room in every cinema within two years.
Business orientation	This type of objective relates to general positions the company seeks to adopt. For example, a university might need to become more research-oriented and therefore sets an objective that 60 per cent of its academic staff should become research-active within a two-year period.
Business organisation	Objectives relating to the structure of the business might be set during a reorganisation. For marketers, this might include reorganising the salesforce, or it might include a more radical conceptual organisation of the status of marketers and marketing within the company.
Public responsibility	This type of objective takes account of the impact of the company's activities on the general public, and indeed on stakeholders in general.
Performance evaluation	An objective to reduce response times between customer complaints and action to rectify the problem would be an example of a performance evaluation objective.

- **Competitors**. These objectives might be set at a strategic or at a functional level. They are concerned with the company's performance within the market relative to its competitors. For example, this could be as simple as gaining a level of **market share** compared with its closest rival.

- **Markets and distribution**. Approaching specific markets and obtaining distribution for products are key objectives. Aiming to get the product into two major super-market groups this year would be a reasonable, measurable objective.

- **Technology and products**. Using new technology in the business is almost always a functional decision.

- **Production capability**. Setting targets for output of particular items is always a marketing decision, because it is actually a function of deciding what the demand is going to be for specific products. To an extent, demand can be driven or at least directed by marketing activities, but in the main demand is decided by consumers.

- **Finance**. Since financial objectives are easy to quantify, they are often set by companies. In almost all cases they are marketing-led.

- **Environment**. Objectives for dealing with the firm's external environment might be set at any level, but they are likely to be difficult to quantify.

In setting objectives, one should move from the general to the particular, from the broad to the narrow, and from the long-term to the short-term (McDonald 1984). This means that objectives will tend to become more focused and therefore more attainable.

Marketing objectives

According to McKay (1972) there are only three basic marketing objectives: to enlarge the overall market, to increase share of the existing market, and to increase profitability (see Figure 2.2). These objectives might be seen as strategic, long-term objectives: they would need to be broken down into sub-objectives, and even sub-sub-objectives. This might give rise to a set of objectives as follows:

- Enlarge the overall market: increase **product innovation** (either through improving existing products or through developing new products), or increase **market innovation** (either through developing existing end-use markets or through discovering new end-use markets).

- Increase market share: either by emphasising product development and improvement (performance, quality or features), or by emphasising persuasion (sales effort, or advertising, or sales promotion), or by improving customer service (after sales, better credit and collection, or better availability and delivery).

- Improve profitability: either by increasing sales volume (more sales effort, stronger advertising and sales promotion), or by eliminating unprofitable activities (prune product range, prune sales coverage, cut customer services), or by improving prices (raise prices, or use price differentiation), or by cutting costs (improved effectiveness of marketing tools).

Some of these objectives might cause disquiet among marketers. Some seem sales-oriented, and the view that advertising is a strong force for persuasion might seem a little odd to some academics. However, the general principle that strategic objectives give rise to a number of sub-objectives still stands.

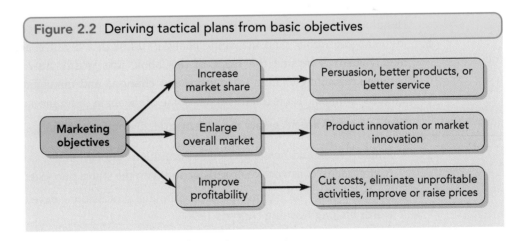

Figure 2.2 Deriving tactical plans from basic objectives

Enlarging the overall market is probably worthwhile only for the biggest firms in the market. For smaller firms, increasing share by taking customers away from other firms is probably a better strategy unless it creates a more cut-throat competitive environment. Improving profitability is an option any firm can pursue, but it is often not as easy as it might seem: cutting costs and raising prices will always meet with resistance from other departments and from customers.

Complexity and objective setting

Objective setting is often made more complicated by the fact that every problem impinges on every other problem. Complexity in decision making has three main characteristics:

1 Any policy-making situation comprises many problems and issues.
2 These problems and issues are usually highly interrelated: solving one problem usually creates another problem elsewhere, and there is rarely a global solution.
3 Few, if any, problems can be isolated effectively for separate treatment.

Complex problems do not have simple solutions (in fact, there is a common saying that there is a simple solution to every complex problem, but the solution is always wrong). Because the solutions create problems elsewhere, the organisation itself creates barriers to solutions: solving a problem in one department or for one individual is likely to create a problem for another department or individual, who will quite naturally resist the change. Coordination is lost and the problem grows worse.

TALKING POINT

> *If solving problems simply creates more problems, why not just learn to live with them? To use an analogy, if it's not raining, you don't need to mend the roof, and if it is raining, you can't go up there to mend it anyway.*
>
> *Why not leave things alone and hope the problem will go away? After all, many problems will just disappear if we ignore them – the colleague we don't get along with might leave or drop dead, the customer we want to sell to might buy anyway and if not, another one will be along shortly. What's the big deal with solving problems?*

Handling change is a constant factor in business – some commentators refer to managing changing rather than managing change. Although a detailed account of change management is beyond the scope of this book, it is worth drawing a comparison between managing change (**discontinuous change**) and managing changing (**continuous change**). Table 2.4 illustrates some of the main differences.

Three elements are necessary for incremental, discontinuous change to happen:

1 Employees should be committed to continuous improvement. Everyone should be committed to constructive dissatisfaction with the status quo (Stacey 1993).
2 Everyone must be committed to continuing professional development, in other words lifelong learning (Argyris 1990).
3 Everyone must be committed to continuous adaptation. This assumes that there will be flexibility in the firm's structures and systems, and there will be a tolerant working culture.

These three elements define the evolutionary organisation. If an organisation is evolutionary, adaptation to changing circumstances is relatively straightforward because change happens all the time anyway. There is therefore less likelihood of staff resistance to change.

Table 2.4 Continuous versus discontinuous change

	Discontinuous change perspective	Continuous change perspective
Emphasis on:	Revolution over evolution	Evolution over revolution
Strategic change as:	Disruptive innovation/turnround	Uninterrupted improvement
Strategic change process	Creative destruction	Organic adaptation
Magnitude of change	Radical, comprehensive and dramatic	Moderate, piecemeal and undramatic
Pace of change	Abrupt, unsteady and intermittent	Gradual, steady and constant
Fundamental change requires:	Sudden break with status quo	Permanent learning and flexibility
Reaction to environment jolts	Shock therapy	Continuous adjustment
View of organisation crises	Under pressure things become fluid	In the cold everything freezes
Long-term change dynamics	Stable and unstable states alternate	Persistent transient state
Long-term change pattern	Punctuated equilibrium	Gradual development

Source: From 'Strategy: Process, Content, Context', Bob de Wit and Ron Meyer, Copyright 1998, Thomson Learning (EMEA) Ltd. Reproduced by permission of Cengage Learning.

Understanding the wider implications of how organisations deal with constant change is an important contextual dimension that underlies the way that marketing planning is undertaken. Changes in environmental forces and within the organisation itself are inevitable, and the rapidity of change in contemporary markets has had a significant effect on the way that marketers approach the task of fulfilling customer requirements and delivering value. With this in mind we will move on to examining some of the key drivers of change and the impacts that they have had on shaping the marketing planning process within organisations.

Summary

The relationship of the marketing plan to the overall organisational aims depends on the status of marketing within the organisation. In many companies marketing is seen as a function, so the marketing plan will be seen as subsidiary to the company's philosophy and aims. This may create conflict if the corporate plan goes against the principle of the marketing concept, however.

The key points from this chapter are as follows:

→ There are four basic corporate objectives: profitability, growth, shareholder value and customer satisfaction. Only the last one is directly related to the marketing concept.

→ Some organisations aim to achieve a broader set of objectives that encompasses more than just financial outcomes.

→ Marketing objectives will be subsidiary to corporate objectives unless the firm as a whole embraces the marketing concept.

→ Corporate strategy derives from mission, vision and strategic intent.

→ Visions are associated with specific goals, whereas missions are associated with behavioural norms.

→ An aim is a general direction; an objective has measurable outcomes.

→ Complex problems can be solved only at the cost of creating new problems.

Launching on the AIM requires companies to satisfy a Nominated Adviser that the company is on a sound financial footing, that the directors are fit people to run the company, and that the company has a long-term future. The objective is to have everything in place within five years, which leads to a sub-objective of setting up a preliminary meeting with a potential Nominated Adviser to find out what the requirements will be in detail. This would be the key to generating a list of sub-objectives.

Mike and Hugh also spent some time formulating the corporate vision, the final version of which ran as follows:

The Eden Garden Tools Company Ltd will be the leading company in horticultural innovation in the UK. This will be achieved by a policy of continuous innovation, coupled with sound engineering and a focus on customer need, whether for the amateur gardener or the professional grower.

Following on from the meeting with the Nominated Adviser, Mike and Hugh came back to the company with a list of objectives. Heading up the list was a requirement to reduce the company's debt ratio and increase the sales turnover by 40 per cent.

The increase in the sales turnover could be achieved provided the tree-pruning equipment succeeded in the market, but the company needed a fall-back position, since many new products fail. At this point, the partners decided they would need to recruit a professional to handle their marketing, and possibly another one to handle sales. This was added to the list of sub-objectives and given a timescale of three months, in view of the timescales involved in increasing sales in the medium term.

Another factor in their thinking was the company's limited resources. Although they could borrow some money from the bank, the ongoing credit crunch meant that any bank lending would be limited, and in any case there would be a conflict with reducing the company's debt ratio. In the end, Hugh and Mike agreed that this was unavoidable in the short term if they were to fund a recruitment exercise and increase the investment in their brand.

Review questions

1 *Why might customer satisfaction be a more appropriate objective than profitability?*

2 *Under what circumstances would corporate strategy and marketing strategy be identical?*

3 *Why might a company seek to help its competitors by increasing the overall market for the product category?*

4 *How might a hairdressing chain define what business it is in?*

5 *Why might a company reduce its product range?*

 ## Case study Richer Sounds

When Julian Richer was only 14 he began buying and selling hi-fi separates. By the age of 17 he had three employees, and at age 19 he opened his first store, at London Bridge. That was in 1978. This store entered the *Guinness Book of Records* for having the highest sales turnover per square foot of any retail outlet in the world.

By 2009, the company had 49 stores throughout the UK, with 10 in London alone; the company has a set policy of not expanding too quickly, but rather going steadily in terms of its growth. Because the company is entirely owned by Julian Richer, there are no shareholders to make their wishes heard. Richer can therefore do whatever he wants with the business.

The result is a very individual approach to shifting hi-fi equipment. Richer has a reputation for a 'pile it high, sell it cheap' approach to retailing, but in recent years the company has begun to stock equipment for hi-fi enthusiasts (called audiophiles) and also LCD and plasma-screen TVs. Richer says that staff are chosen on the basis of enthusiasm and friendliness rather than high-powered salesmanship, but this is not the whole picture – most Richer Sounds staff are friends or relatives of existing employees. In other organisations this would be regarded as corrupt practice, but in Richer Sounds it is seen as a good way to develop and maintain a corporate culture, and especially to make it easy for new staff to fit it. Staff are usually music enthusiasts, and they are encouraged to advise customers but not to adopt a hard-sell approach.

Julian Richer has a ten-point plan which he published in his book, *The Richer Way* (Richer Publishing 2009). He is happy to share the plan with others; probably few other business managers would have the charisma to make it work. The ten points are as follows:

1 Talk to your staff and managers. Change is always greeted with suspicion, even cynicism. Tell everyone you are seeking improvement and why, so everyone is infected with enthusiasm.

2 Examine your mission statement. If you do not have one, form a working party to draw one up.

3 Organise an attitude survey. Find out what employees really think, to set a baseline.

4 Think about fun. How can you liven up the workplace and create a happy atmosphere? Look at reward structures.

5 Revise the rule book. Get rid of outdated regulations and meaningless traditions.

6 Set up a strategic customer service group. Examine your customer service and how it can be improved.

7 Ask your customers what they think. Find ways of inviting their comments at each point of contact.

8 Launch a suggestion scheme. Get the backing of the top person in the organisation and allow ideas from everyone.

9 Review your recruitment. What happens on the first day in the job? Do motivation and communication start from day one?

10 Review the values you deliver. Are you happy with the value for money of your service or product? Could the quality be improved or the price lowered?

Julian Richer personally answers every customer complaint and meets every new staff member. This would clearly be impossible if the company had a high staff turnover, or a high rate of complaints, so Richer must be doing something right. It may be because of Richer Sounds' unique feedback system – customers are invited to comment on the shopping experience, and the comment cards are sent straight to Richer. Staff and customers are encouraged to 'shape the shopping experience' by commenting directly to Richer or to his store managers. Staff are empowered to solve customer problems instantly rather than refer them to a call centre or a head office address.

Richer Sounds is far from being the biggest hi-fi retailer in the UK, but there is little doubt that it is one of the most profitable for its size. It is a great company to work for, and also a great company to do business with – Julian Richer does not see these objectives as being incompatible, in fact quite the reverse.

Questions

1 *Which type of corporate objective does Richer appear to be aiming for?*

2 *What appears to be the relationship between corporate objectives and marketing objectives at Richer Sounds?*

3 *What are the marketing implications of Richer's slow-growth policy?*

4 *What appears to be Richer's strategic intent?*

5 *What has been the role of vision in developing Richer Sounds?*

References

Anderson, E.W., Fornell, C. and Lehmann, D.R. (1994): Customer satisfaction, market share, and profitability: Findings from Sweden, *Journal of Marketing*, 58 (July) pp 53–66.

Argyris, C. (1990): *Overcoming Organisational Defences: Facilitating Organisational Learning* (Boston: Prentice-Hall).

Campbell, A., Devine, M. and Yeung, D. (1990): *A Sense of Mission* (London: Hutchinson Business Books).

Campbell, A., Goold, M. and Alexander, M. (1994): *Corporate-level Strategy: Creating Value in the Multi-business Company* (New York: John Wiley).

Collins, J.C. and Porras, J.I. (1994): *Built to Last: Successful Habits of Visionary Companies* (New York: Harper).

Copeland, T., Koller, T. and Murrin, J. (1995): *Valuation: Measuring and Managing the Value of Companies* (New York: Wiley).

de Wit, B. and Meyer, R. (1998): *Strategy: Process, Content, Context* (London: Thomson).

Elkington, J. (1994): Towards the sustainable corporation: win-win-win business strategies for sustainable development. *California Management Review*, 36 (2) pp 90–100.

Financial Times (1991): Clues that warn of collapse. 26 May, p 3.

Gupta, S. and Zeithaml, V. (2006): Customer metrics and their impact on financial performance, *Marketing Science*, 25 (6) pp 718–39.

Hamel, G. and Prahalad, C.K. (1989): Strategic intent. *Harvard Business Review*, 67 (3) pp 63–76.

Homburg, C., Koschate, N. and Hoyer, W.D. (2006): The role of cognition and affect in the formation of customer satisfaction: a dynamic perspective, *Journal of Marketing*, 70 (3) pp 21–31.

Kaplan, R.S. and Norton, D.P. (1992): The balanced scorecard – measures that drive performance. *Harvard Business Review*, January–February.

Lam, S.Y., Shankar, V., Erramilli, M.K. and Murthy, B. (2004): Customer value, satisfaction, and switching costs: an illustration from business-to-business service context, *Journal of the Academy of Marketing Science*, 32 (3) pp 293–311.

Marsh, P. (1990): *Short Termism on Trial* (London: Institutional Fund Managers Association).

McDonald, M.H.B. (1984): *Marketing Plans* (London: Butterworth-Heinemann).

McKay, E.S. (1972): *The Marketing Mystique* (New York: American Management Association).

Rust, R.T., Moorman, C. and Dickson, P.R. (2002): Getting return on quality: revenue expansion, cost reduction, or both? *Journal of Marketing*, 66 (4) pp 7–24.

Stacey, R.D. (1993): Strategy as order emerging from chaos. *Long Range Planning*, 26 (1) pp 10–17.

Chapter 3

Drivers of marketing planning

THE EDEN GARDEN TOOLS COMPANY LTD

Eden Garden Tools had emerged from the recession battered, but in better shape than many: although there were no cash reserves, and considerably more debt than was the case in 2007, the company remained essentially viable as business picked up.

Hiring some specialist personnel went fairly well. Here the recession had helped, since some very good people were unexpectedly available due to redundancies among competing firms. Hugh and Mike recruited a former marketing manager of a rival lawnmower manufacturer, Umar Sayeed. Sayeed came with knowledge of the amateur gardening market and some insights into business-to-business markets. With his help, the company recruited salesman John Peters, a former sales rep for a manufacturer of cider-making equipment. Although he had little direct experience of dealing with small-scale cider makers, he had a number of contacts with agricultural suppliers, and was known slightly by some of Mike's family.

Umar's first task was to explain to the directors what the key issues were in formulating a marketing plan. Having looked at the very rough outline of where the company needed to be in five years' time, and also having considered the company's vision statement, he outlined what he saw as the main influences they would need to keep in mind when deciding what to do about the firm's marketing.

After reading this chapter, you should be able to:

→ Explain how internal and external environmental factors may affect marketing planning.

→ Identify some of the key drivers of external environmental change.

→ Explain the role of developing resources in creating a high-performance strategy.

→ Describe the process of creating business capabilities from resources.

→ Explain the role of knowledge in creating capabilities.

→ Describe different categories of capability.

→ Explain how individuals, groups and corporations hold competencies.

→ Describe the likely outcomes of management of core competencies.

→ Explain why organisations sometimes become market-driving rather than market-driven.

Introduction

This chapter sets marketing planning against a backdrop of environmental change and examines contemporary and emerging issues that should set the direction of marketing objectives, plans and the planning process.

A coherent approach to environmentally driven and resource-based planning is essential if the organisation is to have any realistic chance of success in marketing. Ignoring forces in the external environment and the resources and capabilities an organisation has available for meeting its objectives is clearly unrealistic, yet it is surprising how many people believe that 'resources should be made available' when the organisation quite clearly does not have the resources at all.

Both the external and internal perspectives on planning are considered here, along with how they contribute to the marketing planning process both separately and together. In particular we identify some of the key drivers of external change in the marketing environment, and from an internal viewpoint the way in which the resource-based view influences planning of marketing activities.

Planning and the marketing environment

Understanding the external marketing environment is essential for any organisation striving to be successful in the task of marketing. Delivering value to customers can be achieved effectively only if marketing organisations are familiar with changes in the external environment and build these into how they affect consumer and competitor behaviour and consequently shape the way in which the marketing offer is constructed for customers. Even more, marketing planners are attempting to identify how change in the environment is going to affect buying behaviour and competitive marketing in the future. They do this by considering current trends and projecting whether they are likely to continue to be important, or identifying whether there are other, as yet unpredicted changes that may be of significance in the market as time progresses. Alternatively we can view change as cyclical – 'what goes around comes around'. As in the case of the 2008 recession, the question was always going to be, when will the economy crash rather than will it crash at all? Similarly, fashions change, with old styles often being replicated in the future, and 'retro' is often seen as a reinvention of the past in markets such as clothing and music.

In a sense we can see change as being both cyclical and following a pattern, or as evolutionary change which is more sudden and unexpected. In either case it is important for marketing planners to be able to take account of these changes when developing plans, setting objectives, formulating strategies and developing marketing programmes. Clearly, unpredictability is difficult to handle in such situations and the marketer must make the best attempt at foreseeing how wider forces will influence market behaviour into the future. Assumptions are therefore extremely important in marketing planning and the basis for how the plan is developed. With uncertain change guaranteed in all markets, planners need to be able to assume that certain changes will occur, patterns and trends will continue, or not, and that this will form the basis of how the plan is shaped. At the same time, assumptions need to be made about internal factors such as the availability of financial resources, staff and technology, and these also need to be built into any plans. Critically, it is vital to be aware of the assumptions that underlie the plan, so that when change occurs that affects performance, the plan can be revisited and realigned with how the future will look at another point in time.

Drivers of change therefore exist externally to the organisation and internally within it and they need to be assessed not only in terms of their likelihood of happening but also in terms of the potential effects and impacts they will have on the markets that the organisation is operating in now or is intending to enter in the future.

Such drivers of change may be considered at different levels of the environment: macro factors, micro factors and internal factors. The first two of these comprise the external environment and can be associated with the concept of environmentally driven marketing strategy, or as a market-orientation perspective on marketing planning. This suggests that marketing plans should be built around wider external forces that shape consumer and competitive behaviour in the market.

Macro forces are often classified through the use of basic analysis tools to cover the full range of external factors that may affect marketing behaviour. A typical way of doing this is using a STEP analysis – Socio-cultural, Technological, Economic and Political – or alternatively a PESTEL analysis – Political, Economic, Socio-cultural, Technological, Ecological and Legal. These will be considered in more detail in a later chapter when we look at analysing the external environment.

Micro forces are also usually classified in a range of ways using models and frameworks such as Porter's Five Forces Model (Porter 1990), or something as straightforward as the 3Cs framework, which considers the micro-environment as comprising customers, competitors and channels. Again we will discuss this further as more detailed analysis of the external environment is undertaken later in the book.

As indicated, the process of externally driven strategy is based on the view that wider macro forces affect the marketplace in terms of their ability to drive changes in micro factors, including consumer behaviour, the way that competitors are able to operate, and the influences on the market of suppliers and intermediaries. Thus marketing planning that takes such an approach will inevitably emphasise what is going on outside the organisation and is consistent with an 'outside-in' perspective.

Contemporary marketing planning has some major factors operating in the external environment that have become key drivers of change. Marketers now need to incorporate these influences into their strategic and operational decisions, as they have become very important in terms of their impacts on the way that customers make buying decisions and how competition takes place in markets.

Using a basic STEP analysis provides us with a useful starting point, and the following external influences may be considered to drive change and hence marketing planning:

- **Socio-cultural**. This factor includes culture, fashions in thought, attitudes, social class issues, and consumer behaviour, which is constantly evolving as a consequence of wider influences. In addition there has been major demographic change throughout the world, leading to an ageing population in many countries, and significant changes in migration patterns. Social mobility resulting from mass education has also become an important factor in affecting consumer attitudes, expectations and behaviour.

- **Technological**. This factor includes engineering breakthroughs, new technology, availability of specific technologies (for example, some communications technologies are unavailable in some parts of the world) and shifts in processes brought about by new ways of doing things. Of major significance has been the growth in use of new information, computing and communications technologies, by both consumers and organisations. The subsequent effects on buying behaviour and the production and supply of goods and services have been revolutionary.

- **Economic**. This includes the general state of the national economy, the wealth and income of the company's customers, and economic barriers such as tariffs or availability of foreign currency. Economies go into recession approximately every seven or eight years, for example, which affects savings and availability of credit, which has a knock-on effect for consumers' capacity to purchase and businesses' ability to invest.

- **Political**. The political climate of the country can change dramatically according to which party is in power. Some political parties are more pro-business generally, and are prepared to help organisations both through legislation and through direct help. Different parties also have different policies on spending priorities – a government which is in favour of increasing defence spending will obviously be a good thing as far as a shipbuilder or aircraft manufacturer is concerned.

Beyond this we can identify some very broad considerations that can be regarded as drivers of change, such as globalisation and corporate social responsibility.

- Globalisation in recent decades has meant that organisations have to deal with consumers that do not fit neatly into country segments but into transnational customer groups that straddle the boundaries of nations or even regions throughout the world. At the same time organisations have to develop their production, supply chain and distribution models to take account of global economics and shift the way that they have traditionally operated by using new business models such as outsourcing.

- Corporate social responsibility (CSR) has become another important factor in influencing marketing behaviour and planning. Organisations are now not only expected to act in the best interests of their customers but also to be seen to be socially responsible in the way that their business impacts on employees, the wider community and the environment. As a consequence, we have become familiar with some of the key issues around this, such as ethical consumption, sustainable business and stakeholder relations.

These factors do not include market forces such as the effect of increasingly more intensive competition. Competitive behaviour also impacts strongly on organisations – a new competitor entering the market, or a more aggressive stance taken by an existing competitor, can make a significant impact on the company's chances of success.

All in all, changes in the external environment have an enormous part to play in determining the way that organisations go about planning their marketing effort, and the significance of some of the key drivers in shaping strategy and plans cannot be understated.

Alternatively, the organisation can be viewed from an internal or 'inside-out' perspective that emphasises that strategy and planning should be predicated on the distinctive or unique resources that it is able to call upon to shape the way that it delivers value to customers in the market. The internal factors include corporate culture, mission, resources and capabilities. The effects of limited resources on the organisation's objectives are widespread, since the organisation cannot do everything it might want to do if the resources are not available. This has led to a rethink among observers and the development of the resource-based view of the organisation.

TALKING POINT

We have considered some of the key drivers of change from an external perspective and some of these are clearly going to be important to the future and be incorporated into the marketing planning process. But who is to say that the factors that we have identified now will be important in the future? What have we missed out and how might these affect marketing planning?

Is it really worth spending time and effort factoring these influences into our plans when we don't really know what is going to happen in the future and whether what is relevant to consumers and organisations in the present day will be of any significance as time progresses?

The resource-based view

The resource-based view of the organisation suggests that a high-performance strategy depends on historically developed resource endowments. **Resource-based marketing** tries to develop a good fit between the needs of the market (i.e. customers and consumers) and the ability of the organisation to produce benefits for them (i.e. to compete effectively in the market).

This is something of a departure from the traditional marketing-orientation paradigm, in which the company seeks to respond to market needs by using high-quality, organisation-wide marketing intelligence. By including the idea that the organisation has to operate within its resource constraints and competencies, the resource-based model is much more in line with real-world experience.

The resources of the organisation are not static, of course, and will develop over time in order to meet market needs more accurately. Opportunities are identified and exploited when the organisation has a specific competence that enables it to pursue the opportunity more effectively than other companies are able to. This means that some market needs will be left for other companies to pursue.

Organisations are driven by many different forces, not just a desire for increasing shareholder value. Other stakeholders have an input into the equation, and some of these stakeholders represent part of the resources of the organisation: employees, suppliers and even customers (or at least the relationship we have with them) can all be regarded as resources. Organisations need to conduct an audit of the resources and capabilities at their disposal if they are to know how best to respond to market opportunities.

Resource categories are (in general) as follows:

1 **Technical resources**. Technical skill is a key resource for many organisations in both manufacturing and service industries, because it enables the company to develop new products and processes as the market's needs change. Technical resources also extend to intellectual property rights such as patents: Pilkington Glass made more from licensing its patented float-glass technique than it did from making glass in its own factories.

2 **Financial standing**. The degree to which the company has access to working capital will determine its ability to respond to opportunities. Equally, the credit standing of the organisation will be a key factor in securing supplies. Marketers within the organisation will always have to ask for a budget in order to carry out any activities, from developing a new product through to attending a trade exhibition. Obviously wealthy companies are in a much better position to commit financial resources to marketing than are less cash-rich organisations.

3 **Managerial skills**. Top-flight, experienced managers can direct and motivate staff to create the maximum efficiency in operations. They can also be creative in getting the maximum use from physical resources such as buildings, equipment and vehicles.

4 **Organisation**. Organisational structure makes a significant difference to the effectiveness of the organisation. The traditional pyramid or hierarchical structure of organisations is extremely effective in markets where change is slow: the mechanistic approach enables organisations to gain maximum efficiency through division of labour. In more volatile market conditions, where change is rapid and unpredictable, a **matrix** (or organismic) **organisation** is probably better since it can respond more flexibly to changes. The drawback of organismic organisations is that

communication takes up a much greater proportion of time than is necessary in pyramid organisations.

5 **Information systems**. Having accurate, up-to-date information to hand can create a strong competitive advantage in itself. For example, the barcode readers in super-markets provide instant information on which products are selling well, allowing the supermarket to ensure that stocks are held at the optimum level. Coupled with the loyalty card data, the supermarket is able to build up a clear picture of each customer's shopping habits and preferences, and can also (by using customers' postcode data) analyse shopping preferences geographically, thus knowing which products might sell well in new stores opening in those areas.

Figure 3.1 shows a resource-based model for competing in a global environment. In this model, resources create **competencies**, which in turn create **capabilities**. Capabilities create a sustainable competitive advantage, which in turn leads to superior performance in the marketplace.

The basic resources, both tangible and intangible, that the organisation has available need to be managed effectively in order to develop capabilities. Developing resources in an appropriate manner is a longer-term proposition, but at every stage management input is essential to the creation of a capacity to operate effectively. A capability is the result of bundling together a set of processes, and should be more than the sum of the individual processes: synergies should result, meaning that the whole is greater than the sum of its parts. This will not happen if the processes are inappropriately linked or are mutually damaging in some way (Stalk et al. 1992).

TALKING POINT

So much for the marketing concept. Here we are, talking about marketing as if we were doing everybody a bit of good, as if marketers are the greatest philanthropists the world has ever seen, and then we come up against reality – we simply don't have the resources to do what we think we ought to do.

So are marketers really doing good in the world? Or are we simply like someone who writes a big cheque for a charity, knowing it will bounce?

Having the competence to do something does not necessarily mean that the organisation is now capable. Capabilities arise out of competencies plus knowledge and attitudes (Durand 1996). Knowledge (in turn) is the set of rules (know-how, know-what, know-where and know-when) and insights (know-why) that is used to make sense of information (Dretske 1981). Knowledge is contained in the heads of employees, but it is also collective: technological expertise and understanding of the market are two examples. Corporate attitude is the shared tendency to behave in a particular way in response to stimuli. Some organisations are known for their caring attitude, some for being particularly litigious, some for being aggressive competitors. Such attitudes can represent considerable assets (or liabilities) to the organisation (Barney 1986).

Capabilities lead to sustainable competitive advantage when they offer something that differentiates the organisation effectively from its competitors. If the capability leads to better value for money for the customers than that obtaining elsewhere, the company

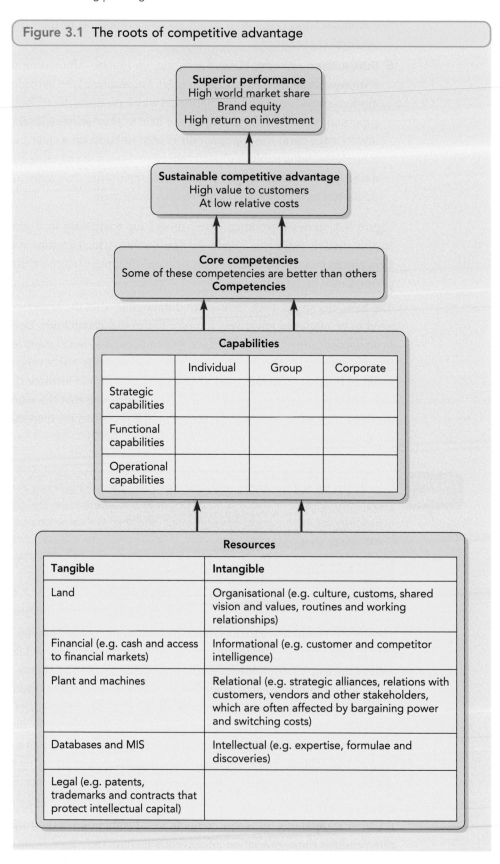

Figure 3.1 The roots of competitive advantage

will have a sustained competitive advantage. If other organisations develop capabilities which are better for customers, the competitive advantage will be eroded and may disappear entirely.

Capabilities can be seen as strategic, functional or operational. Strategic capabilities define the organisation's overall direction, and include the organisation's capacity to learn, as well as the dominant philosophy which guides the senior managers. Ability to manage the strategy is also a key capability.

Functional capabilities include marketing capabilities, financial capabilities and operations management capabilities. They address the ability of the organisation to carry out basic functions effectively and economically.

Operational capabilities are concerned with individual tasks in the overall process which leads to customer satisfaction. This might include efficient use of equipment, individual skills of workers, application of IT, efficient order processing, and so forth.

Competencies often lie with individuals, with teams within the organisation, or at the corporate level.

1 Individual competencies reside within the individuals who work for the organisation. This might include such necessary skills as those of a doctor, specialist learning derived from a research specialism (as might be the case in a university), or even a skill such as glass-blowing, which is, nowadays, possessed by a very few people. For example, a university might run a course in sales management which relies heavily on one individual's research interests. Such a course might prove difficult to run if that individual left or retired.

2 Group competencies can arise either from formal teams within the organisation or from informal groups. A formal team might be, for example, the research and development team which has responsibility for developing new products. If this team works well together and has complementary skills, there will be synergies which help in creating better working conditions. An informal group might arise, for example, among administrators responsible for customer-facing activities such as invoicing or dispatch. If a 'can-do' culture develops, greater efficiency in meeting customer need will arise, even though the company may not have formed a specific team. Often, the informal network in a organisation (i.e. colleagues who become friends) is more powerful in getting things done than is the formal network, especially when something unexpected comes up.

3 Corporate-level competencies arise from the corporate culture. They relate to the ability of the organisation as a whole to carry out the necessary tasks, and may relate to the degree to which the company learns as a whole (rather than relying on individual memory).

Important resources and competencies develop throughout the company's history. The process is usually a slow one: companies cannot develop a competency overnight, nor can resources be acquired instantaneously. Equally, it can be difficult to decide what the core competency of a firm actually is. Prahalad and Hamel carried out a study of successful international companies, concluding that any organisation is likely to be world class in only five or six areas of activity (Prahalad and Hamel 1990). For example, they discovered that Black and Decker's true core competency lay in the development of small electric motors which could be used to run DIY power tools.

Prahalad and Hamel proposed three tests for identifying core competencies:

1 A core competency should be difficult for competitors to copy. If competitors can easily copy it, it isn't core to the organisation – it is common to all organisations.

2 A core competency provides potential access to a wide variety of markets. A core competency in, say, fibre-optic cable would enable a company to access telecommunications markets, aerospace markets, railway signalling markets, defence markets, and so forth.

3 A core competency should make significant contribution to the benefits the customer derives from using the product or service. The competency is worthwhile only if it contributes to customer welfare – a criterion which is very much in line with the marketing concept itself.

The key issue is whether the competency can be combined with other factors within the organisation to create unique value for customers. Grouping core competencies with other competencies (i.e. those which the organisation is good at but which are not unique to the organisation) should add to customer satisfaction, otherwise there is little point in the exercise.

The implications of this view are wide ranging. Management of core competencies is likely to be a driver for corporate planning and consequently marketing planning, which in turn is likely to lead to the following outcomes:

1 Greater emphasis on alliances with other companies, with each company bringing a core competence to the alliance. An example would be the construction of the Eurotunnel, which involved companies with core competencies in mining, in large-scale concrete structures and in railway construction.

2 Divestment of non-core businesses and brands, accompanied by their sale to companies whose core competencies relate better to those businesses and brands.

3 Organisational changes away from strategic business units and towards a more overarching strategic architecture. This would mean that the organisation would tend to use the core competencies to drive everything within the organisation, rather than letting it sit in a subdivision or department.

Competencies do need to be something very specific. Saying that the organisation has a 'quality product' or has a 'strong competitive position' is missing the point – these are attributes that derive from core competencies. The core competency of Toyota, for example, is the organisation's ability to retool rapidly to produce different vehicles from the same stamp mills. This means that the company can respond very quickly to shifts in demand for vehicles, and can also launch new models much faster than its US and European competitors. A side benefit is that the stamp mills are used more intensively – an important consideration, given the high capital cost of buying them.

The list of competencies is likely to be short, perhaps even one or two items. Management will need to be agreed on what the competencies are, of course, and this will not necessarily be obvious. Dissent among managers might mean that the core competencies are not effectively leveraged, i.e. they do not underpin everything the company does. Misidentification of competencies will have a similar effect, in that managers will try to play to strengths that the company does not have.

Collaboration with other organisations is a likely outcome of correct identification of core competencies. Being able to leverage the organisation's unique competencies by linking them with another organisation which has complementary competencies is an excellent way of strengthening both organisations.

The following approach adds further insight into the dilemma of whether the organisation's environment or resources should dominate marketing planning decisions.

The market-driving approach to strategy

The marketing concept implies that organisations can, and should, plan around customer needs. Marketers frequently tell people that this is what they do, whereas in fact many organisations operate on a **market-driving** principle, seeking to shape the market and influence customer decisions.

Table 3.1 contrasts the two approaches.

The **market-driven** paradigm is more closely related to market orientation, whereas the market-driving view is more closely related to the resource-based view. This is because organisations which begin by looking at what they can do for the market rather than what the market needs per se will almost always have to make some kind of proactive approach in persuading people that what is on offer will, in fact, meet their needs.

Although on the face of it the market-driving paradigm does not equate well with the marketing concept, it remains the case that organisations which seek to lead the market are likely to produce innovative products. 3M's invention of Post-It notes was a clear example of a product in search of a market: customers did not know that they had a need for Post-Its until the product appeared, yet now there are few offices which do

Table 3.1 Market-driven vs. market-driving

	Market-driven	Market-driving
General	Organisation acts within the framework and constraints of existing market structure and characteristics.	Organisation can and will act to induce changes in the market structure and changes in the behaviours of the players (customers and competitors).
Customer orientation	Adaptation.	Be at the cutting edge of new customer needs.
Identifying, analysing and answering to the customer	Predict which technologies are likely to be successful given customer needs and preferences. Respond to market structure.	Shape customers' behaviour proactively. Pioneer. Predict how customers' needs and market boundaries evolve with various technical features.
Competitor orientation	Continuous benchmarking. Imitation.	Shape the market structure proactively. Identify and develop difficult-to-imitate internal and external competencies. Discontinuous disruption.

not use them in their thousands. The same is true of almost all breakthrough inventions – home video recording, mobile telephones, television, aircraft, and many other products had no market whatsoever until they became available.

Market-driven organisations, meanwhile, will be more heavily influenced by changes in consumer behaviour (rather than driving the changes by offering something new), by competitive innovations (often resulting from organisations which are market-driving), and by relationships within distribution chains (which a market-driving organisation is likely to control).

It is interesting to make the contrast here between these two different perspectives on strategy, which are akin to the market-oriented and resource-based views. It cannot be denied that the resource-based view adds an important dimension to marketing planning, which extends decision making about the development of objectives, strategies, programmes and plans into the context of the organisation's actual position – rather than simply suggesting that it should be governed by external forces that affect market behaviour.

It is clear that the reality of marketing planning success encompasses a degree of consideration of both 'outside-in' and 'inside-out' perspectives. The extent to which each perspective is influential in such decisions will obviously be determined by the circumstances and priorities of the organisation that has to embark on developing a marketing plan.

Summary

Although the marketing concept represents an ideal to which companies should aspire, most organisations are unable simply to give customers everything they want. Resource constraints will determine what an organisation can and cannot do. Many organisations take this a stage further and seek to influence the market by what they do, rather than being reactive.

The key points from this chapter are as follows:

→ Objectives cannot be set in isolation: external and internal factors will constrain decision making.

→ Key drivers of change exist in the wider environment that have shaped marketing strategies and plans.

→ A high-performance strategy relies on developing resources effectively.

→ Resources create competencies, which in turn create capabilities.

→ Capabilities arise from competencies plus knowledge.

→ Capabilities can be strategic, functional or operational.

→ Competencies might lie with individuals, with groups, or at the corporate level.

→ Management of core competencies is likely to lead to strategic alliances, to divestment of non-core activities and to overarching strategic architecture.

→ Organisations are often market-driving rather than market-driven, due to resource constraints and availability.

Umar explained that the company would need to assess the environment thoroughly, and would need to be clear about the company's strengths and weaknesses. He planned to carry out an analysis over the next few weeks, but in the meantime he explained what he thought were the key drivers for the marketing plan, based on the corporate vision and the initial objectives the directors had already put in place. These drivers (in no particular order) were as follows:

- Innovation. The Eden Garden Tools brand is based on an innovative approach to the amateur gardening market and should be extended to the commercial grower market as well.
- Social responsibility. The Eden Garden Tools Company Ltd has a mission to make gardening easier for the infirm or disabled, and has a range of products which will help in doing that.
- Globalisation is clearly an issue for the company, at least regarding the new tree-pruning saw, and in fact is an issue anyway. This area of the market had been neglected, since the company's business outside the UK is handled by export houses rather than directly from the company itself. Umar flagged up the potential problem of foreign competition entering the UK market, a danger the directors had not considered.
- The current emphasis on sustainability in consumer thinking could be a major boost for the firm since more and more people were looking to grow their own food.
- Stakeholder relations, in particular those between shareholders (Mike's family business, Mike and Hugh themselves, and of course the venture capitalists if and when they came on board), would be of paramount importance.

The directors began to feel that things were moving ahead, but if they were to start to put the flesh on the bones of the corporate and marketing plans, they would need to have a much more detailed analysis.

Review questions

1 *What is the difference between a competency and a capability?*
2 *How might a company set objectives relating to resources?*
3 *Why does management of core competencies often lead to strategic alliances?*
4 *How does the market-driving philosophy relate to the resource-based view of the organisation?*
5 *Why do resource constraints militate against the marketing concept?*

Case study Toyota

Kiichiro Toyoda was born in 1894, the son of the inventor of the automatic loom. Toyoda inherited his father's engineering commitment and skill, and devoted his life to developing cars. In 1929 he travelled around Europe and the US finding out about car production, and in 1935 launched his first passenger car and a light pick-up truck based on the same chassis and engine.

In 1936 the company ran a public competition to design a logo, but Risaburo Toyoda (who had married into the family) pointed out that changing the company name from Toyoda to Toyota made the logo simpler and easier to pronounce.

The Second World War interrupted the production of private vehicles, and it was not until 1947 that Toyota began production for private motorists again. Within ten years the company had entered the US market, and by 1972 had established a factory there. Originally, Toyota vehicles were branded as 'Toyopet', but this branding was rapidly dropped in the US because of the combination of 'toy' and 'pet' which seemed inappropriate for a vehicle.

Since Japan has virtually no natural resources of its own, manufacturing needs to be lean and efficient. This meant that Toyota cars were much smaller than their US counterparts, but luck played a part in Toyota's destiny when the 1973 oil crisis forced many Americans to look for cheaper, smaller and more economical cars. Toyota pioneered the just-in-time stock system, whereby components arrive at the factory just as they are needed – the company keeps no buffer stocks of parts. The company also developed rapid interchange of stamp-mill dies, meaning that production of body parts can be switched rapidly between models. The company's competency in production techniques is regarded as world-beating, and has helped Toyota become the world's fifth largest corporation, producing around 9 million vehicles a year.

The company has invested heavily in environmentally friendly cars, having developed the Prius hybrid petrol–electric car. This is an advanced piece of engineering: the car runs on electric power only at speeds below 31 miles per hour, but at higher speeds the petrol engine automatically starts, in order to provide extra power. The petrol engine also charges the battery, so there is no need to recharge the battery from the mains. The result is a car that will average over 70 miles to the gallon and will (when in electric mode) have no emissions. Toyota hopes to offer a hybrid option for all its vehicles by 2012 and to produce all-electric vehicles during the decade.

Toyota also has an interest in robotics, having produced a robot which can play a trumpet, and a wheelchair which is controlled by thought alone. The company's aim is to produce robots which can be used for the care of the elderly and infirm, and also for automated manufacturing processes.

Toyota has a truly global approach to business, with production subsidiaries in 26 countries. In many cases, production of specific components such as transmissions or engines takes place in one country, with the components being shipped to several other countries for assembly into the finished cars.

Environmental issues play a prominent role in Toyota's thinking. The company follows the two concepts of 'zeronise', which means removing the negative impacts of vehicles such as pollution and traffic congestion, and 'maximise', which means increasing the positive aspects such as fun and convenience. The company aims to introduce more sustainable factories as well as making the vehicles more environmentally friendly: production plants use wind and solar power, and greenery is planted around the production sites to increase biomass. From 2005 Toyota had a five-year environmental plan, which was directed at 'the arrival of a revitalised, recycling-based society'. The plan was intended to build on the company's previously issued Eco-Vehicle Assessment System, which included four elements: fuel efficiency, emissions and noise during vehicle use; disposal recovery rate; the reduction of substances of environmental concern; and the total CO_2 emissions throughout the vehicle's lifecycle, from production through use to disposal.

The underlying theme of Toyota's corporate philosophy is that the company is working to build the world of tomorrow. This is reflected in the strapline for its UK advertising, 'Today, tomorrow, Toyota', but it is embodied in the corporate data book for 2008, in which the company has four objectives for shaping the future:

1 Opening the door to unexplored areas.

2 Starting new cycles of industry.

3 Expanding research into a variety of areas.

4 Building up human resources and organisational strength as the foundations of manufacturing.

These objectives, and indeed the whole Toyota corporate philosophy, are conveyed to employees through the Toyota Institute, a university established by the company in 1981 for the purpose of developing employees' skills and knowledge.

Toyota has come a long way since 1935: in that year, the company built only 20 vehicles and made an overall operating loss. Now the world's largest vehicle manufacturer, Toyota has no intention of resting on its corporate laurels. The company is continually looking to the future – today, tomorrow, Toyota.

Questions

1 *To what extent is Toyota market-driven?*

2 *Why are environmental values so important to the company?*

3 *What are the drivers behind the creation of the hybrid car?*

4 *What are Toyota's key competencies?*

5 *What are Toyota's key capabilities?*

References

Barney, J.B. (1986): Organizational culture: can it be a source of sustained competitive advantage? *Academy of Management Review*, 11, pp 656–65.

Dretske, F. (1981): *Knowledge and the Flow of Information* (Cambridge, MA: MIT Press).

Durand, T. (1996): Revisiting key dimensions of competence. SMS Conference, Phoenix, Arizona.

Porter, M.E. (1990): How competitive forces shape strategy. *Harvard Business Review*, 57 (2) pp 137–45.

Prahalad, C.K. and Hamel, G. (1990): The core competence of the corporation. *Harvard Business Review*, May–June, pp 79–91.

Stalk, G., Evans, P. and Shulman, L. (1992): Competing on capabilities. *Harvard Business Review*, March/April.

Part 2

ENVIRONMENTAL ANALYSIS

All business is conducted within a competitive, legislative and economic environment. Business is not only about money – it is also about people, and for marketers this is especially true since marketing is so intimately involved with meeting people's needs. Planning is, above all else, the art of the possible – whatever we plan to do must fit in around the environment in which we operate. So this section of the book looks at how planners can analyse the environment within which the business must operate, survive and (we hope) grow.

Key in this analysis is the marketing audit, which is the subject of Chapter 4. The audit enables us to develop a 'snapshot' of the company's current position regarding its marketing. The following two chapters look in more depth at analysing the internal and external environments, and Chapter 7 brings the environmental analysis together by looking at ways of identifying suitable strategies.

Chapter 4

The marketing audit

THE
**EDEN
GARDEN
TOOLS**
COMPANY LTD

Umar Sayeed knew that he had a somewhat daunting task ahead of him – carrying out a full marketing audit for a firm which had few systems in place for assessing its marketing activities could be very time consuming, and he had a fairly tight deadline to meet if the company were to be able to meet its targets for negotiation with the venture capitalists.

Thinking about the practicalities of conducting the audit, he came to the following conclusions:

1 The audit would need to be carried out about once a year, since the company did not have sufficient resources to carry it out more frequently, and in particular he would not have time to do it on a regular basis since he would have to do all the work himself as well as carry out the rest of his duties as marketing manager.

2 The audit itself would probably be fairly straightforward as the company carried out relatively few marketing activities – very limited advertising, no PR, and so forth.

3 He would have to take entire responsibility for the audit the first time round, but might expect some help from John Peters once he had had the chance to get out and interact with customers. That would make the following year's audit easier, anyway.

4 There would be a need to revisit the audit in between full audits, because the company itself was going through a period of rapid change.

Having outlined the main issues for himself, Umar moved on to consider the detail of how he would conduct the audit.

Objectives

After reading this chapter, you should be able to:

→ Describe the basic elements of the marketing audit.

→ Explain how the audit helps in forward planning of marketing.

→ Assess the frequency with which the audit should be conducted.

→ Explain some of the problems in carrying out the audit.

→ Show how the audit helps in focusing the thinking of managers.

→ Describe some of the drawbacks of the audit.

Introduction

Any planning process needs to be framed within the context of the planner's present circumstances. Knowing where we are enables us to plan for where we are going: without this vital information, we cannot make realistic decisions.

In financial planning, planners begin by knowing what assets the organisation already has and what is currently being done with those assets. Accountants carry out audits to find out what is owned, what is owed, and what is due to be paid to the organisation. Marketers can carry out a similar type of audit that sets out to examine what the company's current marketing situation is. The marketing audit is therefore an important platform in developing the company's forward planning.

In this chapter the main elements of the marketing audit are explained and some of the practicalities associated with undertaking an audit are discussed.

Elements of the audit

The marketing audit is a comprehensive review of the organisation's strategies, tactics, objectives, performance and activities. The purpose is to provide managers with a complete overview of the organisation's current position – a 'snapshot' view – so that they can plan for moving the organisation forward. In effect, the audit evaluates the organisation's effectiveness in terms of the 7Ps of the extended marketing mix (Band 1984).

The audit is pivotal to the marketing planning process and supports decision making relating to strategic and tactical resource allocation in marketing. The marketing audit broadly has two components, external and internal, although it is commonly sub-divided into a number of elements.

The elements of the marketing audit are shown in Table 4.1. Some of the elements may be difficult to assess – information may not be readily available, or may be expensive to obtain – but the aim is to find out as much as possible about what the organisation is doing in each of the areas identified. This will help to show up any weaknesses in the corporate marketing policy, and should provoke creative thinking among managers as problems are identified.

Each of these elements will be dealt with in more detail in this chapter.

Table 4.1 The marketing audit

Main areas	Sub-sections	Issues to be addressed
Marketing environment audit *Macro environment*	Economic–demographic	Inflation, materials supply and shortages, unemployment, credit availability, forecast trends in population structure.
	Technological	Changes in product and process technology, generic substitutes to replace products.
	Political–legal	Proposed laws, national and local government actions.
	Cultural	Attitude changes in the population as a whole, changes in lifestyles and values.
	Ecological	Cost and availability of natural resources, public concerns about pollution and conservation.
Task environment	Markets	Market size, growth, geographical distribution, profits; changes in market segment sizes and opportunities.
	Customers	Attitudes towards the company and competitors, decision-making processes, evolving needs and wants.
	Competitors	Objectives and strategies of competitors, identifying competitors, trends in future competition.
	Distribution and dealers	Main trade channels, efficiency levels of trade channels.
	Suppliers	Availability of key resources, trends in patterns of selling.
	Facilitators and marketing organisations	Cost and availability of transport, finance and warehousing; effectiveness of advertising (and other) agencies.
	Publics	Opportunity areas, effectiveness of PR activities.
Marketing strategy audit	Business mission	Clear focus, attainability.
	Marketing objectives and goals	Corporate and marketing objectives clearly stated, appropriateness of marketing objectives.
	Strategy	Core marketing strategy, budgeting of resources, allocation of resources.
Marketing organisation audit	Formal structure	Seniority of marketing management, structure of responsibilities.
	Functional efficiency	Communications systems, product management systems, training of personnel.
	Interface efficiency	Connections between marketing and other business functions.
Marketing systems audit	Marketing information system	Accuracy and sufficiency of information, generation and use of market research.
	Marketing planning system	Effectiveness, forecasting, setting of targets.
	Marketing control system	Control procedures, periodic analysis of profitability and costs.
	New product development system	Gathering and screening of ideas, business analysis, pre-launch product and market testing.

Table 4.1 continued

Main areas	Sub-sections	Issues to be addressed
Marketing productivity audit	Profitability analysis	Profitability of each product, market, territory and distribution channel. Entry and exit of segments.
	Cost-effectiveness analysis	Costs and benefits of marketing activities.
Marketing function audits	Products	Product portfolio; what to keep, what to drop, what to add, what to improve.
	Price	Pricing objectives, policies and strategies. Customer attitudes. Price promotions.
	Distribution	Adequacy of market coverage. Effectiveness of channel members. Switching channels.
	Advertising, sales promotion, PR	Suitability of objectives. Effectiveness of execution format. Method of determining the budget. Media selection. Staffing levels and abilities.
	Salesforce	Adequate size to achieve objectives. Territory organisation. Remuneration methods and levels. Morale. Setting quotas and targets.

Source: Adapted from KOTLER, PHILIP, *MARKETING MANAGEMENT*, 11th ed., © 2003. Reproduced by permission of Pearson Education Inc., Upper Saddle River, New Jersey.

In order to carry out the audit, a large number of individuals will need to provide information; in some cases, these people will not be part of the marketing department and may need to be persuaded to help. In most cases, people will want to understand how the audit will benefit them, or make their lives easier. Marketers will need to satisfy them on these points, and will also need to make the provision of information as simple as possible.

Marketing environment audit

This part of the audit is concerned with the various elements which surround the company and affect its activities. The macro environment is those elements which affect all organisations in the industry (and contains many elements which affect all organisations, whatever their industry).

These elements are often called PESTEL elements (see Figure 4.1):

- political factors such as current government policy and the stability of the political climate;
- economic factors such as demand in the national economy, interest rates, credit availability, and so forth;
- socio-cultural elements such as language, social trends, and shared beliefs of the society in which the organisation operates;
- technological elements such as new products on the market, communications technology, or scientific breakthroughs;

Figure 4.1 The marketing environment

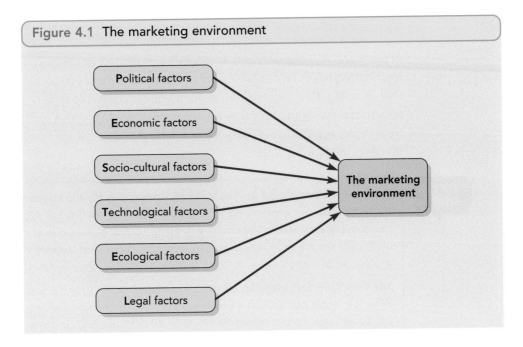

- ecological elements such as conservation of natural resources, concerns about pollution, and availability of sustainable supplies of raw materials; and

- legal factors such as legislation and court decisions.

Most of the information regarding the macro environment is easily available through published sources such as newspapers, government statistics, journals and books. The difficulty with auditing the external environment is that it changes rapidly: new laws are passed, fashions change, and the economy can go through boom and bust quite suddenly (as was seen in the autumn of 2008). This may mean that this part of the audit needs to be updated regularly, perhaps through a **management information system**.

The task environment consists of those elements which affect the immediate task at hand, in other words those factors which aid or inhibit the tactical processes the organisation is undertaking. In a marketing context these will normally be associated with satisfying customer requirements and reaping the rewards from doing that. Task environment elements include markets – these are all the actual and potential customers for the organisation's products. The audit results for this element should include the size of markets (both existing and potential) and the organisation's share in those markets. Customers are another element in the task environment: types of customer, market segments, needs and wants of the customers, and (perhaps crucially) their attitudes towards the company and its products are key pieces of information. This type of information can be collected through internal sources such as the salesforce and the invoicing department, and by carrying out market research with customers.

Auditing competitors must begin by identifying who those competitors are. This can be more difficult than it appears at first because a competitor might be any organisation which competes for our customers' business. For example, a nightclub competes not only with other nightclubs but also with cinemas and restaurants. In a broad sense, fashion stores also compete with nightclubs since they target the same groups of customer. Finding out the objectives and strategies of competitors is clearly extremely difficult and will probably rely heavily on speculation on the part of managers. Some information might be available from competitors' former employees, but this information is unlikely to be reliable. In some cases, competitors may even make public announcements about how they see the market moving, which may provide clues as to their focus; in other cases, corporate statements intended for shareholders and other investors might offer clues.

TALKING POINT

If competitors might be anybody who is competing for the customers' money, is there any point in even trying to find out what they are up to? After all, pretty much every business in the country is trying to get money out of people, so ultimately we are competing with everybody! There's no way we could possibly analyse all of them.

Yet if we take that attitude, what's the point of auditing the environment at all? With the world being such a volatile place, things changing all around us, why would we want to put ourselves through it? Why not just go back to bed, pull the covers over our heads and wait for it all to pass?

Distributors, dealers and suppliers form the rest of the supply chain or marketing channels of which the organisation is part. Auditing the supply chain is relatively easy compared with finding out about competitors' plans: suppliers and distributors are more likely to provide at least some information about their intentions, at least as far as the specific supply chain is concerned. Audit considerations might include power relationships in the chain, possibilities for recruiting new suppliers, or entering new markets currently served by other distributors. Auditors should be asking whether the existing supply chain is the best that can be found, and if not, whether it is better to try to adjust the existing arrangements or find new ones.

Facilitators and marketing organisations might include logistics companies (firms which ship our goods for us), advertising agencies, or consultancy businesses. Information about these should already be available within the company files, but again most of them would be happy to provide missing information. The question here is whether these are the best facilitators, given the organisation's current circumstances.

Publics means anybody who is impacted by the organisation's activities. This includes neighbours, the general public, government departments, pressure groups such as environmentalist organisations, and so forth. Publics are (not surprisingly) the subject of public relations, or PR. The audit should consider what the current relationships are with each of these publics, and should be able to flag up possible opportunities as well as providing an assessment of the effectiveness of current PR activities.

Marketing strategy audit

The overall marketing strategy should be audited with a view to determining whether, in the light of competitive and other activities, it remains the correct one. Strategies often shift as a result of meeting with reality. Even if top management has set a strategy, the actual strategic thrust can be changed as the plan is implemented, for the following reasons:

1 Market conditions turn out to be different from what was anticipated. For example, when Honda first entered the US market, the strategy was to sell large motorbikes because these dominated the US market. These bikes flopped dramatically – but Californians became interested in the 50cc bikes the Honda staff used to commute to the Honda factory, and these became a great success (Pascale 1984).

2 Middle managers' personal agendas cause them to alter the strategy.

3 Competitors force a change of direction. A competitor entering a key market can devastate the strategic plan.

The audit should look at the business mission. Many missions have a very specific end point – for example, a company may want to become the biggest in the industry. If the mission has either been attained or is close to being attained, a revision might well be necessary and a new mission outlined.

Marketing objectives should be clearly stated and appropriate, but like the business mission they may be close to being attained and should therefore be revised – the audit will help in doing this.

Finally, the budgeting and allocation of resources should be considered. This is a difficult area, since every departmental manager would like an increase in budget and can, of course, make a strong case for the increase. Any organisation relies on all its departments – each one is essential to the smooth running and even the survival of the organisation, otherwise it would simply be closed – so managers can always point to the vital importance of their work.

Marketing organisation audit

Checking the organisation structure is important because the structure determines the function of most departments in most companies. In some companies, the organisation structure might be organismic, in which case the structure flexes according to the task facing the company at any specific time; in other companies there is a rigid hierarchy, with each person's task being carefully delineated. Such bureaucratic structures work well in situations where the company operates in a stable business environment.

The question for the auditors is whether the existing structure is appropriate for the conditions and tasks the company finds itself in. For marketers, the position of market-ing in the overall organisation structure is also of great interest – if marketing and marketers generally occupy low-level positions in the structure, the priority given to marketing is also low. Even if the marketers are unable to do anything about it, it does at least indicate what their position and expected role are.

The structure of the organisation goes beyond the formal structure shown on the organisation chart, of course. There is also the informal structure, which comprises the network of social interactions within the organisation. These social interactions happen in many contexts – casual conversations near the photocopier, groups of colleagues who meet for lunch periodically, chance encounters in the corridor, and so forth. The informal network is extremely important in making up for shortcomings and communication failures in the formal network, but it is also virtually impossible to audit because of its inherently chaotic nature. What can be considered is the degree to which the organisation encourages the informal network and facilitates social interaction between colleagues. Many companies do this by organising social events, by including personal news in the staff newsletter, by having 'For Sale' notice boards on the premises, having company clubs and sports societies.

Functional efficiency is about the effectiveness of internal communications, training systems and product management systems. Good administration should provide the right support for the people who are doing the 'real' work – efficient office staff and administrators contribute greatly to this. Of course, no system is ever perfect: what is appropriate for one group of staff may be wholly inappropriate for others. For example, marketing managers may need a constant stream of information from front-liners such as the salesforce, but the salespeople resent taking time away from making sales in order to fill in a lot of statistical information on forms. Good administration and new electronic information systems minimise this type of conflict.

The final element in the organisation audit is interface efficiency. This looks at the connections between marketers and other departments and colleagues, and would be most concerned with the possibilities of conflict and the ways in which conflict is resolved when it happens. Conflict is not necessarily a bad thing, since it often leads to creative solutions (Ruekart and Walker 1987), but conflict-resolution methods need to be effective. (Unfortunately, in many organisations conflict resolution is conspicuous by its absence.)

Marketing systems audit

The systems audit looks at four main areas: information systems, planning systems, control systems and new product development systems. Each of these systems represents a set of procedures which is always followed (perhaps with some flexibility in the system) in order to ensure consistency. The question is whether these procedures are the most efficient, and whether they can be streamlined to improve their effectiveness.

Marketing information systems are there to provide a constant flow of information to decision makers about key factors. A good marketing information system should provide up-to-date information on sales, market share and competitive behaviour, but will provide a great deal more information depending on the decision makers' needs and the constraints of the industry. From the viewpoint of the audit, the questions are whether the right information is being supplied, whether the information is being analysed and disseminated correctly, whether the information is accurate, and whether effective market research is being carried out. One of the problems with auditing the information systems is to ensure that a good balance is obtained between the cost of collecting information and its usefulness to decision makers. Often, information is collected and carefully collated into reports which remain unread on managers' desks, or which are referred to only when things go wrong.

The marketing planning system should be capable of setting appropriate targets and forecasting outcomes. Clearly, it needs to be efficient in terms of using planners' time well:

keeping expensive executives in meetings all the time is not productive, yet this is exactly how many organisations behave. The audit should flag up inefficiencies in the system.

The marketing control system follows on from the planning system, since control should feed back into planning. Control systems should examine factors other than profit and turnover; marketers should, ideally, measure success in terms of customer outcomes such as customer satisfaction rates, market share and customer retention. Whatever measures have been laid down by the planning system, the control and information systems should combine to provide managers with clear feedback on the degree to which marketing activities have been effective in helping to hit targets.

New product development (NPD) is the lifeblood of most companies, since a lack of new products will (eventually) leave the company with only obsolete products to sell. Ensuring that ideas are collected correctly, that the screening process results in the most marketable products coming through (not merely the easiest to produce, or the managers' pet ideas) and that effective pre-launch tests are carried out are the key features of a good NPD audit.

Marketing productivity audit

The marketing productivity audit is intended to ensure that the set of marketing activities the company is undertaking (the marketing mix) is generating optimum outcomes. Marketing is not necessarily only about profitability, of course – organisations may have many different aims – but showing a surplus of income over outgoings is a prerequisite for staying in business. The first part of the productivity audit is therefore a profitability analysis.

Profitability should be analysed in several ways. Companies often tend to analyse profit in terms of the success of individual products, but while this is important in some ways, it certainly does not provide a full picture. The marketing audit therefore requires the auditor to assess the profitability of each market territory, distribution channel and target **segment** as well as entry and exit costs for markets as yet untouched.

Assessing the profitability of marketing territories allows the organisation to decide whether specific territories should be dropped or downgraded, so that resources can be diverted elsewhere. For example, a ferry company operating from Dover would probably find that most of its customers come from the south-east of England, so promoting heavily in northern England or Scotland would probably not be cost effective, whereas a ferry company operating from Humberside or Newcastle would find the reverse is the case. In most circumstances, the differences between territories may not be nearly as obvious. The costs of servicing a rural territory may be high, since salespeople may have to spend more time on the road, but equally some cities might be expensive to service because of traffic delays, greater costs attached to expenses claims for meals and parking, and greater competition.

The profitability of distribution channels is another area which has hidden implications. There is a tendency to believe that shortening a distribution channel will improve profitability, since each member of the channel adds on a profit margin. However, it is often the case that shortening the channel reduces efficiency, since it reduces the gains made by having specialists at each point in the chain. Where an organisation has multiple distribution channels, it should be possible to compare their profitability, but again the company will need to be somewhat circumspect in making decisions to change channels. Even if a channel is less profitable than others, it may be the only way to reach a given target market, or there may be other issues attached to changing it – for example, the distributors may be successful in handling some of the company's other products, and might be annoyed to find their range reduced if a product is moved to another distributor.

For marketers, the profitability of a market segment should be central, due to the concept of customer centrality. Considering the needs of our most profitable segments should be paramount because it focuses us on generating ideas for selling more to the segment and for ensuring that competitors do not lure our customers away. In some cases, unprofitable segments can be dropped, or ways can be found to reduce the amount of resources devoted to them. Some companies have even divested themselves of unprofitable market segments by selling them to competitors – for example, banks sometimes sell off unprofitable loans or loan divisions to specialists who are able to make them pay.

TALKING POINT

Most definitions of marketing include somewhere the words 'profit' or 'profitability'. Indeed, if you ask most people what they think a company is for, they will answer 'to make money'. But is that really the case? After all, many companies operate in industries where margins are very narrow – the package holiday business is one – rather than in businesses where the profit margins are high, such as organised crime.

Is profit really all we are concerned with, as business people? Or is profit just a means to an end, a way of staying in the game while we do something that we think is really worthwhile?

Finally, companies need to look at the entry and exit costs for specific segments. A segment might be identified as profitable but require high investments for entry; perhaps, more importantly, a segment may not be very profitable in itself, but may be so cheap to enter that the business might as well pick up what profit there is. There are many examples of market segments which have been passed up because organisations believe the segment is not profitable, but which have been so cheap to enter that other organisations have scooped a large share at very little cost. Equally, a segment may be losing profitability but be expensive to leave (perhaps because the company has contractual obligations to customers, or long-term servicing agreements). Often these will be business-to-business markets, but there are examples of consumer markets which are expensive to leave – the second-hand car market is one, since car dealers have large amounts of capital tied up in cars which would be difficult to sell quickly without dropping the price dramatically. Some organisations might have large amounts of capital tied up in manufacturing equipment or business premises, with little chance of recovering the money in the event of leaving a market.

Marketing function audit

The marketing function audit is concerned with the marketing mix itself. This part of the audit originally looked only at the 4Ps model (product, price, promotion, place), but since the widespread adoption of the 7Ps model, which includes people, process and physical evidence, the audit is in need of revision.

The product audit is concerned with additions to the product line and to managing the product portfolio. This is an extension of the marketing systems audit, in which new product development systems were considered, but actually is more concerned with strategy than with the mechanics of generating new products. Deciding which products to keep and which to drop is the basis of product strategy, and is a set of decisions which needs to be made in the light of customer needs and wants. In some cases, of course, products cannot be offered because there is no production or marketing synergy with the existing product range; without some linkage of the company's existing range, the chances of success in the market are dramatically reduced (Calentone and Cooper 1981).

Auditing the product range does not necessarily mean cutting out any products which do not show a profit. Such products may be necessary for retaining customer loyalty, or attracting new customers, or may be expensive to drop (see the profitability analysis). In some cases, products may even be kept in the portfolio because of historical or sentimental reasons – one example is Heinz Salad Cream, which suffered declining sales for many years and was eventually scheduled to be discontinued by Heinz. Public outcry at the loss of what was regarded as a British icon and a nostalgic product linked to many people's childhoods resulted in the company shelving the plans (in fact, sales increased once people became afraid that they might be about to lose the product).

The price audit includes considerations of customer attitudes towards the company's prices. This may include customer perception of quality, value for money, or competitive positioning. People rarely, if ever, buy the cheapest product in every category of goods they buy: most people make decisions based on what they consider to be value for money (the relationship between quality and price) rather than on simple money cost. However, since price also relates to profitability, the audit should include an assessment of whether the prices charged are sufficient to cover costs, at the very least.

Distribution issues include whether there is appropriate support for the supply chain (especially retailers) and whether the distribution chain is the most suitable for reaching the specific customer base. Market coverage is another issue in distribution: is the organisation reaching all the segments of the market that it could or should be reaching? In some cases, channel members may need more support, or may be less than efficient. The management of the channel should also be looked at in terms of the degree of control the company is able to exert over its members. In some cases, a channel may be dropped because one or other channel member has too much power.

The promotional audit includes all the communication tools the organisation has at its disposal. Auditing communications effectiveness is notoriously difficult – many organisations try to audit their advertising in terms of increased sales, for example, whereas there may be many other factors which influence sales. In general, communications activities can be measured only by communications outcomes. For instance, an advertising campaign intended to increase brand recognition will not necessarily increase sales, since recognising the brand and wanting to buy it are two completely separate issues. Even though it seems likely that increasing brand awareness will mean bringing the brand to the attention of people who will want to buy it, there is still no guarantee that they will do so – an economic downturn or a competing product entering the market could have a powerful effect in reducing sales. Such a campaign could be assessed by measuring brand awareness before and after the campaign, however: this could be linked to sales if a connection could be established between brand awareness and sales, of course.

The advertising audit should go further than simply seeing whether a campaign has been cost effective. The auditor should also consider whether the objectives are themselves appropriate, whether they are reachable, and whether they have a high degree of fit with the overall marketing strategy. The execution of the advertising itself should also be audited. Does the advertising achieve what it claims to achieve? Is the production of the advertisements what it should be? Are there cheaper ways of achieving the same impact, through producing less expensive advertising? A company, for example, might achieve as good a result by filming an advertisement locally as it would by filming it at an expensive overseas location.

The advertising budget should not merely be audited in terms of cost effectiveness, however. The basis for budgeting should also be re-examined. For instance, a company might be using a percentage-of-sales budgeting method, whereby the budget is calculated on the basis of the sales created last year. This method has the advantage of being easy to apply, but it suffers from the drawback that as sales reduce, the budget also reduces, whereas in fact there is a strong argument for increasing the budget if sales start to fall. The audit is intended not to set the budget but to assess the basis on which the budget is set.

Media choice is also a subject for the audit. In some cases, the medium may have worked well for years, but changes in audience tastes may have rendered the medium less effective. If people no longer buy a particular newspaper, or our target audience no longer watches a specific TV show, this should be picked up in the audit and the necessary changes should be made. Also, new media may appear: the Internet was an obvious example which many organisations failed to exploit adequately. In some ways, the advertising audit includes an external audit: watching for new developments in communication is clearly an important aspect of the audit.

Obviously the problem is much more complicated when it comes to measuring public relations efforts. PR is essentially about making people feel good about the company, and although there is almost certainly a link between this and many good outcomes (sales being only one of them), PR is extremely difficult to audit. Market research can help here, but it should be carried out with all stakeholders, not just customers. For example, one effect of PR is to encourage better-qualified employees to apply for jobs with the organisation. A good PR image also helps in motivating existing staff, in opening doors for the salesforce, and in improving the morale of suppliers. Good PR also eases the organisation's relationship with government departments. All of these factors are hard to measure, and in some cases may be impossible to measure (it is difficult to see how one might approach an MP with a questionnaire). In some cases, organisations assess their PR according to the number of column inches of press coverage they obtain, but this is an extremely crude measure. Apart from the fact that newspaper coverage is only one aspect of news reporting, the quality of the coverage and its impact on the organisation's publics are clearly much more important. A positive story of only ten lines is likely to be worth more than a fearless exposé of the company's activities which covers three pages.

Sales promotions, however, do have a fairly direct impact on sales. Running a good promotion can be measured directly by its effect on sales, but for the purposes of the marketing audit it would certainly create a fuller picture if the company could also assess the sales promotion's impact on brand values. In some cases promotions have a positive effect (the Tesco 'Computers for Schools' promotion is a fine example) whereas in other cases the promotion devalues and cheapens the brand (for example, Pizzaland's 'Pizza for a Penny' promotion meant that people went to Pizzaland only when they had a voucher, so the brand was devalued). Promotions which associate the brand with something upmarket are usually a good way to avoid devaluing the brand: a piggy-back promotion in conjunction with a leading brand can be extremely effective. Simply cutting the price will, of course, encourage brand switching, but such switches are temporary, they damage profitability, and they usually hurt the brand image as well.

The salesforce audit is perhaps among the most complex to carry out, not least because salespeople will try to avoid being made to look bad, and sales managers will certainly not want them to become demotivated. This is a very real danger when people's performance is being assessed, since they tend to feel threatened.

The salesforce as a whole can be audited in terms of the amount of business it brings in compared with the overall cost of running the group. This should provide a benchmark for assessing individual performance, but care needs to be taken: there may be perfectly good reasons why a particular salesperson has lower sales and higher costs than another, for example because he or she is covering a widely separated geographical territory. Individual effectiveness may be affected by many other factors: level of training, level of motivation, age, suitability for selling to specific customers, and so forth. A good sales manager should be on top of these issues, and the audit should help provide further information for managing the salespeople generally.

Ultimately, of course, individual salespeople might be identified as needing extra training, motivation or help: in the last analysis, poor salespeople need to be removed from the salesforce, of course, but care should be taken that this is not perceived as the purpose of the audit. If salespeople come to think that they are likely to be fired as a result of the audit, they are extremely unlikely to cooperate with the process.

The front-line people who have direct contact with customers should also be part of the audit. Even when such individuals do not have a sales role, they do form part of the customer experience, particularly in terms of the service aspects of the product. Truck drivers, receptionists, telephonists, warehouse people and so forth all have a role in creating customer satisfaction. Auditing how they feel about what they do, and what can be done to improve their performance, is of course a key aspect of the audit.

Practicalities of undertaking a marketing audit

Some of the issues associated with conducting a marketing audit in practice revolve around its frequency, the stages involved and how it should be performed effectively.

The timing of an audit depends on a number of factors, including the type of business, the length of the planning cycle and the rapidity of environmental change. In fast-moving markets it is probably better to have more frequent audits than when there is a relatively stable set of market conditions. If the organisation has an annual planning cycle, the audit will take place in sequence with this, or alternatively over some other time period.

It is particularly helpful to have a standard approach to auditing as comparisons can be made with previous periods. A common set of stages includes: the pre-audit, information collection, data analysis, recommendations and an implementation programme. The findings of the audit go forward to the next stage of the marketing planning process, and the more rigorous the audit systems in place, the better the basis will be for forward planning.

Kotler and Keller (2006) identify that for a marketing audit to be effective it should be:

- *comprehensive*: covers all the main elements;
- *systematic*: conducted in a structured and logical manner;
- *independent*: undertaken by someone who is unbiased and will be honest in their assessment of the situation;
- *periodic*: carried out at regular intervals, not just when there is a problem with marketing in the organisation.

With this in mind the audit should be led by a senior manager who will have an audit team in support that will liaise with any eternal auditors who are employed to conduct the audit. Using a balanced group of internal and external auditors in the process will ensure objectivity as well as strategic organisational focus.

Summary

The marketing audit is a template for assessing the organisation's current position in terms of its marketing activities. It provides a comprehensive system for examining everything that impinges on the organisation's marketing planning, but it is not in itself a provider of answers. If anything, the marketing audit generates questions rather than answers and is therefore more an aid to thought than a definitive tool.

There are some very real drawbacks to the audit, of course. These are as follows:

- It is time consuming if it is carried out thoroughly.
- Some aspects of the audit can seem threatening for staff.

- Managers will sometimes 'shade' their responses to audit questions to make themselves look good, or to follow a personal agenda of some kind.
- Much of the audit is subjective: it relies on judgement on the part of the auditor.
- By the time the audit has been carried out in its entirety the world has moved on and the information may be out of date.
- A full audit will require market research, which is expensive and does not provide answers very quickly in most cases.

Because of these very real drawbacks, companies need to make a judgement as to how often the audit should be carried out, and also how assiduous they should be in carrying out a full audit. Carried out properly, the audit will focus the minds of decision makers and often generates creative solutions; carried out poorly, it can easily mislead decision makers and create more problems than it solves.

The key points from this chapter are as follows:

→ The marketing audit has a number of basic elements which, if followed correctly, cover all aspects of the organisation's marketing activities.

→ The audit is a key starting point for all forward planning because it tells us where we are now.

→ The audit should be carried out as frequently as time and resources allow: this may be relatively infrequently, of course.

→ The audit is by no means straightforward: it requires effort, resources and a large degree of objectivity.

→ The audit's strongest benefit lies in focusing the thinking of managers, so managers should be involved fully in carrying out an audit.

→ The nature of the audit process adopted revolves around a number of organisational and market factors.

→ The audit has a number of drawbacks, many of which can be overcome if staff and managers 'buy into' the process.

Having spent a day or so familiarising himself with the company's files, administration and customer records, Umar Sayeed felt able to plan out the audit process for himself. He knew he would have to be objective, but as a new kid he knew this would be easy – the following year it might be harder, as he would be expected to audit his own performance.

He decided that the audit should encompass a future-oriented perspective, and that he would be relying fairly heavily on internally held information. There simply would not be the time to conduct any formal, primary research into the market, but he would be able to use published research fairly easily – amateur gardening is an extremely popular hobby in the UK, since most people live in houses with gardens attached, and many people also have allotments where they grow their own vegetables. Commercial growing might be harder to research, but since the company currently does not seek out commercial growers, this was less of an immediate issue.

Finding out about the competition should also be fairly straightforward, especially considering the experience Mike and Hugh had, plus some input from John Peters: there should also be some information available from Stephanie Walters' records, even though this would be seriously out of date and would need some research to update it.

The basic tasks therefore appeared to be as follows:

- Trawl through the customer records to find out who buys what, when and in what quantities.
- Interview Hugh about his approach to selling the products.
- Look at the company's advertising and compare with company records to see whether there are any identifiable outcomes.
- Find secondary sources of information.
- Identify competitors.
- Evaluate the overall business environment.
- Aim to finish the above within three weeks.

The last task was perhaps the one that would be the hardest to carry out, especially as there was no way of knowing in advance how long each of the other tasks might take, but Umar knew he had to get on with the job if the company were to hit its deadlines and if he were to be able to start on any actual marketing.

Review questions

1 *Why is technology considered as part of the external environment?*
2 *What is the main problem with carrying out a salesforce audit?*
3 *How might a company decide how often to conduct an audit?*
4 *Who should be responsible for carrying out the audit?*
5 *What are the main benefits derived from carrying out a marketing audit?*

Case study Thomson Holidays

Thomson Holidays was founded in 1965, as part of the Thomson Travel Group. The company was one of the early players in the air package holiday market. During the 1960s, air transport regulations meant that scheduled flights were too expensive for ordinary holidaymakers, but charter flights could get round the regulations provided hotel accommodation was bought at the same time.

Thomson Holidays went from strength to strength, expanding by acquisition. During the early 1970s, a damaging price war caused Thomson to restructure the company and buy out the Lunn Poly chain of travel agents, thus giving the organisation a place on the high street and effectively integrating the distribution channel.

The package holiday business has continued to be very price competitive, and in recent years there has been further pressure on the industry due to the deregulation of air transport. This has opened the way for low-cost airlines to sell flight-only deals at low prices, resulting in an explosion of independent travel to foreign destinations. Many holidaymakers now book their flights and their hotels independently, thus increasing their choice and saving money as well. Package holidays are therefore in decline, despite the increase in leisure time that most people in Europe are now enjoying.

Consumer protection legislation in the package holiday industry has also increased dramatically. In the early 1970s, the cut-throat competition resulted in several package holiday businesses going bankrupt, leaving holidaymakers stranded at their holiday destinations. A combination of legislation and industry initiatives means that people can be flown home in the event of a tour company going bankrupt, but the situation is less clear-cut if an airline disappears. This has given something of a competitive advantage to package tour operators, because their customers have a greater degree of security than would be the case if they travelled independently. Yet the greater degree of control has restricted tour operators and increased their running costs.

Despite the competition from independent travel, the greater legislative controls and the narrow profit margins in the travel business, Thomson floated on the London Stock Exchange in 1998, with a valuation of £1.7 billion. The company was subsequently acquired by another business, which is now called TUI AG, and Thomson Holidays is a division of this company to this day.

Thomson has around one-third of the UK's package holiday market and employs 3,000 people (most of whom work outside the UK). A sister company in the TUI AG group is Thomsonfly, which was formerly Britannia Airways. Thomsonfly operates partly as a low-cost airline and partly as the carrier for Thomson's package holiday customers. In effect, spare capacity on the aircraft is sold off to independent travellers, giving the company a foothold in the low-cost airline market. Thomsonfly is the UK's third largest airline.

Thomson Holidays also has its own cruise line, plus six subsidiary brands which offer specialist holidays such as skiing, lakes and mountains holidays, and self-catering holiday homes.

The company has come a long way since the early days of flying planeloads of tourists to the sun. The market has changed dramatically in that time, competition has increased, customer tastes have changed, leisure time has increased, and legislation has been introduced. Thomson has managed to ride out all these storms and remain at the forefront of the holiday and leisure industry.

Questions

1 *What external environment changes have occurred to affect Thomson?*
2 *What might be the problems facing Thomson if it were to conduct an internal audit?*
3 *How might Thomson define its competition?*
4 *What social changes should Thomson be monitoring?*
5 *What ecological factors might be of most interest to Thomson?*

References

Band, W.A. (1984): A marketing audit provides an opportunity for improvement, *Sales and Marketing Management in Canada*, March pp 24–6.

Calentone, R.J. and Cooper, R.G. (1981): New product scenarios: prospects for success. *American Journal of Marketing*, 45 (Spring) p 480.

Kotler, P. (2003): *Marketing Management*, 11th edition (Upper Saddle River, NJ: Pearson Education Inc.).

Kotler, P. and Keller, K.L. (2006): *Marketing Management*, 12th edition (Englewood Cliffs, NJ: Prentice Hall).

Pascale, R.T. (1984): Perspectives on strategy: the real story behind Honda's success. *California Management Review*, XXIV (3) pp 47–72.

Ruekart, R.W. and Walker, O.C. Jr (1987): Marketing's interaction with other functional units: a conceptual framework and empirical evidence. *Journal of Marketing*, 51 (January) pp 1–19.

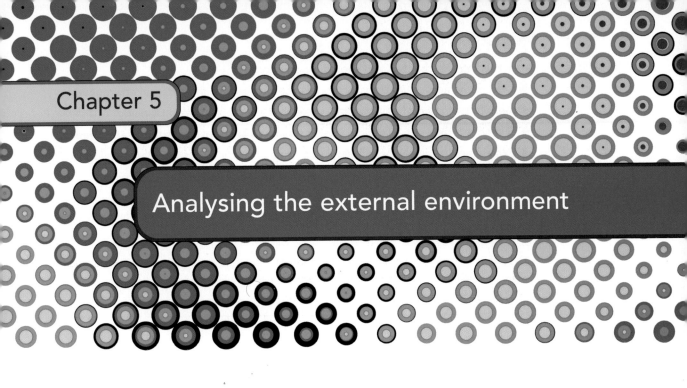

**THE
EDEN
GARDEN
TOOLS
COMPANY LTD**

Umar decided that he should start by assessing the external environment, since this would have a bearing on the company's past marketing activities and the appropriateness of its current activities. He began by identifying sources of information, both internal and external, but quickly rejected the idea of carrying out primary market research because of the cost and the time it would take. After all, the company still had only very limited money to spend – until the venture capitalists injected new funding (assuming that they did), Eden Garden Tools Company Ltd would have to cope on a shoestring.

Umar found some published research from Mintel. This comprised three reports: 'Garden Products Retailing' from 2008, 'Gardening – The Consumer' from 2004 and 'Gardening Review' from 2007. From Datamonitor he found a report from 2009 on gardening and DIY retail futures. In addition, Umar trawled the Internet for information on government legislation and court cases involving gardening supply companies.

Internal sources included sales records, levels of late payment and default on invoices, trends in sales of different items in the product portfolio, and discussions with Hugh about the general feel of the market. Umar knew that other sources might be needed – but this gave him enough sources to be able to make a start.

Objectives

After reading this chapter, you should be able to:

→ Discuss the appropriateness of models used to analyse the external environment.

→ Identify the range of external influences that affects marketing planning.

→ Distinguish between the micro (task) and macro levels of the external environment.

→ Explain how competition influences an organisation's marketing plan development.

→ Illustrate some of the main ways in which external factors affect marketing planning in practice.

→ Show the importance of marketing information systems and explain how they are developed.

Introduction

The external environment is the sum total of all the factors which affect an organisation from the outside. External factors include competitors, the government, the technological environment, the industry structure, the wider economic situation, and the ecology, amongst others. These factors comprise the broader situation in which the organisation has to function. In general, the external environment can be influenced, but typically cannot be controlled, except by the very largest organisations, and only then to a limited extent. Organisations therefore have to plan within the confines of this larger picture, taking account of these forces on the market. Analysis of the external environment is a critical aspect of the marketing audit and the marketing planning process. Information from this analysis provides, along with an understanding of internal factors, one of the main platforms from which marketing strategy and operations are determined and subsequently contribute to the development of the marketing plan.

Modelling the external environment

The macro environment includes those wider forces at play outside the market. There are several models for analysing the external environment at a macro level. Some of these are very similar, being only incremental changes to earlier models. Perhaps one of the best known is the STEP (or PEST) model, as follows:

- Socio-cultural factors.
- Technological factors.
- Economic factors.
- Political factors.

This model has been expanded to create the PESTEL (or PESTLE) model, as follows:

- Political factors.
- Economic factors.
- Socio-cultural factors.

- Technological factors.
- Ecological factors.
- Legal factors.

This variation of the standard model includes ecological factors (those relating to the natural environment) and separates legal factors from political factors. This is a logical development, since the law often operates independently of politics – although governments pass laws which affect business, it is often the case that judges make decisions in interpreting the law which affect business even more strongly. Legal factors include the civil law, which again can be interpreted in different ways by judges.

As is generally the case with models, the above do not cover all the possibilities. Neither of them mentions competitors, nor do they consider suppliers or customers. Analysis therefore needs to be undertaken at the next level, which we have already identified as the task or industry environment but is often commonly recognised as the micro environment.

An attempt to consider all of these factors is Porter's Five Forces Model (Porter 1990). The model seeks to explain how competitive power and competitive advantage (the bases for strategic advantage) come about as a result of environmental factors. The five forces are as follows:

- **The bargaining power of suppliers**. If suppliers in the industry hold much of the power, they will be able to control the competition and dictate competitive positions. This means that competitive forces will be strong unless the organisation is on very good terms with the suppliers.

- **The bargaining power of customers**. If customers hold all the cards (for example, if a large car manufacturer outsources components from small engineering companies), they will seek to play one supplier off against another, thus creating strong competitive pressures.

- **The threat of new entrants**. If new companies can enter the market easily, the competitive picture can change very rapidly indeed. If, however, there are strong barriers to entry, competition is likely to be limited and the market will be stable. The washing-powder market is an example. There are essentially only two washing powder manufacturers in the UK, Unilever and Procter & Gamble. This is because the capital cost of the equipment needed to manufacture powdered detergent is extremely high. The cost of setting up a pizza delivery service, however, is relatively low, so new entrants to the market are fairly common.

- **The threat of substitute products and services**. If close substitutes are available, the competitive position can again become intensive – pizza delivery companies compete with many other types of take-away food, for example.

- **Rivalry among current competitors**. Some industries are oligopolistic, in that companies have a tacit agreement not to encroach on each other's territories. In other industries competition is fierce, with companies battling it out for each customer. Of course, companies are not allowed to collude in order to divide up markets between them, but in industries such as the petroleum business, the major companies refrain from doing anything too dramatic to change the market, for fear of retaliation.

The danger of new organisations entering the market is limited by the following factors:

- **Economies of scale**. In the washing-powder example above, only organisations which can capture a very large chunk of the market could justify the capital costs needed to enter.

- **Product differentiation**. If products can be copied easily, competitors can enter, but if they are either too technically advanced or are protected by patents or strong branding, the potential for entering the market is reduced.

- **Capital requirements**. If the capital needed to enter the market is significant, fewer potential competitors will have the resources to enter. An example is the airline industry, which for many years was the exclusive domain of a relatively few national carriers. As second-hand aircraft became available on lease, and as the regulatory framework eased, new airlines were able to enter the market.

- **Switching costs**. If customers find it prohibitively expensive to change suppliers, competitive pressures will reduce.

- **Access to distribution channels**. If the distribution network is already tied up, new entrants will be unable to access the market. For geographically large markets such as the United States, obtaining distribution is critical. However, the Internet has made strong inroads into distribution because it bypasses wholesalers and retailers for many products.

- **Cost advantages independent of scale**. If an organisation has access to cheap raw materials, or has patent protection on a cost-effective manufacturing process, other companies will find it difficult to enter the market.

From the viewpoint of analysing the external environment, managers need to be aware of possible changes which might affect these factors. For example, if a competitor has a good way of reducing or obviating switching costs, this will change the competitive environment very quickly. Equally, if a technological breakthrough eliminates the need for a high capital requirement, this will give an advantage to entrants.

Analysis at the micro level of the external environment is often also undertaken using an alternative framework based around the 3Cs (customers, competitors and channel members) – see Table 5.1. These are the main actors at the industry level and can enable the marketing planner to form a picture of the dynamics of the market environment.

Table 5.1 The 3Cs framework

Micro environment component	Details
Customers	Information about customers in the market; market trends in demand; seasonality and cycles; composition of the market: needs and wants, benefits sought; demographics, and other segmentation characteristics.
Competitors	Identification of competitors; market presence; size, strengths and weaknesses; strategic groups; response profiles. Pattern of competition adopted: price and non-price dimensions.
Channel members	This relates to suppliers and intermediaries. Importance and reliance for procurement and service. Market coverage. Relationships and power balance.

Macro-environmental influences on planning

The political environment

Political issues often affect business. A change of government can mean a change in the taxation structure, changes in legislation affecting business, even increased help for some sectors of industry. Governments do not entirely run the country, of course; what they do is set the climate in which the country operates, and individuals make decisions within that climate.

Governments in liberal democracies operate as clearing houses for pressures. Politicians try to seek compromises between the various pressure groups that confront them, all the time being aware that the electorate has the power to remove them from office at the next election. This means that they can run the country only provided they have a broad consensus from the people they govern.

Political factors influence marketing planning because planners need to take account of changes in the political orientation of the country. Some political parties are in favour of free trade, others are protectionist; some favour the workers over the employers, others favour the employers over the workers; some favour direct taxes, others favour indirect taxes. Being aware of what might happen if there is a change of government is part of the general anticipation needed for effective planning.

TALKING POINT

If politicians do not run the country, what are they good for? We elect these people in the hope that they will make decisions and enforce laws that will, ultimately, benefit the nation as a whole, but we are now told that in fact they only set a general climate, and it is the citizens of the country who make the real decisions.

Yet perhaps that's how politics works. Negotiating to create an equality of dissatisfaction may be the only way we can get along without resorting to violence – and even then, we still have to live with an element of terrorism. How can businesses respond? By ensuring that they are part of the negotiation, of course. This then begs the question: what is to stop the largest and most powerful firms from wielding the most power in influencing government?

The political environment includes local government and intervention by regulatory bodies. In the UK, the Advertising Standards Authority tries to ensure that adverts are legal, decent, honest and truthful. It has no powers of compulsion, but is generally obeyed because advertisers and the media know that, without it, government regulations might be brought in which would inevitably be tougher and less flexible.

The economic environment

The economic environment comprises two parts: the micro-economic environment and the macro-economic environment. The micro-economic environment is concerned with demand for products and is largely about questions of supply and demand; the macro-economic environment is about demand in the economy as a whole.

The micro economy is therefore about the relationship between what customers want and what is available for them to buy. To an extent, this involves competitors: if competitors are producing close substitutes for what we make ourselves, we will quickly find that supply has increased in the market. The laws of supply and demand usually mean that we will have to lower our prices in order to compete, as Figure 5.1 shows. In the diagram, as price falls, demand will increase but supply will fall because producers find it less attractive to supply the market. If prices rise, demand will fall but supply will increase. If the market is in equilibrium, the amount supplied and the amount demanded will be the same and the market is stable with the price fixed at point A. If, however, the supply curve moves to the right, due to an increase in supply from competitors, supply curve B will require a price fall to price B for supply and demand to equalise.

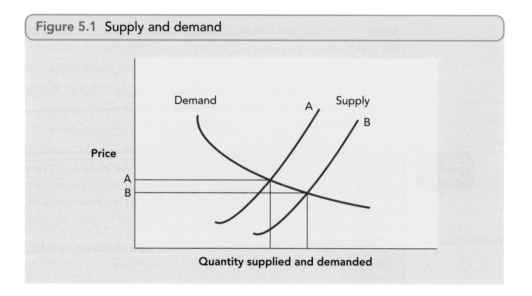

Figure 5.1 Supply and demand

This is, of course, a somewhat simplistic view. It assumes that the products concerned are all identical, for one thing, yet there are likely to be differences in design or quality, or even in the service elements supplied by the organisations concerned, that will differentiate the products in the minds of customers. However, if the substitutes are close there will certainly be some effect, if only among customers who are ready brand switchers.

Likewise, changes in demand for the product might also be assumed to have an effect on price – changes in consumer tastes, changes in the technology and changes in the wealth of customers would all have an effect in those circumstances. Reduction in price leads to a reduction in supply as suppliers decide the market is not worth the effort, so low-cost suppliers will still be able to show a profit and may even gain market share.

Another concept from microeconomics which affects the micro-environment is the concept of economic choice. Customers have only a limited amount of money to spend and therefore have to make choices in their expenditure. Cash spent on one item cannot be spent on another, in other words, so if the demand for one category of product rises, we might expect the demand for all other categories to fall. For example, if there is an increased demand for foreign holidays (perhaps because the pound strengthens against other currencies, making holidays abroad cheaper), we might expect that people will spend less on other items in order to save up for a holiday. For marketers, this is an important consideration because it means that every company is, ultimately, in competition with every other company for the consumers' hard-earned cash. It means that those companies which focus only on competitors which produce close substitutes are very likely to miss seeing a competitive threat coming from somewhere else.

Macroeconomics, meanwhile, deals with overall demand in the economy. There are many factors which contribute to determining demand in the economy – the overall supply of money, the cost of imports and exports, average earnings of people in the country, and so forth. In general, governments like to keep demand growing, because this increases wealth and improves job security as well as increasing revenue from taxation. They therefore try to control overall demand in the economy by regulating the supply of money.

This policy went badly wrong in 2008 when banks found themselves unable to lend due to a high level of bad debt. This resulted in a rapid reduction in the supply of money, which limited people's ability to spend and companies' ability to invest. The global economy quickly went into a downturn, continuing into recession, in which millions of people worldwide lost their jobs. The effect of this downturn in demand was that companies were unable to sell their products – in the case of major capital purchases such as cars, the market virtually disappeared and car manufacturers were in the lead in terms of laying workers off and cutting, or even halting, production.

Managing demand in the economy is regarded as one of government's prime responsibilities, along with defending the country and ensuring internal peace and stability. If the economy takes a major downturn, people often suffer great hardship, losing their jobs and even their homes.

The socio-cultural environment

Socio-cultural forces fall into four categories (see Figure 5.2):

1 **Demographic forces**. **Demography** is the study of the structure of populations, in terms of age, gender, wealth, educational attainment, income distribution, ethnicity, race, and so forth.
2 **Culture**. Culture is the set of shared beliefs, attitudes and behaviours of a large population group. Culture includes religion, language, customs, behaviours and beliefs.
3 **Social responsibility and ethics**. This area derives in part from culture, since it forms part of a collective belief system. It affects organisations because people within a given culture have views about how companies should behave, and in particular what constitutes ethical marketing and what does not.

4 **Consumerism**. In the past 20 or so years, power has steadily shifted away from companies and towards consumers. In part, this has been driven by the Internet, since people can shop around more easily, but it has also been driven by many other factors, including increased consumer understanding of marketing techniques, much greater availability of goods and services, and tougher competition resulting from globalisation of supplies.

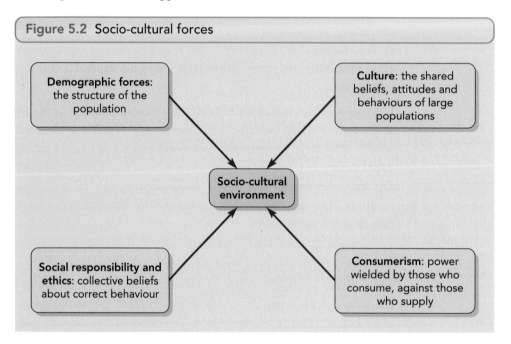

Figure 5.2 Socio-cultural forces

Demography is affected by immigration and emigration, by shifts in the wealth and income distribution among the population, and by changes in the birth and death rates. Some of these shifts are well known: the dramatic increase in immigration into Britain from Eastern Europe has resulted in many new businesses springing up to serve the needs of Poles, Czechs, Hungarians and Slovaks. Over time, some of these migrants are likely to return home, but many will stay, adding to the cultural mix of the UK.

Another well-publicised demographic change is the shift in age distribution in Western Europe caused by increased longevity and a reduced birth rate. At the time of writing the birth rate is less than the death rate, so the population would be shrinking if it were not for immigration from outside Europe. In some countries the situation is near crisis point, with countries such as Spain actively encouraging immigration from Latin America. A falling population means shrinking domestic markets for all goods, which in turn means that businesses will have to contract unless they can find new export markets. At the same time, the increasing age of the population means there are fewer people of working age, trying to support an increasing population of pensioners. In the UK, this has resulted in the government seeking to raise the retirement age.

In 2002 the European Union published 'The Cruijsen Report', an influential report on the demographic changes expected within the 15 member states (by 2009 there were 25 members). With substantial immigration, virtually no emigration and a reduced birth rate the member states were experiencing a drop in the under-25 age group, and increases in both the working population (due to immigration) and the elderly population

(Cruijsen et al. 2002). Entry of the Eastern European states changed the situation in the short term, since these countries have lower life expectancies. However, these countries have themselves experienced lower birth rates since 1990 (when communism collapsed in Eastern Europe), probably due to economic dislocation and worsening health care.

The report goes on to say that there would be the following demographic changes in the 15 states as a result of allowing the 10 new states to join:

1 Population decline would occur several years sooner.
2 Population ageing would be slightly suppressed.
3 Population dejuvenation (reduction in the proportion of under-25s) would become stronger in future decades.
4 The expected decline in the working population would be delayed.

So far, these predictions have been borne out, but since the report attempted to predict changes over a 50-year period it is still too early to tell whether the authors will be vindicated. Technological changes in the care of the elderly could well mean that the calculations are severely affected, since the authors assume that people are unlikely to live much beyond 100 years of age.

For marketers, this shift in the age structure of the population means new opportunities. Retired people have greater leisure time, and since many elderly people retire on substantial occupational pensions, they have money to spend on enjoying themselves. On the other hand, age does bring more physical problems: sales of hearing aids, spectacles, walking frames, powered wheelchairs, and so forth are likely to increase, even though improvements in nutrition and health care mean that 70 year olds in the 21st century are as fit as 50 year olds were in the 1960s.

Income and wealth distribution vary from country to country. For example, there are more millionaires in India than there are in the UK, even though the average wealth per head of the population is much lower. This is due to greater wealth concentration, and of course a bigger population. Wealth concentration also changes over time – in the UK the wealth is much more evenly distributed than it was even 50 years ago. This has meant that people in lower income brackets can easily afford products that would have been out of their reach in the 1960s: cars, foreign holidays, domestic equipment such as dishwashers and even washing machines, entertainment systems, and so forth would not have been affordable for the average person in 1960.

Culture is the set of shared beliefs and behaviours that characterises a group of people. Almost all human behaviour is learned, and the majority of it is culturally based because we need to fit in with the people around us. Polite behaviour differs from one culture to the next, simply because of differences in the learning process. For example, time sense differs between agrarian societies and industrial ones: in agrarian societies, each day is the same as the one before it and the one after it, so there is a belief that it does not matter much if tasks are not completed in one day, since the day will be given back again in the morning. In industrial societies, each day is unique, and once it has gone it can never be repeated. This accounts for the sometimes frustrating 'mañana' attitude prevalent in rural areas worldwide, as well as for the stressful 'no time to waste' attitude prevalent in urban areas.

Culture is extremely important to marketers in the international context because it dictates consumption patterns. What people wear, eat, drink and do for entertainment are all culturally based. In some countries (notably Turkey and the United States) even the poorest people eat out in restaurants on a regular basis, usually daily. In the UK, this is less so because restaurants are much more expensive, but people frequently have cooked food delivered to their houses in a way that would seem bizarre to a French person.

Consumerism has grown rapidly over the past 20 or so years, with the advent of the Internet. Consumerism has its roots in the 1960s, when campaigners began to question the quality and safety of products. Ralph Nader's book, *Unsafe At Any Speed*, for instance, publicised the dangerous nature of the design of some cars, in particular the Chevrolet Corvair. By the 1990s the Internet was giving consumers a global voice, and shadow websites (sites which exist to carry complaints about companies) now appear close to most corporate websites. Consumers expect to have the power in the relationship between themselves and suppliers, and in many cases they exercise the power almost without restraint, backed by consumerist legislation and regulatory bodies.

The technological environment

Technologies change regularly. In recent years the emphasis has been very much on electronics and communications technology, with the rise in the use of computers, mobile telephones and fibre-optic communication systems leading to a revolution in the way information is stored and exchanged. However, technology also includes breakthroughs in other areas of engineering. For example, car manufacture was revolutionised by Toyota's invention of interchangeable stamp-mill technology, enabling the company to re-tool a car factory within hours instead of the months it was taking its American competitors.

The technological environment can change rapidly if there is a major scientific breakthrough. Even 15 years ago the Internet was a minor consideration in most marketers' thinking; now it is absolutely central to marketing communications.

The technological environment is not limited to immediate competitors within the same industry, either. Technological change can render whole industries obsolete, as the Internet threatens to do to postal services and as the car did to horse-drawn transport.

The ecological environment

In the past 20 years or so, the ecological environment has come to the forefront of people's thinking. Although there is considerable debate about the best course of action to take to preserve the natural world and protect the physical environment, there is little doubt that we cannot continue to use up the planet's natural resources indefinitely.

Concerns about the **ecology** spill over into political and socio-cultural areas because people and their governments have begun to take action against corporations which are seen to be damaging the environment excessively. Legislation has been introduced in many areas to reduce industry's impact on the natural world, and pressure groups have sprung up to protest about what is seen as corporate irresponsibility. Marketers cannot ignore these pressures.

The sources of environmentalist pressure are as follows (see Figure 5.3):

1 **Customers**. Many customers in developed countries use some environmentalist criteria in at least some of their decision making. Consumers may show concern about the energy efficiency of the products they buy and often are concerned about the industrial processes used in manufacture.

2 **Green pressure groups**. Pressure groups conduct campaigns to influence planning, both public and corporate, and to publicise their cause. Green pressure groups such as Friends of the Earth and Greenpeace lobby government for changes in legislation and apply pressure to companies (mainly through PR stunts and protests) to influence their decision making. Sometimes direct action is taken – hammering steel spikes into trees to damage chainsaws, or sailing across the bows of ships at sea, for example.

3 **Employees**. Sometimes employees become 'whistleblowers', taking their environmental concerns to the news media. In other cases employees are in a position to act directly, in their work as engineers or researchers, to influence policy towards more environment-friendly alternatives.

4 **Legislation**. Politicians respond to pressure groups, and in some countries (notably the Netherlands and Germany) ecological political parties are influential in their own right. In some cases, politicians are lobbied by the industries themselves: organisations which want to be eco-friendly sometimes like to ensure that other organisations have to compete on an equal footing.

5 **Media**. The news media are often interested in stories about species threatened with extinction, or organisations which intend to carry out environmentally damaging projects. In 2008, the news that a colony of 2,000 orang-utans had been found in a remote part of Indonesia made headlines worldwide; 20 years ago this would not have rated a mention in the news.

6 **Ethical investors**. Many private investors like to be reassured that their savings are not being invested in environmentally damaging projects. Therefore, many banks and trust funds now offer ethical investment packages for ecologically aware clients.

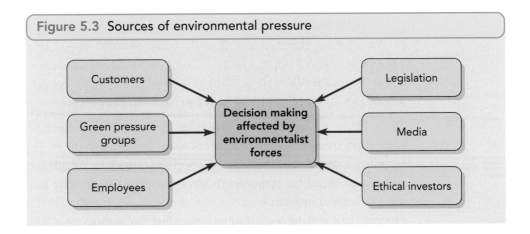

Figure 5.3 **Sources of environmental pressure**

Companies need to consider ecological issues when developing products, so monitoring the climate of opinion about the environment is as important as monitoring any other aspect. The difficulty for marketers is that product planning often takes place months or years ahead of launch, so there is a need to anticipate swings in public opinion. Also, ecological awareness is patchy and disjointed – people are concerned, but opinion on what is and is not environmentally friendly is divided. For example, older cars are often less fuel efficient than newer ones, but scrapping an old car and making a new one is clearly wasteful.

TALKING POINT

Why should companies have to take individual action to be environmentally friendly when consumers clearly don't care? Litter in the streets, people using their cars to travel when walking or cycling would be perfectly feasible, people burning their rubbish or dumping it in beauty spots, and even throwing away perfectly good products simply because they have grown tired of them, all show that most people actually don't care.

How many of us actually avoid buying over-packaged products? How many of us buy disposable products rather than ones which can be used over and over again? How many of us sell our unwanted goods rather than simply dumping them?

Clearly it is more profitable for a company to ignore environmental issues – after all, company directors have a legal responsibility to shareholders to look after their interests. Unless there is an equal liability to look after the environment, why should boards of directors do anything?

The legal environment

The legal environment is created in two ways: first, through legislation passed by governments (and therefore part of the political environment) and second, through the interpretation of legislation by judges, also known as case law.

Legislation is, in general, a somewhat crude tool. No parliamentary body can anticipate all the possible effects of a new piece of legislation, so courts have to decide how the legislation applies in actual cases. Sometimes judges can rely on precedent (previous decisions by other judges) but in many cases they have to interpret the actual circumstances in the case before them.

Once a judge has made a decision in a specific case, it becomes part of precedent: other judges are then expected to follow the same decision in similar cases, although of course it is always open to a judge to interpret the precedent as not applying. Lawyers will argue for specific precedents to be followed, but since there are so many it is quite possible for a judge to be faced with two conflicting precedents.

The problem for marketers in analysing the legal environment is that decisions are being made every day, and they are not always reported in the trade press. Some industry journals do monitor the courts for decisions which might affect companies, but it is still often difficult for managers to know what the law actually is on a given issue. At the same time, ignorance of the law is not an excuse for breaking it – we are all expected to know the legal position regarding any actions we might take.

The law divides into criminal law and civil law. Criminal law is concerned with activities which are damaging to the common good and which are punishable by fines or imprisonment; civil law is concerned with making reparations to the injured party. Taking money from someone for a product which does not exist would come under the criminal law (fraud), but selling someone a product which is faulty would come under the civil law. In most cases, civil law is likely to cause the most problems, since people can sue for damages; provided one runs one's business honestly, the criminal law is unlikely to come into play.

Competitor analysis

As part of any environmental analysis it is critical to have a detailed understanding of the competition that the organisation faces in the markets that it operates in and those that it is planning to enter in the future. It also involves assessing the level of competition and whether competition is direct in terms of offering the same or similar products, or indirect where there is competition for the same 'share of the wallet' in a different market.

A key element of any marketing strategy will be the relationship that the business has with its competitors and the way that it positions itself against competitors in the market. In particular it is essential to identify who the competitors are, and what strengths and weaknesses they have, their strategic positioning and source of competitive advantage, and the way that they are likely to respond to a competitive move by the organisation. The competitive response profile is also a major factor in any analysis. This latter aspect of competitor evaluation requires an understanding of how they are likely to respond tactically and strategically when the organisation undertakes a marketing initiative such as launching a new product, reducing its prices, or embarking on a sales promotion campaign. Some competitors will respond slowly, or not respond at all (**laid-back competitors**), whereas others may respond in an aggressive manner in terms of speed and weight of response (**tiger competitors**). This can be viewed as a continuum based on speed and level of response, and sometimes may simply classify competitors as unpredictable (**stochastic competitors**), therefore making planning for their response much more difficult to achieve.

A further level of analysis can be undertaken in terms of strategic groups or competitive marketing strategy types. This classifies all the competing businesses in the industry as a whole according to the emphasis that they place on particular marketing strategies, clustering together different types based on the position that they take in the market. Once key factors have been identified to distinguish one type from another, the competitors are brought together into strategic groups and usually mapped, enabling possible gaps in the market, and therefore exploitable sources of competitive advantage, to be identified. A number of variables have been used to develop strategy group types, including size, market share, geographic market coverage, product range, price positioning and branding. Such information can be of tremendous help to marketing planners when making decisions relating to where they are going to position the organisation in the market or making specific decisions about strategy.

Researching the marketing environment

A **marketing information system** consists of four elements:

1 Internal continuous data.

2 Internal **ad-hoc data**.

3 **Environmental scanning**.

4 Market research.

Internal continuous data is collected through customer feedback (both positive and negative), sales records, individual performance records for salespeople, profitability calculations, and so forth. This information may provide an advance warning of an environmental shift – for example, a drop in sales in a particular market may be as a result of a competitor entering the market, or may indicate a change in consumer tastes. In many organisations, managers will regularly calculate the profitability of a specific product, but it is relatively rare for organisations to calculate the profitability of a market segment, even though this is probably a more logical approach for a marketer.

Internal ad-hoc data is information collected for a limited period to check on a specific issue. For example, a new product launch might necessitate collecting data on how the sales of the product are affecting other products in the range, or how they are impinging on competitors. This might be linked to an external scan on what competitors are doing to retaliate.

Environmental scanning should be a large part of any marketing information system. Ideally, it should be carried out in a formal way, by checking the national press, the business press, the trade journals, and business programmes on TV. There are also websites which provide valuable information about current business issues; most of these are run by newspapers or other news agencies and are therefore fairly reliable. Environmental scanning can also sometimes be bought in – there are commercial research organisations (and even trade associations) which offer data on how the market as a whole is performing. In many cases organisations are prepared to provide information on their own marketing successes or failures in exchange for corresponding information about competitors.

One of the drawbacks of environmental scanning is that it can be time consuming. It is difficult for a junior member of staff to recognise what might or might not be important, and the same is true for subscriptions to cuttings agencies (organisations which will send any newspaper cuttings about you or your competitors, or indeed anything else you brief them to send).

Market research about the environment might be carried out in the following ways, depending on the specific problem facing the organisation:

1 **Secondary, or desk, research.** This would be appropriate as a starting point for assessing the environment for a new market (e.g. a foreign country).

2 **Primary research.** This is original research carried out to answer a specific problem, for example running a focus group to find out people's attitudes to a new product line. Again, this is likely to be necessary when entering a foreign market because it will assess cultural issues.

3 **Environmental scanning**. This is the process of monitoring the key issues in the environment on a continuous basis.

Secondary research is carried out by using already published data. It is always cheaper than primary research, sometimes provides all the answers, and even if there are still gaps in what needs to be known, secondary research will at least cut down on the amount of primary research needed. It is therefore always the starting point in any research programme. Sources of secondary data include government publications, country guides, commercial market research such as that published by Mintel and Keynote, and journals (including newspapers – for example, the *Financial Times* frequently publishes detailed guides to doing business in specific countries or regions). Research on the Internet is extremely common nowadays, of course, but is not necessarily reliable – there are few, if any, controls on what can be published on the Internet, so people are quite capable of putting false information on there as a way of furthering their own agendas.

Secondary research is useful in checking the legal, economic and political environments in foreign markets, and can also be helpful in checking the technological environment. Secondary research will usually provide good information on a country's demographics, but it tends to be less reliable on cultural and social issues – for those, primary research is almost always necessary.

Primary research is designed to answer specific questions, usually those which the secondary research has left unanswered. Good primary research can help organisations avoid basic errors in planning – for example, using a brand name which is inappropriate for the country being targeted. Many cultural gaffes could have been avoided simply by checking with local people – Euro Disney's disastrous start in Paris which eventually resulted in the theme park rebranding itself, and McDonald's failure to establish itself in Fiji, to name but two.

It is beyond the scope of this book to go into a detailed description of research methods, but primary research can be carried out either qualitatively or quantitatively. Quantitative research (typified by surveys) is good for telling us what, when, where and how things happen. Qualitative research (typified by interviews and focus groups) is good for telling us why things happen. In recent years, qualitative research has come to the forefront much more, partly because so much quantitative data is easily obtained through secondary research, and partly because surveys have been growing much harder to administer, as people refuse to participate. It has also been found that many people deliberately give false information on surveys, to the extent that (for example) exit polls have failed to predict the outcomes of the last four general elections in the UK.

Whatever the drawbacks of research systems and techniques, the fact remains that information is extremely important for decision making. Without a clear idea of the environment in which the company operates, there is little chance of making correct decisions: like driving a car in fog, correct business decisions cannot be made without some idea of what lies ahead.

Summary

Assessing the external environment means finding out about it and modelling it so that different decisions can be judged ahead of their implementation. Failure to analyse the environment correctly will inevitably lead to errors of judgement; equally, creating or using the wrong model will lead to errors.

The key points from this chapter are as follows:

→ Analysing the environment requires managers to apply the appropriate model. However, all models are flawed since they are abstracts of the real world.

→ The political orientation of the country affects planning, even if legislation does not.

→ Consumerism has become a major force – consumers wield a great deal of power, and are educated enough to know how to use it.

→ Environmentalism is widespread and is not confined to pressure groups: customers, legislators, employees, the media and ethical investors all have some input.

→ Analysis of competitors and other marketing channel members is a key dimension of the marketing audit and marketing planning.

→ Marketing information systems provide a continuous flow of information on which to base decisions, provided they are designed correctly.

THE
**EDEN
GARDEN
TOOLS**
COMPANY LTD

Altogether Umar spent just over £7,000 on the published reports, which was a considerable sum from the budget but he got most of the information he needed. He was able to fill in the gaps from the Internet and from the internal sources.

At the end of the first week he was able to answer many of the questions embodied in the external audit. The economic–demographic part of the audit was straightforward enough – the newspapers provided plenty of answers. Credit availability was still limited, unemployment still rising, the population would continue to age (a good outcome for Eden Garden Tools, given that older people have more time for gardening and more need for tools for the infirm).

The technological audit was also relatively straightforward, since Eden Garden Tools was in fact driving the market to some extent, as the most innovative company in the industry. However, new technologies in production and process might come along. Umar's discussions with Mike on the technological aspects indicated that the tree-pruning saw would need some fairly innovative technology, since the battery life would need to be long enough for the saw to be used for most of an eight-hour working day.

No particular legal changes came to light, but the new pruning saw would certainly have to meet health and safety regulations. Ecological concerns would probably be helpful for Eden Garden Tools, given the business it is in.

Review questions

1 *Why does choosing the right model affect analysis of the external environment?*

2 *How might a company counteract a shadow website?*

3 *How should a company monitor changes in the law relevant to its own operations?*

4 *What are the key factors in developing a marketing information system?*

5 *How might the political orientation of the country affect planning?*

 ## Case study BAE Systems

BAE Systems is a defence manufacturing company based in the UK. It is the third largest defence contractor in the world, and can trace its history back to 1560 and the Royal Gunpowder Factory in Waltham, Essex – in the 16th century, making gunpowder was about as high-tech as it got. Over the ensuing centuries, various other companies were brought into the fold: ship-builders such as Yarrow, gun manufacturers such as Bofors, aircraft manufacturers such as Vickers (later the British Aircraft Corporation), and electronics companies such as Marconi. The complex series of mergers, demergers, nationalisations and privatisations which led to the creation of the modern BAE Systems is often difficult to follow: successive governments in the UK have decided that important defence industries should be owned nationally, or alternatively have decided that they should be free to pursue commercial objectives.

Few companies are involved in defence work exclusively for the national government; most also make products for civilian use, and many also manufacture for overseas governments. This can cause problems: apart from the obvious fact that no government wants its enemies to be as well equipped as its own armed forces, and will therefore seek to restrict exports of some items, peace activists see the international arms trade as being inherently wrong and will seek to have it stopped. Meanwhile, a company which has managed to develop a powerful new weapon will naturally want to sell it as widely as possible in order to obtain **economies of scale**.

From the government viewpoint, supplying foreign powers is a double-edged sword. On the one hand, having overseas soldiers using British-made weapons against British armed forces is undoubtedly a political hot potato, raising all kinds of moral issues; on the other hand, a country which has entirely British-made armaments is unlikely to start a war with Britain since this would inevitably lead to problems in obtaining ammunition, spares and servicing. Modern weaponry is extremely complex, and in some cases almost fragile: soldiers need to be highly trained to use it and such training is best provided by the manufacturer.

According to BAE Systems, the defence industry is driven by customer demand for greater capability for less money (not unlike most other industries). In the defence industry, this means more complex systems because a reliance on electronics, automation and communications technology improves the capability of the weaponry, but at the same time it tends to increase the training and servicing requirements. Also, modern armies need weaponry to be compatible – in the past, this may have meant only that ammunition should be standardised at least in terms of calibre, but nowadays it means that communications, radar and guidance systems should also be compatible. For example, ground forces need to be able to pass information to aircraft, so radio and computer systems must be compatible.

At the same time, weaponry needs to be upgradeable. This means that buyers will be compelled to enter into a long-term relationship with BAE in order to obtain the latest upgrades, which in turn militates against conducting any military adventure which might jeopardise relations with the UK.

BAE's code of conduct is a substantial document, covering all the ethical issues any employee might encounter, from workplace bullying through to breaches of security – these can happen accidentally or deliberately, and are controlled by the criminal law. For example, an engineer might correspond by e-mail with a customer's engineering department in another country about projects they are both working on. This could well break the law, since sensitive information might be passed without either engineer realising that they are doing anything wrong: e-mail communication is not secure.

Clearly, business practice differs in other countries. Bribes might be offered in some countries, or special rules might apply to the import and export of armaments. BAE has been accused of bribing foreign government officials in order to make sales, but since every defence manufacturer in the world has had such accusations levelled at it, the company is probably not especially worried.

BAE Systems operates in a complex environment, producing complex products. Even though people campaign for peace, and almost all of us would rather live in a world without war, BAE has a bright future. Few companies in the defence business have the wide range of products BAE can offer, which means that few have the opportunity or capability to provide fully integrated defence systems.

Questions

1 *What would be the result of a PESTEL analysis for BAE? What factors would be included?*

2 *How might political orientation affect BAE?*

3 *What types of information should BAE collect via a marketing information system?*

4 *How does environmentalism affect BAE?*

5 *What ethical issues affect BAE and how can the company address them?*

References

Cruijsen, H., Eding, H. and Gjatelma, T. (2002): Demographic consequences of enlargement of the European Union with the 12 candidate countries. Statistics Netherlands, Division of Social and Spatial Statistics, Project Group European Demography.

Nader, R. (1965): *Unsafe At Any Speed* (New York: Grossman Publishers).

Porter, M.E. (1990): How competitive forces shape strategy. *Harvard Business Review*, 57 (2) pp 137–45.

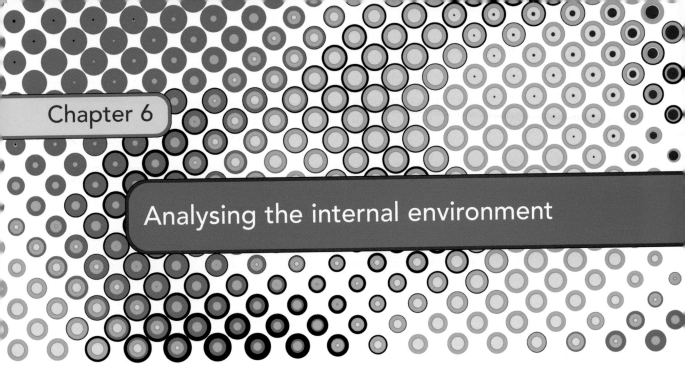

Chapter 6

Analysing the internal environment

THE EDEN GARDEN TOOLS COMPANY LTD

Having completed his assessment of the external environment, Umar Sayeed turned to the internal environment. This, he knew, would be the crucial one: the company was in for a period of rapid change, with new products and new disciplines coming to the forefront. If everything went well, the company could expect to see some fairly rapid organic growth in the future, which would mean new roles and responsibilities for existing staff as well as hiring new staff.

Umar knew that he would have to consider the internal marketing of the firm and the resources available, as well as looking at the product portfolio and potential life cycle of products. This would involve using internal sales records, interviews with staff, and discussions with Mike about the technical aspects of the products.

Objectives   After reading this chapter, you should be able to:

→ Explain the role of organisational culture.

→ Describe ways of managing change.

→ Explain how information systems can be constructed.

→ Show how information systems can be used to encourage customer loyalty.

→ Describe ways of monitoring and auditing strategy.

Introduction

The internal environment comprises those factors which make up the organisation: its strategy, its culture, its structure, its management style and its information systems, amongst other things. The internal environment is what makes the organisation what it is, and it derives from the people who are its members, and other characteristics that it has. In particular its resources, competencies and capabilities need to be evaluated, especially in terms of how the organisation is able to respond to changes in the environment.

Undertaking internal analysis

The purpose of an internal audit is much the same as that of a financial audit: it provides a 'snapshot' of the current state of affairs within the organisation. In some ways, the internal audit is the easiest to conduct because all the information is (or should be) readily available from staff working in the organisation. The problem is that staff will often feel that the audit is intrusive, or is perhaps an attempt on the part of management to find fault with their work. In order to reduce the risk of this happening, the following policies might be adopted:

1 Avoid using anything uncovered in the audit as a means to criticise staff.

2 Ensure that the audit process is transparent, in other words make it clear exactly what the information is to be used for, and make it available to staff whenever possible.

3 If possible, use outside consultants to carry out the audit. This will reduce the tendency for people to give politically motivated responses.

Since the audit relies heavily on honesty and openness, it could be distorted by wishful thinking, or even by deliberate attempts to pervert the outcome by individuals with a political agenda. This is less likely to happen if the process is seen as supportive rather than punitive. Outside consultants are extremely useful in carrying out audits – because they have no political ambitions within the organisation, they are seen as impartial, and they are often able to help by asking the right questions. A good consultant (in this context) is not someone who gives answers but rather one who asks the right questions and causes the directors and managers of the organisation to examine what they are doing in an objective manner.

Assessing the organisation's strategic position

Evaluating where an organisation is in terms of its strategic situation begins with looking at the mission statement. The issue here is whether the mission is clearly stated and whether it is attainable. The mission must also have a clear focus: some mission statements contain little more than platitudes, which are unhelpful when it comes to the day-to-day running of the organisation.

The marketing strategy should have clear objectives and goals. This means that the corporate and marketing objectives should be clearly stated, and the objectives should be appropriate in terms of meeting overall corporate objectives. The theory behind management by objectives is that only that which is measured will be achieved. This means that a failure to set objectives will lead to a failure to achieve anything worthwhile.

Assessing the strategic situation should examine the core marketing strategy, the budgeting of resources and the allocation of resources. Budgeting resources is possibly one of the most contentious areas for the organisation, since it is the area where each manager will want to maximise his or her budget in order to take advantage of the resources available for the department's tasks.

Carrying out an internal strategic audit is usually a matter for the directors of the company or the senior marketing managers. In some cases, 'think tanks' of individuals from different departments are used as a task force to examine the organisation's objectives and strategy. This has the advantage of keeping ownership of the process within the organisation, while maintaining some objectivity. If undertaken in this way, the audit is less likely to be regarded as the domain of any one department.

In whichever way it is accomplished, the strategy evaluation should provide answers to the following questions:

1 Are the objectives appropriate?
2 Are the major policies and plans appropriate?
3 Do the results obtained so far confirm the critical assumptions on which the strategy has been based?

The issues which complicate strategic assessment surround the uniqueness of each strategy (in other words, comparisons are difficult), the evaluation of goals and objectives (which are easier to set and even achieve than they are to evaluate), and the perceived threat to managers inherent in any kind of review of their activities.

It is impossible to say that a particular strategy is absolutely correct: circumstances change too often to allow for this. However, it is possible to say that a strategy is flawed. For a strategy to be considered viable, it must fit within the criteria shown in Table 6.1.

Strategy evaluation is not a purely intellectual task – the issues are too important and there are likely to be too many political ramifications involved for the evaluation to take place in an 'ivory tower'. This means that auditing the strategy is likely to be an organisational process, probably undertaken as part of the normal planning, reporting, control and reward systems of the organisation.

Table 6.1 Criteria for successful strategy

Criterion	Explanation and examples
Consistency	Many strategies have not been specifically formulated, but have simply grown up as a result of adoption of a set of tactical actions. This means that 'the way we do things round here' can achieve the status of a strategy without ever having been examined. Indicators that the strategy is inconsistent are first, problems in coordination and planning, especially if these are issue-based rather than staff-based; second, if success for one department is interpreted as failure for another; and third, if operating problems are being constantly referred to senior managers for resolution. All these difficulties indicate that the strategy is not performing its coordinating function effectively.
Consonance	The business must match and be adapted to its environment and at the same time compete with other organisations which are trying to match to the environment. The first aspect of strategy therefore deals with the basic mission of the business, the second aspect deals with the organisation's special competitive position or 'edge'. The difficulty in evaluating consonance is that most of the threats to a business come from outside and threaten the entire industry, whereas managements are more usually preoccupied with their competitive position relative to other organisations within the industry. The key to evaluating consonance is to understand the underlying reasons for the organisation's (and the industry's) existence. Understanding the basic social and economic reasons for the organisation's existence enables managers to decide which types of change are most crucial.
Advantage	Generic strategy focuses on the common missions of an industry. Competitive strategy focuses on the differences between organisations rather than their similarities. For example, supermarkets have almost entirely replaced traditional grocery shops where assistants would weigh out goods and collect goods from the stock room for customers. As a generic strategy, the supermarket concept has been wildly successful, but an individual organisation in the supermarket business needs to go further than this and differentiate itself from other supermarkets if it is to compete successfully. The three main forms of competitive advantage are superior resources, superior skills and superior position.
Feasibility	Financial resources are usually the easiest to quantify, and in some ways are also the easiest to control, but feasibility of strategies also depends on human resources and physical resources. To assess feasibility, the organisation needs to be assured that first it has the necessary problem-solving and special competencies for the strategy, second it has sufficient coordinative and integrative skill, and third the strategy can challenge and motivate key personnel and is acceptable to them.

Organisational structures and systems

Organisations have both a formal and an informal structure, each of which influences its performance. The formal structure is the one which appears on organisation charts. In the case of a hierarchical, bureaucratic structure there will be fixed lines of communications and clear distinctions regarding roles, responsibilities and reporting. The informal structure does not exist as an organisational chart because it comprises myriad personal relationships which build up over time as people work in close proximity with each other.

Informal structures

An organisational chart might make it perfectly clear that the correct way to obtain information on the company's sales figures is to send a memo to the sales manager; in practice, it might be quicker and easier for all concerned to talk to the sales manager's secretary or personal assistant. The informal structure is important because it is the repository of the corporate culture – the set of beliefs and attitudes which grow up around the organisation. This culture is reinforced by conversations at the photocopier, or over coffee in the canteen, or at people's homes when they invite work colleagues round for dinner.

TALKING POINT

Informal communications at the photocopier or the coffee machine seem to be very effective in cementing the corporate culture. They also seem to be pretty good for passing on hard information – and, of course, unfounded rumours and gossip.

So if the informal system is so effective, why do we bother having a formal system? Everyone knows that most e-mails are written only in order to protect the rear end of the person writing the e-mail – the real work gets done on the golf course anyway. Maybe the formal structure gives us a way of recording and validating what was said. But equally, it may be simply a way of controlling the flow of information in a way that suits senior management. Can we stop the gossip and rumour and just keep the true information? Can we perhaps encourage staff to record their informal talks? If not, maybe we should look at banning such conversations altogether?

Some managers (particularly those that affirm the scientific management school of thought) have attempted to stamp out the informal structure. Some organisations are trying to restrict the use of office e-mail to prevent personal use of the system for exchanging jokes, arranging private parties, or simply chatting to friends at work and elsewhere. This type of restriction is likely to prove counter-productive, since staff will always want to interact with colleagues on a personal level – using the local network for this is probably a time saver over the traditional photocopier or coffee-machine meetings. Wiser managements will try to incorporate the informal structure into the organisation by encouraging interaction between staff members. Organised staff social events, staff social clubs, and a laissez-faire attitude towards workplace gossip help to smooth communications and improve staff loyalty – acting as a potential platform for internal marketing initiatives.

Formal structures

Organisations all differ in their structures, but there are two main types of structure which represent the extremes of the continuum. The first is the hierarchical structure, also known as the mechanistic or bureaucratic structure. This is shown in Figure 6.1.

Wholly hierarchical organisations are somewhat rare nowadays and are usually confined to government departments and traditional industries that are not subject to significant change. The characteristics of a hierarchical organisation are as follows:

1 Members are appointed by reason of their formal qualifications and experience.
2 Communication is assumed to travel up the hierarchy and instructions come down.

Figure 6.1 Example of a hierarchical structure

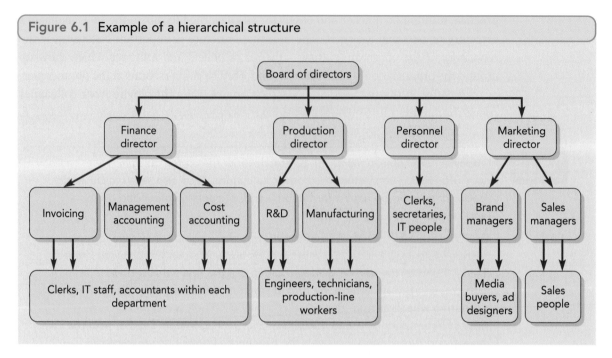

3 The people at the top of the hierarchy are assumed to have full knowledge of everything that happens further down.

4 Roles within the organisation are clearly defined and are generally fixed unless the individual is promoted.

5 Changes in the organisation are made through consultation and on instructions from the top.

Hierarchical organisations are extremely efficient, provided the industry or the environment is slow to change. The efficiency comes from division of labour and specialisation: each individual becomes expert at his or her own part of the job. Little time is wasted on communication because the channels are clearly defined; communication is also smooth, provided nothing unusual happens. The problem with hierarchies is that they tend to be very slow to adapt to changing circumstances – because each person's job is strictly defined, there is resentment at any attempt to change. Communication is slow because it has to go up through the layers of the hierarchy (presumably being distorted at each stage) and then instructions have to come back down from above to the levels below.

At the other extreme is the organismic organisation, as shown in Figure 6.2.

In a fully organismic organisation, communication flows between all the members in a completely open way. No one member is in overall charge – the task of leadership will change according to the task faced by the organisation. This type of structure is again rare in its pure form, but might be typical of some consultancy organisations, research groups, or small professional partnerships.

In an organismic organisation, the formal qualifications of members are not necessarily the only aspect of the person that is taken into account. Because such organisations operate best in rapidly changing environments, all the skills and experience of the members are likely to be brought into play at one time or another.

Figure 6.2 Example of an organismic organisation

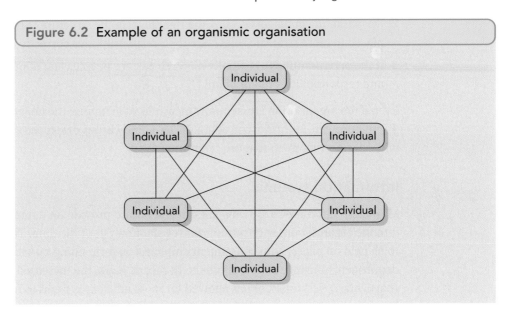

In practice, most organisations will occupy a position on a continuum somewhere between the hierarchical and the organismic. In the future it seems likely that organismic structures will be better able to survive, due to the need to adapt swiftly to changes.

Organisational systems

The functional efficiency of an organisation depends on its communication systems, its product management systems and its training systems.

Communication systems which follow a formal, hierarchical approach tend to be slow and can suffer from distortion. Yet such systems tend to minimise the time spent in communicating and maximise the time spent on tasks. The current trend in communication is to use electronic methods, in particular e-mail, to speed up communication and make all the members of an organisation accessible to each other. The shortcoming of e-mail is that it is too easy to send messages to a global address list: there is a proliferation of messages, which means that members of the organisation often spend inordinate amounts of time ploughing through e-mails that are of little or no relevance to their particular duties. Inevitably this distracts them from carrying out the tasks in hand. Moreover, those who are technophobic, or computer illiterate, or even slow typists will find the system virtually unworkable and will retaliate by ignoring it or by using the telephone instead.

If the formal communication system does not meet the needs of the employees, they will fall back on the informal system, which will result in the most useful organisational business being conducted over the photocopier or coffee machine.

For the purposes of assessing the appropriateness of the organisation of marketing, managers will need to address the following questions:

1 Is the current structural type correct for the organisation's environment and objectives? Should it be more hierarchical or more organismic?

2 Do marketing managers occupy the right level in the structure? Should marketers be placed in more strategic roles? Are their responsibilities correctly allocated?

3 If the organisation is essentially hierarchical, are people clear about what their roles and responsibilities might entail?

Even if the organisation is essentially hierarchical in nature, the negative effects of such a structure can be offset considerably by empowering employees to take decisions without referring them to more senior managers.

Information systems

Marketing information systems are often set up to provide an automatic flow of data into the organisation, with systems for regular analysis of the data. These systems used to be held on paper, with consequent emphasis on form filling by salespeople, logistics departments, finance staff and others. In recent years, the increased use of computers (particularly desktop PCs) has allowed far more efficient systems to be put in place and has reduced the amount of time spent on gathering information (Proctor 2000). There is always a trade-off involved between the value of information and the cost in time, effort and money of obtaining it; by reducing the cost element, computers have increased the possibilities for obtaining useful data and converting it into useable information. Computer-based systems such as these are called **decision support systems** – an example is the electronic point-of-sale (EPOS) systems used by large retailers. These record every purchase made in the store so that the retailer can reorder stock in the correct amounts, can automatically analyse trends and can even (with the use of loyalty cards) track an individual customer's purchases over a period of time (Evans 1994).

Decision support systems need to be user friendly so that managers without training in data analysis can use them. This is the main reason for their popularity over paper-based information systems (Sprague and Watson 1986; Bessen 1994). For example, the ways in which sales management information systems help sales managers are shown in Table 6.2.

As with any other management tool, there are problems attached to the use of sales management information systems. First, there is the problem of information overload –

Table 6.2 Sales management information systems

Functional area	Explanation
Sales reporting and analysis	Collecting and analysing call reports, levels of actual sales compared with budgeted sales, analysis of sales by market segment, and profit dimensions of sales performances. These figures can be calculated according to individual salespeople, teams or the entire salesforce.
Sales planning	Identifying leads, classifying prospects (segmenting the market) and building up customer profiles. These can be assessed across a variety of criteria including organisation type, buying pattern, creditworthiness and size of average order.
Future options and projections	Computer modelling enables the manager to try different options and predict possible future scenarios. Although this is unlikely to provide the definitive answer to problems, it can often help in rejecting some alternatives and in clarifying the manager's thinking.

sometimes so much information is generated that it becomes impossible to wade through it all and arrive at a coherent decision. Second, computers sometimes give a spurious credibility to results which have been obtained from inaccurate input data – this is called GIGO (garbage in, garbage out).

Third, developing the systems usually means that managers have to come into contact with IT specialists. Since neither of them knows enough about the other's specialism to be able to comment or make suggestions, it may take some time for them to work out an optimum system. The exigencies of making the system compatible with the rest of the organisation's systems may compel the IT expert to make inappropriate compromises.

Fourth, management requirements change rapidly. Developments in the market, the type of products being sold, the size of the organisation or the management structure may mean that the information needs change frequently and the system has to change with them.

Fifth, there is the problem of technophobia. Some staff (and managers) do not trust the computer and are almost hoping that the system will fail. This can become a self-fulfilling prophecy as the people concerned do not manage to provide the appropriate information at the right time.

Assessing the costs and benefits of using IT can also be problematical, since the costs are easily identified but the benefits often are not.

A customer information system (CIS) can be structured as a database to maximise the opportunities for developing customer loyalty. Database management is potentially a complex issue. Table 6.3 explains some of the current terminology and features of databases.

Table 6.3 Database terminology

Term	Meaning
Flat database	This is a database in which all the information about a given customer is stored. Management of such databases is easy, since information is easily added or edited, but the possibilities for using the database to drive strategic decision making are limited.
Relational database	This type of database allows information about an individual customer to be accessed under several different categories. For example, a relational database containing details of doctors might be able to list them by location, by medical specialism, by purchasing frequency, by age, or by size of practice.
Data warehouse	This is an electronic storage facility which holds very large amounts of information. The information can be cross-checked against other pieces of information to clean it, and can be manipulated in various ways to generate information for decision making.
Data mining	This process of generating information by the use of advanced statistical processes enables organisations to find significant relationships between customers or chunks of customer information. This information provides almost instant market research, enabling organisations to develop rapid responses to market trends.
Extranet	Extranets allow companies to share some information while retaining their trade secrets. Driven through the Internet, extranets open some of the company's files to authorised outsiders. Trading information in this way can help markedly in ensuring industry survival.

Here is a checklist for ensuring that the customer information system is functioning correctly:

1 Has the system been designed to be state of the art? Beware of setting a technical horizon based on the user's technical knowledge. Often managers will design the system based on their knowledge of what is possible rather than on what a technician would regard as possible.

2 What business needs should the CIS serve? What types of analysis should it be able to handle? Determine the objectives of the system and put these in writing.

3 Involve the major users. They are closest to the system and can identify its strengths and weaknesses better than anyone.

4 Is the system simple, both in terms of collecting information and in terms of providing it?

5 Check that the CIS can sort information in a variety of ways: by customer purchase frequency, by order size, by geographical location, and so forth.

6 Is the system cleaned regularly to ensure that data is still current?

7 Is the system suitably backed up in the event of a computer crash?

8 Is the system secure – but at the same time is it easily accessible for authorised users?

For many organisations, the information systems have become the core activity of the business. More and more organisations are becoming database-driven, using a single database to inform all decisions within the organisation. Integrating all the business's activities around a single database increases the coherence of the marketing communications and increases the possibilities for establishing relationship marketing. A single database puts the company in the position of the small retailer; the organisation knows all its regular customers and can therefore anticipate and satisfy their needs much more effectively in terms of both product and communications.

Assessing marketing productivity

Measuring productivity of marketing is concerned with two areas: profitability analysis – although in non-profit-oriented organisations this may relate to another key objective – and cost-effectiveness analysis.

Profitability can be assessed for each product, each market, each territory or each distribution channel. Most organisations tend to measure profitability in terms of the profit made from each brand or product, because this is relatively easy to calculate. Conceptually this is a flawed approach, at least for marketers, because it is not market-oriented. The most customer-oriented approach is to assess profitability in terms of market segments. This may be expressed in geographical terms (so that territory is the issue), in terms of types of retail outlet (so that distribution channels are the key), or in demographics (so that the consumers are the key). In fact, any form of segmentation method can be the basis for a profitability analysis.

The profitability analysis will affect strategic planning since it allows planners to decide whether a segment is worth entering, or conversely whether a segment should be abandoned. Not all customers are worth having: sometimes resources are better allocated to other segments.

Another approach, and one which may allow for triangulation to determine the most profitable activities, is to calculate the costs and benefits of various marketing activities. For example, the return on using a telesales operation rather than a direct-mail exercise to generate leads might be calculated. The main problem with this type of calculation is that it tends to consider marketing activities in terms of short-term cash returns rather than long-term benefits. It is extremely easy to run a lead-generating exercise which produces a quick result but which at the same time causes future problems. For instance, it is surprisingly common for organisations to run exhibition stands which generate large numbers of potential sales leads and useful contacts. Often these leads are not followed up and the contacts are left uncontacted, which not only wastes the effort that went into their collection but also antagonises potential customers (Blythe 2000). Equally, salespeople might obtain quick sales by using high-pressure techniques at the expense of building longer-term (and hence more valuable) relationships with customers.

Resources, competencies and capabilities

Competency to achieve a given strategic objective is derived from the way resources are combined and utilised. Efficiency in the use of resources is the key to effectiveness in strategic success (usually expressed as competitive advantage). If resources are to be adequately utilised, managers must know what resources are available. In order to ensure that those resources are being used effectively, competency auditing is also essential. Having said that, there are problems in translating theory into practice.

There has been considerable research into the importance of what are broadly termed the resources of the organisation (Penrose 1958; Wernerfelt 1984; Barney 1991), particularly from the perspective of how they contribute to competitive advantage and organisational performance (Grant 2002). There is a problem of definition here, however – some authors prefer not to use the term 'resources' when writing of the range of means at the disposal of the planners and managers, but instead refer to 'assets'. This means that there is no generally agreed classification of resources (or assets) within the field of strategic marketing planning.

Having said that, there are certainly some major distinctions which can be made. First, resources may be tangible or intangible. Tangible resources are those assets such as machinery, buildings, vehicles, stock, work in progress and so on which can be touched and handled. Intangible resources are intellectual property such as patents or software, brand equity, goodwill, and the intellectual resources of the employees. Of the two, it is the tangible assets which are the easiest to identify, value, buy and sell; the intangible assets are more fragile (in that they can easily be lost) and are harder to value (since future income streams can be difficult to predict). Intangible assets often represent the major part of an organisation's stock market valuation, however.

The second classification which can be made is to divide intangible resources into relational resources and competencies. Relational resources are all of the means available to the organisation derived from its relationship with its environment (Lowendahl 1997). These might include special relationships with customers, distributors and consumers, and also the organisation's reputation and brand equity.

From the viewpoint of auditing resources and competencies, there are considerable conceptual difficulties. As far as tangible assets go, accountants have evolved some straightforward techniques for arriving at a value; however, these values are valid only in particular circumstances. For example, a fixed asset such as a piece of machinery might be valued in one of three separate ways.

First, its value in terms of what it can produce, or the income stream that might be expected from it. This is also a function of the business environment, since the value of the production might vary or the demand for the product may shift dramatically. An injection mould which produces plastic components, for example, is valuable only so long as the demand for those components continues – as soon as the demand is removed, the value of the mould drops to zero. Second, tangible assets might be valued in terms of their purchase price and expected life. Thus a vehicle might depreciate by a calculable amount over a given period. The organisation's accountants are usually able to calculate the value of, for example, the salesforce's company cars in this way. Third, tangible assets can be valued according to their resale value. This can be higher than the original purchase price (for example, buildings or office premises) or lower than the original purchase price (e.g. vehicles or machinery), or in some cases might be virtually zero (e.g. some of the tunnelling machinery used to build the Eurotunnel).

Each of these valuation methods will arrive at a different answer. Clearly the difficulties inherent in auditing intangible assets are likely to be greater, particularly if there is pressure to audit in financial terms. Therefore few organisations do this. This is one of the problems faced by marketers when trying to justify expenditures on, for instance, brand building.

Auditing knowledge is likely to be judgement-based, since knowledge has a high rate of decay in a changing environment. A linked audit might be to consider the organisation's ability and disposition towards maintaining its knowledge base. This is a function of the training of staff, of staff development initiatives, and also its propensity to spend money on research and development. This audit can be assessed qualitatively by making benchmarking comparisons with other organisations in the same industry.

Auditing capability is likewise a judgement-based activity, though there may be some objective elements involved. Capability might be judged by events in the recent past (for example, an exceptionally effective new product development and launch) or by assessing the individual capabilities of the organisation and aggregating them to give an overall view of capability (i.e. what we should be able to accomplish). This latter method has the advantage of being more up to date but has the major drawback of not taking account of possible synergies or unforeseen weaknesses.

Corporate attitude is probably subject to more instances of self-delusion on the part of senior managers than any other element in the competencies framework. Often the attitude of senior management is not reflected further down the hierarchy, and (worse) employees may be at some pains to conceal their real attitudes for fear of appearing to be out of step with the management. This is likely to have a severely damaging effect on the coordinating function of the strategy, since employees are likely to act in one way while trying to convince senior management that they are in fact acting in a different way. For this reason, corporate attitudes need to be monitored at grass-roots level. Attitudes are difficult to measure at best, because behaviour is not a good guide and self-reports may conceal political agendas.

Relational resources are even harder to pin down: with whom does the organisation have a relationship, and what is the value and status of the relationship? Relationships often break down – in business as well as in real life. What is the value of the organisation's reputation? This can sometimes be arrived at in general terms by looking at the difference between the organisation's balance-sheet asset value and its stock-market valuation, but this is a somewhat nebulous measure, relying as much on factors such as the general state of the economy, the general state of the industry, and the state of competing investments, as on the current state of the organisation.

Valuing a brand is not as straightforward as might at first appear, either. A well-established brand tends to have a less elastic demand curve; in other words, it is less price-sensitive (Hamilton et al. 1997). This means that a price increase on a strong brand will have less effect than a price increase on a weak brand. This implies that a strong brand will have a much better chance of weathering a recession than a weak brand. This is in itself a valuable characteristic and one that is well worth investing in.

Carrying out a resource and competency assessment is, notwithstanding the conceptual and practical difficulties, an essential activity for any organisation attempting to plan strategy.

The resource audit will cover the areas shown in Table 6.4. It should include all the resources the organisation can tap into, even when it does not actually own these –

Table 6.4 Elements in the resource audit

Element	Examples and explanation
Physical resources	A list of the fixed assets of the organisation, for example machinery, buildings and equipment. The audit needs to include the age and condition of the assets, their location and their capability as well as their financial value (which is often calculated in an arbitrary manner in any case). This is to determine their usefulness in achieving strategic advantages.
Human resources	This can be a problematical area, since much of the value of staff depends on their motivation and commitment rather than on their paper qualifications and the numbers of them within the organisation.
Financial resources	This should include the sources of money (whether equity or loan), the liabilities the organisation has and the possible availability of capital or loans should it become necessary to acquire more funding. This is essentially the organisation's credit rating.
Intangibles	From a marketer's point of view, intangible assets such as brands, patents, reputation and relationships with customers (goodwill) are at least as important as any of the organisation's other assets, since these are the capital from which marketers derive competence.

intangible resources and financial resources which can be called upon if needed fall into this category. Particular weight should be given to unique resources – those resources which competitors are unable to duplicate, for example patented products or other intellectual property.

Competence analysis cannot be measured in absolute terms – it always has to be measured against competitors' provision and customers' expectations. In particular it is important to identify the organisation's core competencies – the particular competencies that ensure that the organisation can outperform its competition in some respects. Competencies can be understood and analysed in two steps: **value chain analysis** and competence bases.

Value chain analysis examines the ways that organisations add value to products as they pass along the chain. This involves analysing both what happens within the organisation itself and what happens in the supplier and distributor parts of the chain. Value chain analysis recognises that each organisation and process in the chain adds value to the product, otherwise there would be no point in their becoming involved in the process. Each increment of value should be greater than the costs attaching to its production, otherwise that part of the chain is not operating efficiently and should be changed or removed. Much of the efficiency gained by effective organisations lies in their ability to manage the linkages between the activities of other organisations.

Within the value chain, there exist categories of activity which are shown in Table 6.5.

Very few companies undertake all the value activities from raw material through to final product. The oil industry is a notable exception. Specialisation of role is therefore the norm, with each organisation adding only part of the value to the product. For example, in the food industry a basic product such as tuna might pass through eight or more organisations on its way from the fishermen to the consumer's larder, each organisation adding something to the product (canning, shipping, delivering, displaying, advertising, etc.).

Identifying core competencies will vary from one industry to another. Threshold competencies are those which any business in the industry would need to have in order to survive. Any car manufacturer needs a threshold competence in engineering and in design, but some car manufacturers have developed core competencies which single them out from the competition. Ferrari, for instance, has a core competence in stylish design, Volkswagen has a core competence in reliability, and Ford has a core competence in low running costs. Core competencies have relevance only when compared with competitors and with market segments.

Core competencies might also be linked to critical success factors. The critical success factor in an industry is the basic elements that have to be right if the organisation is to succeed, rather than merely survive. For example, Internet-based organisations need a threshold competency in information technology, but the critical success factor is likely to be the design of the web page. A well-designed page will encourage business, whereas a poorly designed one is frustrating to visit. Examples of poor design abound. The ill-fated Boo.com had a state-of-the-art animated website which was able to show all the organisation's clothes in three dimensions. Unfortunately, prospective customers needed

Table 6.5 Primary and support activities

Primary activity	Explanation and examples
Inbound logistics	All the activities concerned with receiving, storing and distributing raw materials or other inputs. Warehousing, inbound shipping and materials-handling systems are examples.
Operations	The processes which transform the incoming raw materials into the organisation's finished product. This may, of course, become raw materials or components for another organisation, for example when an electronics manufacturer makes car radios for a car manufacturer.
Outbound logistics	Collection, storage and delivery to customers. Much of this activity might be undertaken by a distributor or transport company.
Marketing communications	Here we are looking at the functional aspects of marketing, in which customers are made aware of the products and fine-tuning of the product offering is made to suit the needs of individual customers.
Before-sales and after-sales service	All those activities which enhance or maintain the product value. For example, installation of equipment, repair of faulty equipment, training, and so forth.

Support activities	Explanation and examples
Procurement	The processes involved in obtaining the resource inputs needed for the primary activities. These would include raw materials purchase, equipment purchase and acquiring suitable spaces (factory, shop or office).
Technology development	Technological advances may reside in the product (through research and development or through product design), with the processes (more efficient production or delivery methods) or with resource improvements (for example making use of a previously ignored raw material).
Human resource management	The activities involved in shaping an effective workforce. These may involve hiring suitable people, offering appropriate training, ensuring suitable motivation and reward structures are in place, and (when unavoidable) firing unsuitable employees.
Infrastructure	The systems of planning, finance, quality control, information management, communication, and so forth. The routines and structures of the organisation often determine the level of flexibility the organisation has – greater flexibility means greater ability to cope with change.

a state-of-the-art computer to download the images in anything like a reasonable amount of time. Most simply got bored and went elsewhere, or found that the connection timed out before they were able to make a purchase. Some airline websites do not give the times of the flights, but require prospective passengers to enter the time of the flight in order to check availability. Wrong guesses mean wasted time where the system says 'There is no flight at that time'. Some cheap flight websites will not offer flights that do not exactly fit the customer's specification. This means that a customer may end up paying more than necessary, simply because the site is not able to mention that a much cheaper flight is available the day before. Such websites lose out to those which develop a core competence in website design, such as easyJet or Amazon.

TALKING POINT

> We are always being told that we need to be different, to develop core competencies which make us stand out from the crowd. But if everybody stands out from the crowd and adds value to the core generic product, who will make the commodity products?
>
> Maybe there's still a market out there for the basic, cheap, simple product. Maybe not everybody **wants** the extra bells and whistles. Although this might be a marketing heresy, could the production of the 'commodity' version actually be a core competency in its own right?

Overall assessment of the resources and competencies of an organisation provides insight into its particular capabilities to compete effectively in the marketplace by providing value to customers, usually through exploiting a particular advantage that it has. Normally such an advantage comes from the valuable capability providing the organisation with a means of meeting the needs of the business environment and being difficult to copy by rival organisations.

Of particular significance in highly volatile contemporary business environments are an organisation's 'dynamic capabilities', which refer to an organisation's ability to integrate, build and readjust internal and external competencies to address rapidly changing environments. The main thrust of the dynamic capabilities framework is that in contemporary, fast-moving markets, organisations are compelled to respond quickly and to be innovative when dealing with rapid change. Three dynamic capabilities are necessary to maintain a competitive advantage in a fast-changing environment. First, in order to meet these challenges organisations and their employees need the capability to learn quickly and to build strategic assets. Second, new strategic assets, such as technology, knowledge and customer feedback, have to be integrated within the organisation. Third, existing strategic assets have to be reconfigured or transformed. Building on the resource-based view of the organisation, the dynamic capabilities approach requires that success comes from more than just selecting resources on which to base competitive advantage; rather it indicates that success will stem only from effective resource development and renewal as external factors change. In the context of marketing planning, therefore, assessing the internal resources of a business needs to be undertaken from a dynamic perspective with the future in mind rather than simply looking at the current situation.

Audit analysis

Finally, the audit process itself should be examined and decisions taken as to whether it is appropriate, feasible and effective. Here is a checklist for determining whether the audit has been correctly carried out:

1 Were the right people involved? Did they have the relevant knowledge, and the necessary objectivity, to carry out the task?

2 Were the right questions asked? Did the questions elicit reliable and relevant answers?

3 Has the process been non-threatening for the people concerned? Might anybody have felt constrained to provide a particular answer in order to avoid losing face or admitting to a problem?

Summary

The internal environment is at the root of corporate strengths. The people who work within the organisation, and the organisation's physical assets, are the basis of its capabilities for dealing with the external environment. In strategic terms, they are the equivalent of the army's soldiers and weapons.

Some of these assets are difficult to assess. Again, to use the military analogy, the soldiers need to be tested under fire before the generals can be sure of their mettle.

The key points from this chapter are as follows:

→ Internal audits provide a 'snapshot'; they do not provide a permanent view of what is happening.

→ Audits should not be used to discipline staff.

→ Introspection, honesty and integrity are paramount. Sometimes it is better to use external consultants or interdepartmental groups in order to minimise political agendas.

→ Hierarchical organisations are efficient, but extremely slow to change.

→ Organismic organisations are flexible, but require more time spent in communication.

→ Information support systems must be user-friendly, or they will be unused or, worse, corrupted.

→ Systems should be designed around corporate need, not perceived technical capability. Technicians can usually rise to the challenge.

→ Resources are harder to define and to quantify than might at first be expected, particularly with regard to the ability of the organisation to adapt to future change.

→ The audit process itself should be audited.

Umar's analysis of the internal environment turned up one or two surprises. First, an examination of the sales figures showed that the Slick Mower was not selling as well as it should have been – sales were still moving upwards, but not as fast as the growth in the market said they should have been. This probably meant that the Slick Mower was heading towards a downturn, becoming obsolete in the face of competition from other mowers. Since the Slick Mower was the company's flagship product and should have been a cash cow, this presented an immediate problem to be solved.

Other products in the portfolio were clearly in the maturity stage, but Umar was unable to identify any stars (see Chapter 8). Equally, there were no dogs, and in fact most products had performed fairly consistently during the recession, none standing out as being worse hit than any other, even though sales across the board were somewhat down. Umar's inference from this was that the company needed some new products fairly quickly, and in particular a new version of the 12-year-old Slick Mower was needed as a matter of urgency.

Analysis of the company's resources showed that the fixed assets (equipment, machinery, factory space, etc.) were in good shape, but the financial position was poor. This meant that there would be very little in the budget for marketing unless the venture capitalists came on board – leaving Umar with something of a problem. The order book looked moderately healthy, though.

Interviews with the staff also revealed something surprising – employees thought the company was somewhat old-fashioned and not especially innovative. This opinion directly contradicted the directors' view of the company and flew in the face of the new vision statement. Obviously the internal marketing had gone badly wrong somewhere!

Review questions

1 How might an organisation in the public sector, for example a local authority, carry out an internal audit?

2 How might an internal audit differ in an organismic organisation as opposed to a hierarchical organisation?

3 How might a database be used for audit purposes?

4 How might an organisation decide the frequency of auditing activities?

5 If an audit is a snapshot, and a decision-support system provides a constant stream of information, how can the one be reconciled with the other?

Case study Iveco

Iveco manufactures trucks, light commercial vehicles, buses and specialist vehicles such as fire-fighting trucks. The company was formed in 1975 through the merger of the commercial vehicle divisions of Fiat, Magirus-Deutz (of Germany), Unic (of France) and several other Italian industrial vehicle makers. The result was the Industrial Vehicle Company, or Iveco.

In 1975 the European Union was not as integrated as it is today, and cross-border alliances and mergers were less common, indeed were resisted by many national governments. The fledgling company therefore found itself in a difficult position at first and had to make considerable efforts to integrate the member companies into a single unit. The first problem was language – Germans find Italian and French difficult to learn, and at the time of the merger few of the

French and Italian managers spoke each other's languages. Iveco management took the unusual step of adopting English as the corporate language, spending thousands of lire, francs and deutschmarks on a dedicated English-language course for hundreds of senior managers. Even the course texts were copyrighted to Iveco. This paid off handsomely later, when Iveco negotiated a joint venture with Ford UK.

During the ensuing years, Iveco focused on developing a single range of vehicles, using the expertise within the member companies to develop a wide range of vehicles which still took advantage of the economies of scale available to the organisation. Officine Meccaniche (OM) provided expertise in light vehicles, Fiat in the area of medium to heavy lorries, and Magirus-Deutz in off-road, heavy-duty and firefighting vehicles.

In 1980, Iveco restructured the company to create greater integration. Engineering, manufacturing, purchasing and administration were integrated under a single senior manager for each function, creating a truly cross-border management system. In addition, separate divisions were created for specialist areas of enterprise: diesel engines, buses and fire-fighting vehicles were each given their own division, again operating across borders.

In the early 1990s Iveco further reorganised itself, in response to market pressures. This time the company reorganised around specific customer types, in an attempt to become more customer-oriented. In 1995, the company's EuroClass luxury coach was voted International Coach of the Year, and the EuroCargo medium lorry became the market leader in the UK, Spain, Bulgaria and Slovenia as well as in its native Italy. In 2000, the Daily light van was voted International Van of the Year.

A renewed focus on customer needs has certainly helped Iveco capture a large share of its chosen markets and the company now outperforms the original parent company, Fiat, which at the time of writing was in some financial difficulties due to the recession. Iveco has a programme of continuous improvement: new models, and new versions of existing models, roll off the drawing board and onto the production line regularly, in response to customer need. At the time of writing, Iveco was testing diesel–electric versions of the Daily with FedEx. Initial results showed a 26 per cent reduction in fuel consumption and a total of 7.5 tonnes of CO_2 per vehicle saved in only the first six months of operation.

Iveco's willingness to organise the company around the market rather than try to change the market to suit its own structure has been an important aspect of its success. However, there is no question that skilled design and engineering have been the key factors in growing the company to become one of the world's largest commercial vehicle producers.

Questions

1 *How should Iveco go about conducting an internal audit? What special problems might there be?*

2 *What type of information should Iveco collect to help its decision making?*

3 *What type of organisation structure should Iveco have?*

4 *What special problems might arise in setting up a decision support system for Iveco?*

5 *What would be the key benefits of adopting English as the official language of the company?*

References

Barney, J.B. (1986): Organisational culture: can it be a source of sustained competitive advantage? *Academy of Management Review*, 11 pp 656–65.

Barney, J.B. (1991): Organisation resources and sustained competitive advantage. *Journal of Management*, 17 (1) pp 99–120.

Bessen, J. (1994): Riding the marketing information wave. *Harvard Business Review*, September–October pp 150–60.

Blythe, J. (2000): Objectives and measures at UK trade exhibitions. *Journal of Marketing Management*, 16 pp 203–22.

Dretske, F. (1981): *Knowledge and the Flow of Information* (Cambridge, MA: MIT Press).

Durand, T. (1996): Revisiting key dimensions of competence. Paper presented to the SMS Conference, Phoenix, Arizona.

Evans, M.J. (1994): Domesday marketing? *Journal of Marketing Management*, 10 (5) pp 409–31.

Grant, R.M. (2002): *Contemporary Strategy Analysis*, 4th edition (Oxford: Blackwell Publishers Inc).

Hamilton, W., East, R. and Kalafatis, S. (1997): The measurement and utility of brand price elasticities. *Journal of Marketing Management*, 13 (4) pp 285–98.

Lowendahl, B.R. (1997): *Strategic Management of Professional Business Service Organisations* (Copenhagen: Copenhagen Business School Press).

Penrose, E.T. (1958): *The Theory of the Growth of the Organisation* (New York: Wiley).

Prahalad, C.K. and Hamel, G. (1990): The core competence of the corporation. *Harvard Business Review*, May–June pp 79–91.

Proctor, T. (2000): *Essentials of Marketing Research*, 2nd edition (Harlow: Financial Times Prentice Hall).

Sprague, R.H. and Watson, H.J. (1986): *Decision Support Systems: Putting Theory into Practice* (Englewood Cliffs, NJ: Prentice Hall).

Stalk, G., Evans, P. and Shulman, L. (1992): Competing on capabilities. *Harvard Business Review*, March/April.

Teece, D.J., Pisano, G. and Shuen, A. (1997): Dynamic capabilities and strategic management. *Strategic Management Journal*, 18 (7) pp 509–33.

Wernerfelt, B. (1984): A resource-based view of the organisation. *Strategic Management Journal*, April/June pp 171–80.

Chapter 7

Identifying marketing strategies

THE EDEN GARDEN TOOLS COMPANY LTD

A month after Umar Sayeed had joined the company, Eden Garden Tools' senior management met to discuss the marketing audit. At this point, Umar was able to provide a fairly complete picture of the company's current situation, even though he admitted that there might well be several gaps since he had been unable to carry out primary research within the time frame.

The purpose of the discussions was to identify where the company needed to make changes in order to get on track for the future. This meant being very clear indeed about where the company wanted to be – not just in vague terms of 'wanting to be successful' or 'wanting to be the best' but in exact terminology which would enable it to know what to do each day and to monitor its progress towards the final goal.

Identifying the gaps between where it wanted to be and where it was now was the key purpose of the meeting.

After reading this chapter, you should be able to:

→ Explain what is meant by the planning gap.

→ Explain the difficulties of identifying underlying problems.

→ Describe the basic strategies for developing the business.

→ Describe the winning strategies of business – and identify the failing ones.

→ Describe value disciplines and explain what is meant by them.

→ Explain how recessions can be good for businesses.

→ Describe the different ways of entering overseas markets.

→ Explain the purpose of SWOT analysis.

Introduction

Knowing where we are is one thing; deciding where we want to be is another, and often rather harder, set of decisions. Between the two lie the decisions on creating appropriate marketing strategies.

This chapter examines the use of the planning gap as a means of identifying opportunities to fulfil the organisation's marketing strategy, and assesses the issues and constraints arising from the marketing audit and their consequences for developing the marketing plan.

Included in this chapter are objectives and the planning gap, generating alternative strategic options, closing the planning gap with new and existing strategies, evaluation of marketing opportunities and competitive advantage, prioritising and executing SWOT analysis, specifying marketing objectives, strategies and plans, and consideration of timescales for implementation.

The planning gap

Setting objectives implies that marketing planners would like something to change in the way the organisation operates. There is an assumption that, without some kind of direct intervention, the business will not reach the stated objectives and will carry on to some other undesired destination. The difference between what the planners expect to happen as a result of the new objectives and what would happen if they did nothing is called the **planning gap** (or sometimes the performance gap). In other words, it is the gap we need to plan for, and fill.

Planners begin by assessing what would happen if the organisation takes no action, basing this projection on available data. This is called a **reference projection** and is the baseline by which the various planning suggestions will be judged. For example, a company may be considering which objectives to aim for in order to increase profit. The reference projection would be based on market growth/decline, previous performance, competitive activity, consumer behaviour, and so forth on the assumption that the organisation continues with present policies. Different possible strategic and tactical programmes would then be modelled to see which (if any) would result in an improved performance in terms of, say, profit at the end of the year. Obviously profit may not be the only objective, but the basic premise still has validity. Whatever aspect of the company's activities is under scrutiny, there is likely to be a planning gap.

The intention of planning is to close the gap, so that the new reference projection accords with the new plan. Objectives might, of course, be revised to direct the company towards the point at which it will arrive anyway, or (more likely) tactics can be developed in order to hit the objectives originally identified, rather than the reference projection.

If the planning gap is large, it would be reasonable to suppose that the organisation has a problem. The fact that there is a problem does not necessarily mean that there is an easy solution to that problem, and still less does it imply that the planners know what the solution is. There may be many possibilities for closing the planning gap, some of which will be wrong. Understanding the full extent of the problem will mean understanding the full extent of the possible solutions. In most cases, solutions create problems of their own, which need to be addressed or at least taken into account as a cost of the solution.

The immediate problem may not necessarily be what needs to be addressed – there may be an underlying problem. For example, an organisation might perceive a competitor's surprise new assault on the market as being the problem, whereas in fact the underlying problem is the organisation's poor information system which did not predict the competitive response.

Closing the planning gap through marketing strategies

There are likely to be many options for closing the planning gap, but the successful ones will necessarily take account of the organisation's resources. Unless the organisation is facing an immediate crisis, in which case something will need to be done very quickly, planning will be guided by the following factors:

1 The situation as revealed by analysis of the planning gap.
2 The manager's understanding of the problem. This will be coloured by the manager's perception of what the real problem is – not necessarily the underlying problem.
3 The historical situation of the company, taken from the marketing audit.
4 Current strategy, tactics, mission and vision.
5 Existing capabilities, competencies and resources as well as those which might be developed or acquired by forming alliances.

Marketing strategy search is likely to be logical and formulaic in part, but there should also be space for inspiration to strike: sometimes one of the planning team will have an idea which goes straight to the heart of the problem. However, it is more common for several possible strategies to be proposed, and the management team will then have the problem of discussing the alternatives and possibly modelling the proposals to see whether they will close the gap or not. The basic difficulty here is that the models themselves are likely to be more than a little subjective – managers have to make assumptions, and are likely to select assumptions which will support their chosen view of what should happen.

Before embarking on discussion of possible marketing strategies, however, it is worth considering what we actually mean by this term and how it fits into the bigger picture of the marketing planning process. A marketing strategy is generally considered to be the identification and pursuit of a marketing opportunity based upon a specific target market and a particular competitive advantage. The marketing strategy needs a clear focus and should be consistent with the organisation's overall goals and needs to take account of the key dimensions of planning: customers, competitors and internal factors.

The marketing opportunity that we identify needs to relate to a target market and should involve adopting a strategy which enables effective positioning through marketing activities to fulfil the requirements of that customer group. Effectively we are concerned with targeting a particular market segment with an appropriate marketing mix. This process will be discussed in detail in the following chapters.

One way of generating marketing strategies is through the contextual application of Ansoff's product-market matrix. Ansoff (1965) identified four basic strategies for achieving growth (see Figure 7.1).

1 **Market penetration**. The company can try to grow by increasing its share of the existing market. This can be achieved either by attracting customers away from competitors or by encouraging existing customers to use more of the product. Taking share from competitors invites retaliation – the competitors are unlikely to stand still while their customers are lured away, and will inevitably try to retain customers, or (better still) try to lure customers away from other organisations. This type of competition usually benefits consumers, at least in the short run, but can be very damaging for companies. Encouraging customers to use more of the product invites copying on the part of competitors – if we have a way of persuading our customers to buy more and use more, competitors will quickly join in. For example, if we discover a new use for a product, our competitors can publicise it in the same way. This strategy often involves price cutting, promotion, or finding new distribution outlets.

2 **Enter new markets**. Taking an existing product into a new market can be an easy way to grow. The new market may be an overseas one, in which case the organisation will face competitive retaliation from local producers, or it may be a new segment in the home country. For example, classical music tends to be more popular with older people, but a concert hall could specifically target a young audience with a different repertoire.

3 **Develop new products**. Products can be entirely new, or can be adaptations of our existing product range. For example, an insurance company might offer an entirely new product (insurance for children) or might adapt an existing product for a new market (specialist car insurance for family motorists).

4 **Diversify**. Entering entirely new markets with entirely new products is a high-risk strategy, but it can be very effective, especially if the organisation contracts an alliance with another organisation in order to enter the new market. Obviously this approach can work only if the organisation's core competencies can be used to good effect in the new market. For example, Honda's capability for manufacturing petrol

engines with a high power-to-weight ratio enabled it to capture the light motorcycle market in the 1960s, but the same capability enabled it to make inroads into the outboard motor market, the portable generator market and the power garden tools market as well.

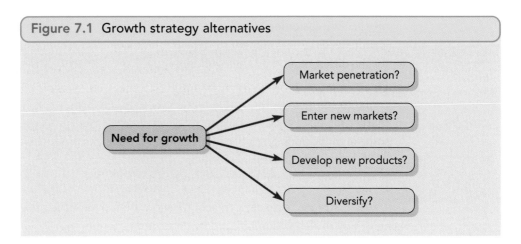

Figure 7.1 Growth strategy alternatives

Various models exist for assessing market potential, i.e. the attractiveness of given markets, but most rely on subjective judgements at some point or another. The maximum attainable usage of a product might be obtained from market research, but the extent to which the product will attain those levels of usage is somewhat harder to assess. Typically, planners will use surrogates – similar products in similar markets – to make these judgements, but often such surrogates do not exist and the calculations amount to little more than guesswork.

TALKING POINT

If marketing strategies are so easy to identify, why is it that so many businesses get this part of their planning wrong? Using a basic tool like the Ansoff matrix should enable all organisations to produce a range of strategic options, whatever type of business they are in. Yet why is it the case that so many fail to identify the best options? Why is it that some organisations always go for complex solutions like product development and diversification, when the more straightforward alternatives of market penetration and development may be much better choices?

Is it because the decision makers ignore the process or that they just have a blinkered view about what needs to be done?

An alternative view of available strategies has been offered by Porter (1985). Porter suggested three potential winning strategies and one failing strategy. The potential winning strategies are as follows:

1 **Overall cost leadership**. A company which succeeds in minimising its production and distribution costs is able to offer a price advantage over its competitors without sacrificing profits. To this end, many companies have moved their manufacturing operations to low-wage economies in the Third World, and many more have streamlined their distribution operations or combined them to create an integrated logistics system.

2 Differentiation. Companies which can show the customers that their products are significantly different from others on the market are able to charge premium prices (provided different equates to better in the eyes of some customers). Differentiation comes from two sources: first, real differences in the features and benefits the product offers, and second, strong promotional efforts to make these differences apparent to prospective customers. Both these sources cost money to implement, so the organisation needs to be confident that the premium which customers are prepared to pay for the differentiated product will more than cover the extra costs.

3 Focus. Here the company concentrates on a few market segments rather than trying to compete in the whole market. Often these will be exclusive markets: the market for luxury yachts falls into this category. In business-to-business markets, some organisations specialise in providing for a specific product type – Novo Nordisk of Denmark specialises in producing industrial enzymes and has become highly profitable by being the best in its chosen specialisation.

The failing strategy is to seek to achieve more than one of the above and thus fail to achieve any of them. Combining low cost with differentiation is impossible, because a differentiation strategy requires higher expenditures on R&D and promotion if it is to work. Combining low cost with focus is also unlikely to work, because low cost requires high volumes in order to attract economies of scale. Focus and differentiation combine well, but there are cost implications. The essence of the problem is to pursue a clear strategy which customers can identify with. If they are unable to recognise whether the organisation is cheap, or best at serving its market segment, or offering the highest perceived value, the organisation's products will not stand out and will thus be relegated to a lower status in the decision-making framework.

Organisations occasionally attempt to carry out more than one strategic approach at a time because of disagreements among top managers. Consensus among managers improves performance at the strategic business unit (SBU) level, especially for differentiation strategies (Homburg et al. 1999), but appears unnecessary if the organisation is pursuing a low-cost strategy, perhaps because this is an easy strategy to understand and relate to, even if disagreements occur elsewhere.

Yet another way of looking at competitive strategies is that proposed by Treacy and Wiersema (1993) – see Figure 7.2. This identifies three strategies or value disciplines aimed at increasing customer value:

1 Operational excellence. Here the company provides better value for its customers by leading the industry in price and convenience. Similar to the cost leadership approach, the organisation tries to reduce costs and create an effective and efficient delivery system.

2 Customer intimacy. Here the company creates value by detailed segmentation, meeting the needs of its chosen customers very precisely. This strategy is likely to be based on developing close relationships with customers, which in turn means empowering staff to make decisions close to the customers, and developing detailed knowledge of customers' needs. Such companies attract customers who are prepared to pay substantial premiums to get exactly what they want, and who are prepared to be loyal to companies which deliver.

3 **Product leadership**. Companies pursuing this strategy offer leading-edge, state-of-the-art products and services, aiming to make the competitors' products (and indeed their own) obsolete. Such companies have large R&D expenditures, staff innovation programmes and systems for getting new products to market quickly.

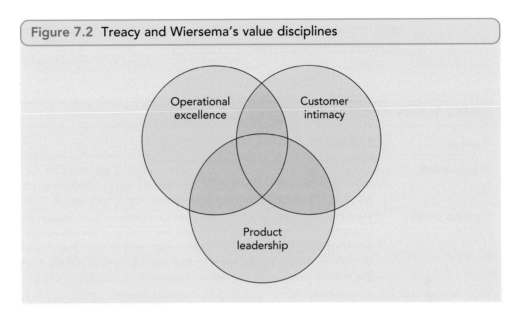

Figure 7.2 Treacy and Wiersema's value disciplines

Unlike Porter's strategy categorisations, the Treacy and Wiersema categories are not mutually exclusive. It is possible to pursue operational excellence and customer intimacy, for example (as easyJet does), or customer intimacy and product leadership (as Virgin does). Pursuing all three is probably somewhat difficult, since the company will be providing exceptional value for money, which is of course likely to lead to reduced profit margins.

Organisations might be **market challengers**, which seek to increase their share of the market by adopting a market penetration strategy. They might be **market followers**, which allow the market leader to make most of the investment in developing a new market, then follow along behind and pick up any segments the leader has not already taken. Finally, an organisation might be a **market nicher**, concentrating on a small segment of the market. This is a typical strategy of a small organisation with few resources, but with a strong competency in one area.

Market challenger strategies

Market challengers are organisations which seek to increase their share of the market, usually through aggressive competitive tactics. Market challengers are in a different position from market leaders in that they have two choices of competitor to attack: they can attack the market leader (a high-risk but potentially high-gain strategy) or they can try to pick off the smaller competitors, either by out-competing them or by taking them over. Attacking the market leader probably means that the organisation will be up against a larger organisation than itself – the market leader probably has the resources and the experience to mount a vigorous defence, whereas the smaller organisations may not be so able to withstand a determined assault. However, beating the market leader would mean becoming market leader oneself – which has quite obvious advantages.

In order to attack the market leader, the challenger must have a clear competitive advantage: a cost advantage, or the ability to provide better value for money by offering a better product. Attacking smaller competitors may only require an aggressive promotional campaign, a short price war, or a takeover policy. The strategies open to a market challenger are shown in Table 7.1.

Table 7.1 Market challenger strategies

Strategy	Explanation
Frontal attack	The challenger matches the competitor's marketing efforts across the board. It attacks the competitor's strengths, not its weaknesses, and in effect enters into a war of attrition. The company with the greater resources usually wins in these circumstances.
Flanking attack	Here the challenger concentrates on the competitor's weaknesses rather than its strengths. The challenger tries to find some portion of the competitor's business which is being poorly served or which it feels able to serve better, and attacks that. Sometimes the competitor will withdraw without much of a fight. A lot depends on the relative resources of the two organisations.
Encirclement attack	This strategy involves attacking from several directions at once. This approach works best when the attacker has more resources than the defender.
Bypass attack	Here the challenger bypasses the market leader completely and targets new markets. This might involve entering new geographic markets, or using new technology to tap into new groups of customers. This has the advantage of not offering a direct threat to the competitor and thus minimising the risk of retaliation.
Guerrilla attack	The challenger makes occasional attacks on the larger competitor, using different tactics each time in order to demoralise and confuse the market leader. For example, a challenger might run a cut-price offer for one month only, followed the next month by a sales promotion, followed the next month by a promotional campaign. This constant switching of tactics does not allow the market leader time to organise a retaliatory strike, but instead forces the leader to become a follower, retaliating after the challenger has moved on to the next tactic. Guerrilla actions work best for small organisations which are able to respond quickly and have the flexibility to move on as soon as their larger, perhaps more bureaucratic, competitors try to retaliate.

Market follower strategies

Most organisations operate with the view that competitors are 'the enemy' and therefore will try to attack their competitors to seize market share. However, challenging the market leader, or indeed competing aggressively at all, is not necessarily the best way forward. The primary task of any organisation is to survive, and retaliation from a more powerful company might well make this difficult.

Market followers allow the market leader to make most of the investment in developing new products and markets, then follow on to pick up on any spare segments which the leader may have bypassed. The follower gains in terms of reduced costs and

Table 7.2 Market follower categories	
Category	Explanation
Cloner	These organisations make almost exact copies of the leader's products, distribution, promotion and other marketing strategies. They can often do this at much lower cost because they do not have the market leaders' development costs or risks. Organisations making exact copies of products are relatively rare, due to patenting and other intellectual property defences, but in some markets (particularly agricultural markets) cloning is perfectly feasible.
Imitator	Here the follower copies most of the leader's strategies, but retains some differentiation. This approach is more common than cloning because it often avoids direct competition with the market leader, and can even help the leader to avoid charges of monopolistic behaviour. Typical imitator strategies would be supermarkets selling own brands which look like the market-leader brands, or burger restaurants which imitate the McDonald's high-speed service system.
Adapter	Adapters go one step further than the market leader, producing improved versions of products or marketing programmes. Adapters can become industry leaders, and are really only one step short of being challengers.

reduced risk, and although followers will never become market leaders, they are often as profitable as leaders (Haines et al. 1989).

Market followers fall into three types, as shown in Table 7.2.

Being the leader always carries risks: the vast majority of new products fail when they reach the market, and the successful products have to pay for all the unsuccessful ones. Followers are able to be much more confident that their products will succeed, since they can copy only those products which are already successful. The same applies to promotional activities and distribution strategies – even though the bulk of the market is likely to go to the innovators, the costs of doing this are great, and the profits often go to the followers.

Market nicher strategies

Market nichers are organisations which concentrate on small segments of the market, seeking to meet the needs of those customers as closely as possible. Nichers operate on a low-volume, high-margin basis, so this is often a suitable strategic position for medium-sized companies (Clifford and Cavanagh 1985).

Competitors are closed out of the niche because the niche company develops an intimate knowledge of customer needs which would be difficult for a new entrant to acquire. Also, the niche is often too small to support more than one company. The key to success in niche marketing is to specialise. Table 7.3 shows some of the ways niche marketers can specialise.

Niche marketers run the risk of their chosen market declining or disappearing. A niche marketer has all his eggs in one basket, which is fine as long as he follows Mark Twain's advice and watches that basket, but even so there is a strong chance of problems arising. For this reason some niche marketers concentrate on more than one niche and so hedge their bets.

Table 7.3 Niche roles

Role	Explanation
End-use specialist	The organisation specialises in meeting all the needs of one type of end user. For example, Maplin's aims to supply all the needs of amateur electronics hobbyists.
Vertical-level specialist	The organisation specialises in one level of the production–distribution cycle. For example, Pickfords specialises in moving heavy equipment and abnormal loads.
Customer-size specialist	Here the organisation concentrates on marketing to organisations of a particular size. Often smaller organisations are neglected by the industry majors, allowing a foot in the door for nichers.
Specific-customer specialist	The organisation specialises in supplying one or two very large organisations. This is typical of small engineering organisations: they offer specialist manufacturing expertise to larger organisations which find it cheaper to outsource than to manufacture in-house. Weber carburettors is an example: the organisation supplies high-quality carburettors to most car manufacturers for their high-performance cars.
Geographical specialist	Here the organisation stays within a small geographical area. For example, Welsh-language book publishers do not operate outside Wales and Argentina, where the Welsh language is also spoken.
Product or feature specialist	The organisation specialises in producing a particular product, or one with unique features. This type of specialisation is often based on a patented system or process.
Quality-price specialist	The organisation operates within a niche at the top or bottom of the market. For example, the market for executive jet planes is dominated by Lear and Cessna.
Service specialist	The organisation offers a service which is unavailable elsewhere. Only NASA offers a recovery and repair service for satellites, and only the Russian space agency offers space tourist flights (albeit at an extremely high price). This is set to change in the next few years, as Virgin Galactic starts commercial space flights for tourists.

Collaborating with competitors

Hamel et al. (1989) propose collaboration with competitors as a way forward in securing markets. Strategic alliances generated through joint ventures, product licensing, or cooperative research strengthen organisations against competitors from outside the partnership by increasing the market coverage, reducing costs, generating greater efficiency and raising the profile of both companies. It can be a low-cost way for organisations to access new markets, and many Japanese organisations have used this approach to enter European Union markets, where they would otherwise have to pay substantial tariffs to import directly from Japan.

Hamel et al.'s research shows that collaboration between Japanese organisations and Western partners often leaves the Western partner worse off in the long run. This they attribute to poor negotiating skills, poor fit between strategic goals and poor protection of sensitive information. More recent research from Hennart et al. (1999) shows that, provided the partnership is well managed, the benefits of collaboration outweigh the risks. Organisations which benefit most from competitive collaboration tend to follow the principles outlined in Table 7.4.

Western companies often enter alliances in order to avoid making investments, either in moving into new markets or in developing new products. Unfortunately this often plays into the hands of the partner organisation, which then has the capability to

Table 7.4 Principles for successful collaboration

Principle	Explanation
Collaboration is competition in a different form	Successful collaborators remember that their partner may well try to take over the whole market later on and become a major competitor. The collaboration may not last for ever!
Harmony is not the most important measure of success	Occasional conflict may well lead to creative solutions for problems: like a marriage, if the partnership is a sincere commitment, arguments will happen now and then. Harmony usually prevails only where neither party really cares about the outcome, or indeed about the relationship.
Cooperation has limits	Strategic alliances often result in substantial transfers of information, perhaps well beyond that originally envisaged by senior management when they hammered out the deal. Successful collaborators will ensure that employees are well aware of what information can and cannot be passed on.
Learning from partners is paramount	Successful collaborators ensure that the new knowledge gained from the partner is diffused throughout their own organisation. This knowledge will remain even if the partnership dissolves.

control the situation to their advantage. Mutual gain is, however, possible if the partners conform to the following conditions:

- The partners' strategic goals converge while their competitive goals diverge. Each partner must allow the other to prosper in the shared venture, but should avoid competing directly.
- The size and power of both partners is modest compared with the industry leaders. The partners should also be of similar size compared with each other. These conditions ensure that neither partner develops a controlling influence, and also ensures that it is in both partners' interests to continue the alliance in order to avoid clashing with the industry leader.
- Each partner can learn from the other, while restricting access to sensitive information.

Collaboration offers a way forward for many smaller companies, and indeed some larger ones as well. Collaboration between Ford, Volkswagen and Seat has produced several car designs, notably the Ford Galaxy multi-purpose vehicle, sold by Volkswagen as the Sharan and by Seat as the Alhambra.

Marketing strategy in a recession

During recessions most markets shrink, and a common response to this is for organisations to retrench, put their expansion plans on hold and wait for the economic climate to improve. In fact, for the astute organisation a recession offers tremendous opportunities for growth, provided the company is prepared in advance. Growth in declining markets is likely to happen through acquisition of ailing competitors, and this is never easier than during a recession. Here is a list of strategies for riding a recession and coming out of it in better shape than when the recession started.

- **Cash is king**. During a recession, credit becomes tighter, so companies with cash reserves are able to force down prices from suppliers or buy out competitors much more easily.

- **Debtors default much more often**. Giving credit to customers is a bad idea during a recession – payment dates stretch out and the debtor organisation may well go bankrupt, leaving the debt unpaid. Debtors can be a useful source of expansion by takeover: some organisations have achieved enviable vertical integration in this way.

- **Deals can be struck with liquidators**. If a competitor, supplier or distributor does go bankrupt, it is often possible to buy the organisation from the liquidators for a fraction of its going-concern value. In fact, some organisations even strike lucrative deals with directors before the company goes under, in order to avoid the stigma of bankruptcy or even to save the directors from the scrutiny of regulators.

- **Markets shrink for suppliers as well**. An organisation which has been a good customer in the past and shows signs of being a good payer is a valuable asset to a supplier, and one which is worth offering concessions to.

- **Good staff often become available unexpectedly**. As organisations go bankrupt, some highly skilled people enter the jobs market, often for salaries below what they might have commanded in their previous jobs.

- **Most financial managers insist on promotional budget cuts when times are hard**. This means that share of voice is easier to achieve, since competitors promote less, but it also means that advertising rates are likely to be cut as media struggle to sell space.

- **Raw material prices drop**. Many organisations destock during recessions. Towards the end of a recession, and indeed when dealing with liquidators, it is often possible to stock up with raw materials or components at very favourable prices.

Such strategies all have implications for marketing and can affect the marketing strategies adopted. Overall, recessions can be viewed as an opportunity rather than a threat. The key to success in a recession is to ensure that the organisation goes in with low financial gearing, and preferably with a cash 'war chest' in order to snap up bargains. Recessions normally last only a few months and are replaced within a year or two by boom conditions, during which it might be advisable to shed some assets while prices are high – in order to have cash on hand for the next recession.

TALKING POINT

If recessions are such a good thing, why do people complain about them? Surely a rattling good recession provides so many opportunities we should be opening the champagne, not crying into our beer!

Maybe recession favours only those who saw it coming, though – and fortune telling is a hit-and-miss business. Or perhaps the downside is greater than the upside, with companies losing business and people losing their jobs.

Of course, recessions might provide a good opportunity for the economy to cull the weak businesses – get rid of businesses that should never have been started in the first place. So are recessions good or bad? Much depends on your viewpoint and your level of preparedness.

International market entry strategies

There are five basic strategies for entering foreign markets, as shown in Table 7.5.

Two basic models of internationalisation are thought to be operating. The first is the stages of development model, in which organisations move through a series of stages as shown in Table 7.6.

In practice, most organisations use a customised approach to markets. Even organisations pursuing a globalisation strategy rarely use an entirely standardised approach across all the target countries (Harris 1996). Of 38 multinational companies surveyed by Harris, 26 claimed to standardise their advertising, but in fact only 4 used completely standardised advertisements.

An alternative view of internationalisation strategy is offered by Dunning (1993), who proposes the eclectic theory of internationalising. According to Dunning, organisations determine their specific competitive advantage over organisations both at home and overseas, and plan their market entry strategies accordingly. This means that an organisation will examine its strengths and weaknesses in relation to the overseas competitors, and instead of beginning by exporting and gradually making a greater commitment to the market, will enter the market by playing to its strengths. For example, IKEA has strengths in managing retail stores at minimum cost whilst also minimising customer

Table 7.5 International market entry strategies

Strategy	Explanation
Keep product and promotion the same worldwide	The advantage of this is that it minimises entry costs. Coca-Cola often adopts this approach, using basically the same advertising worldwide but translating any voiceovers into the local language. The major drawback of the approach is that it takes no account of local customs and attitudes, and tends to lead to a 'lowest common denominator' advertisement which can be understood by everybody and offends nobody.
Adapt promotion only	The product remains the same, but the promotion is adapted to local cultural norms. This is a fairly common approach, since it enables the marketing communications to reach the consumers more effectively while at the same time avoiding a redesign of the product itself.
Adapt product only	This is less common, but has been done by some detergent manufacturers to allow for differences in local water supplies and washing machines. Likewise, the supposedly 'global' Ford Focus is substantially modified for different markets in order to meet local emission standards and road-safety laws.
Adapt both product and promotion	Sometimes it is necessary to adapt both the product and the promotion, as in the case of Cheer washing powder, a Procter & Gamble product marketed in Japan. Cheer was reformulated to allow for the extra fabric softeners the Japanese use, and the promotion emphasised that the powder worked well in cold water (since most Japanese wash clothes in cold water).
Invent new products	If the existing products cannot meet the conditions in the new market, a new product must be invented. For example, the clockwork radio was invented for use in countries where there is no mains power supply and batteries are difficult to obtain.

Table 7.6 Stages of development model

Stage	Explanation
Exporting	This implies the smallest commitment to the foreign market. The exporter produces the goods in the organisation's home country and ships them overseas to be sold through agents or distributors. In the early stages of export, the organisation might even be using a reactive strategy, fulfilling orders only if a foreign distributor actually seeks them out rather than making any deliberate approach to the foreign market.
Establish a sales office in the foreign market	The organisation is now committed to the market, but could withdraw if necessary. Manufacture and decision making still take place in the home country, but some tactical marketing has been transferred into the target country.
Overseas physical distribution	This would involve establishing a warehousing and distribution system in the target country, implying an even greater commitment to the market. At this stage much of the marketing strategy is devolved to the organisation in the target country, bringing the decision making closer to the customers.
Overseas manufacture	Manufacturing the product in the overseas market means that the company can shorten the lines of supply and be more responsive to the customers' needs.
Multinational marketing	The company makes and sells the products in whichever countries are most advantageous. Components might be supplied from several countries for assembly in several others, for onward export to still more countries.
Global marketing	Global marketing means standardising products for perceived global segments. This is the approach taken by major computer manufacturers and other organisations where economies of scale are available for very large-scale manufacture. National boundaries almost cease to exist for such organisations, and their size ensures that their activities transcend national governments.

error in purchasing flat-pack furniture. IKEA therefore entered the UK market with full-blown retail stores, rather than operating concessions within other stores or simply exporting the furniture to other retailers.

Evaluating strategies through SWOT analysis

The above approach looked at how the organisation starts to assess its internal strengths and weaknesses when deciding on its market entry strategy in an international context. When evaluating marketing strategies generally, however, a similar approach is usually adopted and made more comprehensive through the inclusion of external opportunities and threats. Hence we commonly see SWOT (strengths, weaknesses, opportunities, threats) analysis as a key component of the marketing planning process (see Figure 7.3).

In effect the SWOT matrix depicts the marketing strategy process through bringing together the external and internal evaluation of the organisation's situation using information collected from the marketing audit. The process of strategy selection involved

Figure 7.3 SWOT analysis

Strengths	Weaknesses
Opportunities	Threats

requires that the business tries to *match* its internal marketing opportunities with its internal strengths. Alternatively it should try to *convert* weaknesses into strengths and threats into opportunities. Strategising around this is a key aspect of the marketing planner's task and needs to be undertaken through a full assessment of all the information gleaned through the marketing audit using a range of appropriate analysis tools and techniques.

Summary

Choosing an appropriate strategy as a way of closing the planning gap means making a series of complex decisions. Some of these decisions require a degree of subjective input, some are made as the result of sudden insights, most will require discussion with colleagues, and all involve an element of risk. In some cases, decisions are made in haste, in other cases they can be deliberated over for some time in order to calculate an answer.

The key points from this chapter are as follows:

→ The planning gap is the difference between what the company would like to have happen and what will happen if the company changes nothing.
→ Identifying the real problem often relies on managers' subjective perceptions.
→ Growth can be achieved by market penetration, entering new markets, developing new products, or diversification.
→ Winning strategies are cost leadership, differentiation, or niching. Trying to combine these will result in failure.
→ Value disciplines are operational excellence, customer intimacy and product leadership.
→ Recessions can be good, if the organisation is well prepared.
→ Entry to overseas markets can be incremental or eclectic.
→ SWOT analysis is used to facilitate decisions about marketing strategy.

Umar's analysis had identified that the Slick Mower was potentially heading into the decline phase of the product life cycle. The reference projection for the company assumed that, within five years, this product would be obsolescent and therefore a prime candidate for being dropped from the range. This would leave only the hand tools as the company's cash cows, sales of which would almost certainly be inadequate for maintaining profitability or indeed retaining credibility in the Eden Garden Tools brand.

Another problem Umar had identified was the perception on the part of the staff that the company was a traditional, even old-fashioned one. The reason for this perception was unclear – possibly it arose mainly from the feeling that the company was run in an old-fashioned way, possibly it was because few new products had been introduced in recent years.

Stopping the decline would require some drastic action. The basic alternatives were to enter new markets, develop new products, diversify, or increase penetration in existing markets. The audit had shown that Eden Garden Tools had a high share of its markets due to the innovative nature of the products (relatively few direct competitors could match the features and benefits Eden Garden Tools was offering). This meant that increased penetration would be difficult or impossible – Hugh pointed out that he was doing his best anyway and did not feel that John Peters would be able to do any better.

The management team decided that the company's core competency lay in its ability to innovate, even though this had been on the back burner during the recession. The vision statement had already emphasised this, and the group agreed that developing new products was the way forward. The tree pruning saw was only one of many innovative products the firm would need, and the feeling of the group was that, even if the venture capitalists' injection of cash did not materialise, the company needed to spruce up its product portfolio.

This in turn led to a decision about the company's competitive position. Clearly a cost leadership position would be impossible, given that cheap gardening tools were coming in from China at prices lower than Eden Garden Tools could manufacture them. Although the current competitive strength of the firm came (at least in part) from a focus strategy (supplying tools for women and disabled people), this approach had proved to be something of a dead end: there were no new markets to conquer.

The group decided that, if the company was to become a major player rather than a niche specialist, they would have to go the differentiation route.

Review questions

1 *Why is it often difficult to identify the problems that create the planning gap?*

2 *Why is a combination strategy likely to fail?*

3 *What are the main benefits of recessions?*

4 *Explain the difference between the stages of development approach and Dunning's eclectic theory.*

5 *How might companies choose between different strategies when trying to close the planning gap?*

Case study AeroMexico

Aerovias de Mexico S.A., operating as AeroMexico, is an airline based at Mexico City Airport. The airline runs extensive local services throughout Mexico itself and has subsidiary hubs at Monterrey and Hermosillo.

AeroMexico was founded in 1934, with one aircraft. The inaugural flight was from Mexico City to Acapulco, a distance of around 300 km. The company was helped a lot by Pan Am, which owned 25 per cent of the fledgling airline, and after the Second World War AeroMexico grew by acquisition, buying out small airlines such as Aerovias Guest, which at that time owned the routes to Paris and Madrid. Buying up war surplus Douglas DC-3s, the company was able to expand rapidly and by the 1960s began replacing the piston-engined aircraft with fast jets such as the Comet IV-C.

The company was nationalised for a while, along with all other Mexican airlines, but during the 1980s it suffered a major setback following an accident in which a private plane collided with an AeroMexico airliner over Los Angeles, killing all 64 passengers and crew on the airliner and another 15 people on the ground. The pilot of the private plane was blamed for the crash as he had strayed into controlled airspace without permission – but the bad publicity bankrupted AeroMexico. In August 1988 the company was privatised and relaunched, with a commitment to meet high standards of punctuality, trustworthiness and care in the use of the equipment, i.e. the aircraft. In fact, AeroMexico is the second most punctual airline in the world (after, perhaps surprisingly, Aeroflot). In the mid-1990s the company suffered some financial setbacks, and reformulated its approach to make its routes more productive and to generate greater shareholder value by maximising income and reducing operating costs. The company became structured into three market segments (beaches, businesses and borders) in order to compete effectively with the new generation of low-cost airlines springing up. The main plank in this platform was the establishment of AeroMexico Connect, which uses small aircraft as 'feeders' from regional airports such as La Paz and Vera Cruz to bring passengers into the main 'hub' airports of Mexico City and Monterrey. Connect operates in much the same way as any other low-cost airline – tickets are bought online and fares are determined mainly by demand: tickets from Mexico City to La Paz can be bought for as little as £10 (plus airport fees and taxes).

Where Connect differs from other low-cost airlines is that passengers can choose from four separate fare deals, each one of which allows the passenger different facilities and rights to change the fare or the route. This enables people to choose whether they want the cheapest fare with no frills, or to pay extra and have greater flexibility and comfort.

AeroMexico's entry into overseas markets appears somewhat haphazard, with routes being inherited from other companies and sometimes added or dropped arbitrarily. The route to Madrid is an obvious one for a Latin airline to choose, since so many Mexicans live in Spain and vice versa (in the same way as flights between New York and London are an obvious route for British and American airlines). However, the routes to Japan and China are less obvious, even though AeroMexico is the only Latin airline flying to the Far East at the time of writing. AeroMexico has scored well in sharing its frequent flyer programme with Air France, KLM and Delta. This naturally increases the links between these airlines and encourages through-ticketing whereby each airline can accept bookings for the others, thus covering routes which would otherwise not be feasible for any one of the members.

AeroMexico has had a somewhat chequered past, and given the current state of the world airline industry probably has an equally problematic future. In the meantime, the company knows its domestic market well and is making strong inroads into international markets.

Questions

1 *What are the fundamental problems underlying AeroMexico's future?*
2 *What model of internationalisation does AeroMexico appear to be following?*
3 *Which of Porter's strategies is AeroMexico following?*
4 *Which value disciplines might work best for AeroMexico?*
5 *How might AeroMexico best grow its business?*

References

Ansoff, H.I. (1965): *Corporate Strategy* (Harmondsworth: Penguin).

Clifford, D.K. and Cavanagh, R.E. (1985): *The Winning Performance: How America's High- and Midsize Growth Companies Succeed* (New York: Bantam).

Dunning, J.H. (1993): *The Globalisation of Business* (London: Routledge).

Haines, D.W., Chandran, R. and Parkhe, A. (1989): Winning by being first to market – or last? *Journal of Consumer Marketing*, Winter pp 63–9.

Hamel, G., Doz, Y. and Prahalad, C.K. (1989): Collaborate with your competitors – and win. *Harvard Business Review*, January/February.

Harris, G. (1996): International advertising; developmental and implementational issues. *Journal of Marketing Management*, 12 pp 551–60.

Hennart, J.F., Roehl, T. and Zietlow, D.S. (1999): Trojan horse or workhorse? The evolution of US–Japanese joint ventures in the United States. *Strategic Management Journal*, 20 pp 15–29.

Homburg, C., Krohmer, H. and Workman, Jr., J.P. (1999): Strategic consensus and performance: the role of strategy type and market-related dynamism. *Strategic Management Journal*, 20 (4) pp 339–57.

Porter, M.E. (1985): *Competitive Advantage* (New York: The Free Press).

Treacy, M. and Wiersema, F. (1993): Customer intimacy and other value disciplines. *Harvard Business Review*, January–February pp 84–93.

Part 3

MARKETING STRATEGY THROUGH SEGMENTATION

Choosing the right group of customers to target is one sure way of using resources wisely. Adopting a 'scattergun' approach in which marketing effort is spread across a wide range of customers is, however, a sure way of allowing competitors to gain the upper hand.

This section of the book considers segmentation, targeting and positioning in depth. Choosing the right way to segment the market, choosing the right segment to target, and then positioning the company against its competitors in the customers' perception will avoid squandering the firm's resources on chasing people who have no interest in, or use for, the products on offer.

Chapter 8 considers strategic aspects of segmentation. Chapter 9 moves on to a more tactical viewpoint. Chapter 10 is about choosing which segments to target, and Chapter 11 considers positioning.

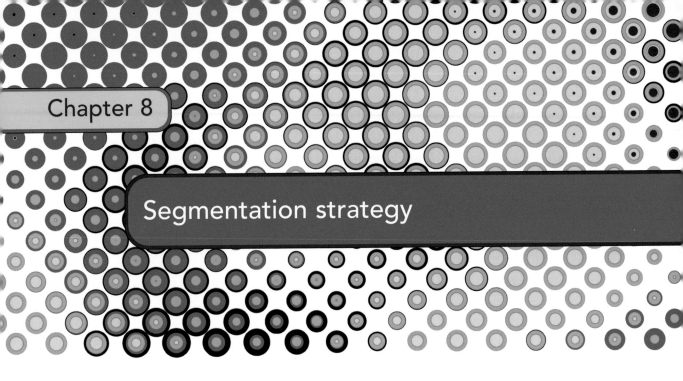

Segmentation strategy

THE EDEN GARDEN TOOLS COMPANY LTD

The senior management of the company (Mike Winton, Hugh Parris, Umar Sayeed and John Peters) met to consider the overall market the company was in. Mike expressed the idea that the company was in the gardening tools business, Hugh said they were in the business of making life easier for gardeners, John said they were in the business of moving engineering products, and Umar said they were in the business of improving the lives of several groups of people, including homeowners and disabled people.

After a certain amount of discussion among the team, they decided that Umar had a point – there were several groups of people that the company served, out of a large overall market which might be defined in terms of 'people who grow plants, either because they like to or because they earn money doing it'. This somewhat clumsy definition of the market helped to clarify their thinking, but did not help much in knowing what they should be doing on a day-to-day basis. What they needed to do was define their customers much more closely – in other words, segment their market.

Objectives After reading this chapter, you should be able to:

→ Explain what is meant by the served market and outline its significance in planning.

→ Describe the different levels at which segmentation works.

→ Explain why people are prepared to pay more for a customised product, and why the one-size-fits-all approach rarely works.

→ Explain why multiple segmentation bases should be used.

→ Describe the difference between strategic value of a segment and tactical value, and evaluate the trade-offs between them.

→ Explain the components of product strategy.

→ Describe the strategic functions of pricing.

→ Explain the integration of the marketing mix in developing strategy.

Introduction

Strategy is about where the company is going, as opposed to tactics, which is how the company is going to get there. In many companies, marketing is seen as an essentially tactical tool, but marketing strategists believe that marketing should be the guiding principle of the business and therefore marketing strategy should also be the company's overall strategy.

Whether or not marketing strategy and corporate strategy are identical, segmentation is a key factor in deciding in which direction the company is going. Segmentation is the process of dividing up the market according to customers' needs, wants and behaviour. It is a crucial aspect of marketing because it indicates where resources can be best directed to achieve the company's objectives.

Defining marketing boundaries

Segmentation is only one of several factors which define the boundaries of a market. For example, there are various ways of cooking a meal: gas cookers, electric cookers, microwave ovens, even electric kettles can be used to boil water for preparing instant noodles. There are devices such as electric griddles, meths-fuelled fondue sets, and barbecues as well. Should all these products be lumped together as a single market, or can they be separated out in some way? After all, most of us would not be able to cope very well if we could cook only on a barbecue or in a microwave.

Traditionally, markets have been defined in terms of product and market space (Srivastava et al. 1981). This leads us to talk about the car market, the book market, or the housing market. Alternatively, we might define the market in terms of buyers, talking about the motoring public, book buyers, or homeowners. In fact, these definitions are not anywhere near precise enough for practical marketing in the complex world of the 21st century.

An alternative approach, originally put forward by Abell (1980), looks at the market from three dimensions: technology, customer function and customer group. Technology refers to the different ways the same function can be performed using different technologies. Using the cooking example, one can deep-fry fish and chips in a pan on an electric cooker, in a pan on a gas stove, or in a deep-fat fryer. In terms of the end result for the customer, the differences are small – other factors such as the type of cooking oil used will be a great deal more important.

Customer function refers to the end result for the customer. In the cooking example, the end result of using all three methods of deep frying is a meal, but there is more to it in the sense that some methods are messier or smellier, or more expensive in terms of fuel use. The customer function is what provides the overall range of customer benefits.

Customer group is what is also referred to as a market segment. It is a group of people with similar needs and characteristics. These groups can be targeted by companies with the necessary technology to provide a customer function.

A market might be defined by any combination of these three factors. For example, an electronics manufacturer such as Samsung has moved from supplying televisions and radios to supplying microwave ovens; the technology is similar, even though the customer function and customer group are different from those the company has addressed in the past. The market boundary for Samsung is defined by electronic technology, cooking function and customers with the money, the desire and the need for a fast way of heating food. (Customers might be defined even more tightly, of course – since many people use microwaves mainly for reheating pre-prepared food, the market boundary on that dimension might be defined as people who can't cook.)

As markets evolve, the boundaries may very well need to be restated. New technology will change the boundaries, as will changing customer need and the changing profile of the segments. New customer groups might enter the market (microwaves were originally owned only by the wealthy – it was some time before they became cheap enough for everyone to own one) and some customers might leave the segment permanently, either because they move on to a better solution for their needs or because the need no longer exists.

This leads to the concept of the served market. The served market is the parts of the overall market that the company is able to serve, in other words the amount of market share the company can realistically capture. The served market is usually a lot smaller than the total market, because of lack of resources and presence of competition. The decision about which parts of the market to serve is based on the following criteria (Jain 2000):

- The managers' perception of which product function and technology groupings can best be protected and dominated.
- Internal resource limitations that force a narrow focus.
- Cumulative trial-and-error experience in reacting to threats and opportunities.
- Unusual competencies stemming from access to scarce resources or protected markets.

In practice, of course, the decisions are not likely to be made in such a calculated manner. Managers end up making decisions in various ad-hoc ways, with limited information and time pressures added to the mix. Strategically, the choice of served market might be based on the following possibilities:

1 **Breadth of product line**. The company might specialise in a particular technology with a broad range of product uses. For example, an electronics manufacturer might produce everything from radios to guided missile systems – the silicon chips used for video games might well be the same ones used for missile guidance systems. A firm might equally specialise in product use, using a wide range of technologies – for example, a firm might specialise in security equipment and offer locks, burglar alarms, security shutters, window bars, security doors, and so forth. Specialising in a single technology with a narrow range of uses is another option, especially for a small, science-based firm – for example, biohazard detection systems using live animals is a highly specialised business. Firms might specialise in a broad range of related technologies and uses, or might (finally) have a broad range of quality and price levels.

2 **Types of customer**. The firm might target a single segment or multiple segments, offering either an undifferentiated or a differentiated treatment.

3 **Geographic scope**. This could be local or regional, national, or multinational.

4 **Level of production**. This could be raw or semi-finished materials, finished products, or wholesale or retail distribution.

For most marketers, the firm's technology is a given factor beyond the control of the marketing department, at least in the short term. Equally, the customer function aspect is beyond the control of the marketer (although it is possible to decide which customer function we intend to address). This means that the main strategic area the marketers will be involved in will be in dealing with segmentation.

Strategic issues in segmentation

The main strategic problem in segmentation lies in choosing the most appropriate basis on which to divide the market. It is easy to make a wrong assumption when choosing a segmentation base. The classic example is nightclubs, which were assumed to be aimed mainly at a segment of young people, so the market was segmented according to age. In fact, nightclubs are used by single people, most of whom are likely to be young, but many of whom are divorced or widowed and looking for a new partner. The result of this insight was the over-30s, over-40s and even over-50s nights which are now a regular part of the nightclub scene.

All very well saying that it is easy to get the segmentation base wrong, but how do we know we are getting it right? If business is good and we have a nightclub full of young people, why should we care that the market is defined as a single market rather than a young market? In any case, it's more likely the bouncers will be excluding people who appear to be too young (under age) rather than people who are obviously a bit older.

If somebody else comes along and opens a nightclub for the over-30s, why should that affect us? After all, young people won't want to go to a club that's got a reputation for being full of old people! The big question, at the end of the day, is whether we need to worry about segmentation at all. In the words of the Kevin Costner movie Field of Dreams, *'Build it, and they will come'. If we offer what we offer, those who like what we offer will spend their money with us, surely?*

Or maybe it's about directing our advertising better?

The same can be true of industrial market segmentation. It may appear that a market segments according to the industry the customers are in, whereas in fact it segments according to the end use of the product. For example, it may be the case that the fishing industry uses a particular type of heavy-weather protective clothing, and thus the manufacturer segments the market according to industry, whereas in fact the clothing might be equally appropriate for other outdoor workers or even hikers.

Segmentation operates at four levels, as follows:

1 **Mass marketing**. This is not really segmentation at all – the firm simply produces something that a very large number of people will want, then produces it in vast quantities at very low prices. Clothing items such as baseball caps and T-shirts fall into this category. In the 21st century, this approach is all but impossible to carry out, since consumer expectations have shifted and people want products which are more nearly tailored to personal needs. Also, there are very few products which everyone wants – and most of those are already in production, meaning that companies in those markets are forced to compete on price.

2 **Segmented markets**. At this level, the marketers have identified substantial groups of people with similar needs, and have also identified a means to satisfy those needs. The company will choose which segments to target, and can direct resources in the most efficient way, at the same time reducing competition.

3 **Niche marketing**. Typically, this approach is carried out by companies with very limited resources or with very high levels of expertise in a given area. Niche marketers focus on a small sub-set of a segment, offering carefully targeted products. The advantage is that these sub-sets are often too small to be economic for a large firm to tackle, so there is unlikely to be strong competitive pressure. The small firm is therefore able to carve out a comfortable living and can often charge premium prices for what is, after all, a specialist service.

4 Micromarketing. At this level the company tailors its products to the exact requirements of each customer. Two hundred years ago, this was how almost all products

were made. Each customer would commission a craftsman to make something exactly to order, whether it was a pair of boots or a bed frame. Micromarketing uses modern production techniques to create tailored products – for example, the optician chain Vision Express manufactures spectacle lenses on-site in each of its shops, so that customers can have an eye test, choose suitable frames and walk out with tailor-made glasses within an hour. Unfortunately, many people are not prepared to pay the premium prices necessary to cover the increased cost of such a service (Bardacki and Whitelock 2004).

In general, people are prepared to pay more for a more customised product, but there are limits. Since most firms operate in global markets, the economies of scale involved in manufacturing a wide range of products mean that most people are able to find almost-perfect products without too much difficulty. At the same time, there is a great deal more choice of supplier, so marketers who do not treat their customers as individuals, with individual needs and wants, will find themselves losing business.

For a larger firm, the degree to which the company will cover a given market is a strategic issue. Abell (1980) offered five basic strategies for market coverage, as shown in Table 8.1.

Table 8.1 Market coverage strategies

Strategy	Explanation	Example
Product/market concentration	This is niche marketing by another name. The company chooses a small, specific group of customers with very special needs.	Pickfords heavy haulage is a company which specialises in moving unusual loads such as large machinery. It has a fleet of special lorries, contacts with the police, and an in-depth knowledge of the road system (for example, where there are low bridges or tight corners which would prevent the load from passing).
Product specialisation	The firm produces a full line of a specific product type.	Campbell's produces soup almost to the exclusion of everything else.
Market specialisation	The company produces everything that a specific group of customers needs.	Titleist produces everything a golfer needs, from clubs to balls to golfing clothing.
Selective specialisation	The firm enters selective niches that are not closely related but are profitable.	British Telecom sells telephone services to private individuals and businesses, and also sells spare capacity on its satellites to TV stations.
Full coverage	The firm enters every possible segment of its potential market.	Honda produces every possible form of private transport, from light motorcycles to cars, including off-road quad bikes and sports motorcycles.

Strategic evaluation of segments

Correct identification of the segments means that marketers can meet the needs of the segment members much more effectively than the competition can. The segment will be profitable provided customers are prepared to pay a sufficiently large premium to cover the extra costs of producing a more tailored product. These costs can be substantial, since narrowing down the segment means a smaller number of potential customers.

The strategic potential of a segment goes beyond its immediate tactical value (see Figure 8.1). Simply choosing the segment which offers the highest immediate profit level is far from adequate. A given segment may have potential in many other ways, as follows:

1 **The segment may have future potential**. For example, some airlines target young backpackers taking a year out before going to university, since these people will (eventually) become professional people who may well travel business class. The same applies to some fast-food restaurants – McDonald's notoriously targets children, even though the margins on children's meals are relatively low and children are likely to be more troublesome than adults in the restaurants.

2 **The segment may have influence over other segments**. Celebrities are an obvious example, but in the business-to-business world it is common for some companies to have influence or even power over others. For example, when Westinghouse invented air brakes for trains, it targeted a railroad which operated out of Chicago and persuaded it to fit the system. This meant that any other railroad company which intended to run trains through Chicago needed to adopt the same system in order to be compatible with other trains.

3 **The segment may open the door to a market for other products in the range**. People who look for a cheap computer printer will need to buy ink cartridges, and likewise people who buy computers are likely to be in the market for software of various types.

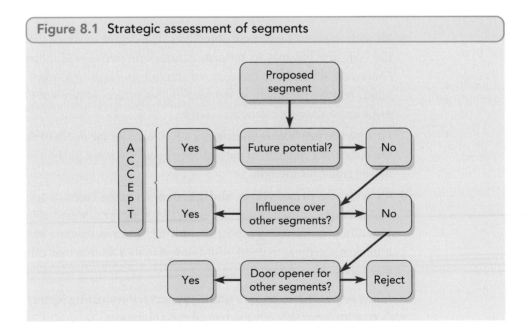

Figure 8.1 **Strategic assessment of segments**

Evaluating segments

Segments can be evaluated against a number of criteria, both internal and external, as follows:

1 **Immediate profit**. A segment which will show a quick profit is, at first sight, attractive. However, managers need to be aware that competitors are likely to enter the market since the segment will appear profitable to them as well. This may not be a major problem, but does require special preparation.

2 **Sustainability**. This is the degree to which the segment will retain its members in the longer term. In consumer markets, there are relatively few segments that remain sustainable long term because individuals pass through various life stages, and in any case fashions alter – the market for top hats is now very limited, whereas a century ago the market was substantial. Business markets tend to be more stable in the long run, because business needs change at a slower rate.

3 **Future potential**. The segment may be growing in size, or it may be growing in spending power.

4 **Current size**. The greater the number of customers in the segment, the less important each individual customer becomes. This allows the company the possibility of making a few mistakes – if it has only one potential customer for the products on offer, the risk becomes very high, in part because the potential customer may not agree to buy anything, and in part because the potential customer will wield a disproportionate amount of negotiating power.

5 **Current spending power**. If the segment members are financially robust, the segment appears attractive. This consideration applies in both business-to-business markets and consumer markets (although marketers need to bear in mind that wealthy individuals are often extremely careful about how they spend their money). In business markets, it may be the case that a particular segment is cash-rich due to special circumstances such as a rise in commodity prices (e.g. oil companies) or interest rates (e.g. banks).

6 **Fit with the firm's strategic objectives**. The degree to which the segment will help the company towards its ultimate strategic objective will influence the decision. Otherwise, it would be too easy for the firm to waste resources chasing segments which may be profitable in themselves, but which simply serve to blur the firm's focus and reduce its competitive edge.

7 **Fit with the firm's core competencies**. The closer the needs of the segment fit with the company's capacity to meet those needs, the more likely it is that the segment will be viable for the firm.

8 **Fit with the firm's vision and mission**. In some cases, a segment might raise ethical issues, or may simply not fit well with the firm's vision of itself and its future. This differs from having a poor fit with the firm's immediate strategic objectives – it implies a general malaise with the segment, a feeling that this would be a poor marriage.

It should be possible to create a scoring system for evaluating segments, but in practice such systems inevitably rely on managerial judgement.

Marketing strategies for marketing objectives

Marketing strategies exist as a means towards meeting corporate objectives. Each of the 7Ps has a strategic dimension, and each of these dimensions has implications for reaching objectives. This section examines some of the implications.

Product

Product strategy falls into two sections: new product development strategy and portfolio management strategy. New product development is driven by innovation objectives, which in turn are driven by the corporate vision. In some cases, the company will see itself as wishing to be at the forefront of technology (e.g. 3M or Sony), where in other cases the company sees itself as exploiting existing technology more effectively.

Basic innovation strategies are as follows:

1 **Imitative**. Here the company simply copies an existing product. This strategy means that the company can be reasonably sure of finding a market, because the product already exists: capturing a section of an existing market is clearly advantageous. Provided the product also has marketing or production synergies (or both), it is likely to succeed, but without these it is likely to fail (Calentone and Cooper 1981). The biggest drawback of this strategy is that it almost inevitably implies competing on price, which of course reduces profits.

2 **Defensive**. This strategy means that the company copies an existing product, but makes some improvements or at least changes it enough to differentiate it. Again, the company may end up competing on price, but it may very well have a product that overcomes some of the drawbacks of the first-to-market product, and of course the company will not have incurred anything like the development costs that the innovating company had to invest. Often a defensive strategy comes about because the company is threatened by new competition and is forced to produce something which offers similar benefits – for example, when low-cost airlines began to make serious inroads into traditional routes flown by major flag-carrier airlines, the flag carriers often started their own low-cost subsidiaries. Such products are often called 'me-too' products.

3 **Offensive**. Here the company takes pride in being the first to market with truly new-to-the-world products. This implies a heavy investment in research and development, and also making considerable efforts to protect the intellectual property of the company, but it does have the advantage that the firm might capture the whole of the market.

4 **Dependent**. A dependent strategy means that the firm produces new products only when told to by a customer. This often happens in business-to-business markets, where (for example) a small firm supplies a much larger firm. The small firm might be asked to supply components made to a particular specification as a result of the large firm bringing out a new model.

5 **Traditional**. This strategy is not innovative at all. The company simply produces old designs, either because it has always produced them or because the products are tried and tested and need no improvement. For example, tin-opener technology has hardly changed in 100 years. Equally, some companies take pride in continuing to produce items that have been in their portfolio almost since the company began – the Acme Whistle Company still markets the same whistles that were supplied to officers on the *Titanic*, and manages to make a very good business of it.

6 **Opportunistic**. This strategy involves marketing new inventions. Most inventions are technology-driven rather than market-driven, so they often fail to find a market, but occasionally something will come along that succeeds in capturing a segment. The clockwork radio (invented by Trevor Bayliss and marketed by his company Baygen is one such example). Companies operating on an opportunistic basis would usually have to take on a lot of new products to obtain a relatively few successes – but such a strategy can provide all the advantages of the offensive strategy without the up-front development costs (which have mainly been borne by the inventor).

In recent years, the traditional strategy has received a boost due to the interest in 'retro' products. 1950s-style household appliances and radios have been launched, and of course the car industry is full of examples – the new Volkswagen Beetle, the Mini Cooper and the Chrysler PSV are all revived designs which have done well in the market.

Whether a new product should go ahead or not rests on four decision dimensions (Carbonell-Foulquie et al. 2004). These are as follows:

1 **Strategic fit**. This is the degree to which the new product will take the company nearer to where it plans to be in the future. Specifically, this will rest on whether the product is effective in meeting the needs of a specific segment the company wishes to target.

2 **Technical feasibility**. This is about offering the product as part of a portfolio, as well as the question of whether the product can be made economically. If making the product will detract from the production of other products in the range, it may not be feasible to go ahead.

3 **Customer acceptance**. Many products are launched each year which fail to find a place in the market. Obviously no marketer should consider launching a product which does not meet a specific need better than the products which are already available, but people do make mistakes – it is far from uncommon for managers to fall in love with a product to the extent that they lose sight of the fact that no one else loves it.

4 **Market opportunity**. This is about the level of competition the firm is likely to meet and other factors in the external environment. Careful monitoring of the external environment will help to inform this decision, but the main elements are the customers and the competitors because these make up the market.

5 **Financial performance**. This does not necessarily mean profit, but firms do have to show an overall profit if they are going to stay in the game. If a product can never be profitable, the firm does need to consider whether it should be launched at all – only an overwhelming strategic argument in favour of launch could make it worthwhile.

Ultimately, it is customer acceptance that is the deciding factor. If customers cannot accept the product, launching it is a waste of time and effort. Almost everything else can be overcome if customers like the product.

TALKING POINT

Launching new products seems to be pretty risky, one way or another. It's expensive to develop a new product, it's expensive to launch it, products can easily be copied by other firms and even then the customers might not buy it. So why bother?

Is it some kind of ego trip on the part of the company's directors? Is it a view that we need to do something the competitors aren't doing? Is it about obsolescence of existing products? Of course, if no one ever produced anything new, the horse would still be the quickest way of getting from one cave to another, but why risk it?

Maybe we should find out how many estate agents are making a living from selling caves, though. People like new products – but should we be the ones who risk launching them?

Portfolio management strategy

Few, if any, companies have only one product to sell. Almost all have several products in the portfolio, so they need to decide how to allocate resources between the various products.

The classic model for doing this is the 1970 Boston Consulting Group Matrix, which sought to trade off market share and rate of growth of the market to decide whether a product was worth keeping. In fact, the Boston Consulting Group now say that the model was never intended to be used in this way, and that it was more about the attractiveness of markets than about the viability of products. Having said that, the model is widely quoted.

In the diagram, a product with a high share of a rapidly growing market is categorised as a star. This product is probably not profitable yet, but it will be eventually – at present it is fighting off competitors and having a lot spent on its growth.

A product with a large share of a low-growth market is a cash cow. This is because it requires very little marketing input: other firms are not very interested in entering the market because it is not growing, so occasional reminder advertising will usually suffice to keep the product in the market. Meanwhile the product can be 'milked' for cash to fund others in the portfolio.

A product with a small share of a high-growth market is a problem child or question mark. This product is worrying because it is getting left behind by other people's stars. Many managers make the error of believing that year-on-year growth in sales of a product mean that it is a success; in fact, if the market is growing faster than growth in sales of the product, the company is falling behind. Building market share is likely to be difficult, since other products are better established, so adapting the product may be necessary. The difficulty for marketers lies in working out why the product is not succeeding when others like it are – hence the 'problem child' label.

Finally, a product with a small share of a low-growth market is called a dog. The implication is that the product has failed and should be dropped. Obviously there may be strategic reasons (or even sentimental reasons) for keeping an old brand that has been superseded, but the theory is that such products should not be kept in the portfolio.

The BCG Matrix considers only markets which are growing. However, markets do not always grow – as the financial crisis of 2008 demonstrated. In 1982, during an earlier recession, Barksdale and Harris (1982) added two more categories to the BCG Matrix (see Figure 8.2). These were the warhorse, which has a large share of a shrinking market, and the dodo, which has a small share of a shrinking market. There would appear to be no imaginable justification for keeping a dodo in the portfolio, but a warhorse might conceivably have some worth since it is extremely unlikely to need much, if any, marketing expenditure and can therefore be allowed to fade away while providing a cash flow, much like a cash cow.

Figure 8.2 Expanded BCG Matrix

		Relative market share	
		High	Low
Market growth	High	Star	Problem child
	Low	Cash cow	Dog
	Negative	Warhorse	Dodo

Source: Barksdale and Harris, 1982.

There are several difficulties with this type of analysis, however. First, the categories are arbitrary: whether a share is 'high' or 'low' demands judgement on the part of the manager. The same applies to growth rates. Second, the purpose of the portfolio management exercise is to allocate resources more effectively. If there are no current outlets for resources (for example, the manager has underspent the budget), the company may well feel that it is worthwhile taking a risk with a cash cow or a problem child. However, a sudden drop in available resources (perhaps because business is worse than was expected) might mean that a promising star has to be cut from the portfolio.

Price

Price is more than just a way of getting money in. Price signals the quality of the product and can help in positioning (see Chapter 11). Setting the right price is one thing; having the right pricing strategy is another.

Pricing strategies fall into the following categories:

1 **Price skimming**. This means charging a high price initially, then steadily reducing it as competitors enter the market and the company's intellectual property wears thin. In some markets price skimming has become so commonplace that consumers will wait until the price falls. The home electronics market is one such example.

2 Demand pricing. This means setting the price at a level that the market will bear, in other words a price level that people see as good value for money, but which returns a profit to the firm.

3 Price penetration. Here the company sets the price low in order to capture a large part of the market before competitors can respond. This strategy is extremely dangerous – it can easily trigger a price war, in which only the firm with the deepest pockets will come out the winner.

4 Customary pricing. This strategy means that the price stays the same but the product gradually shrinks. This is the way telephone companies price calls from public call boxes. The strategy avoids the necessity of resetting the boxes every time the price of a call goes up.

Strategic pricing means setting prices according to the characteristics of the target segment. Being the cheapest product in the market is not usually a very good strategy to follow – apart from the profit implications, it signals poor quality. Most companies concentrate on representing good value for money to their chosen segments, rather than aiming to be cheap.

Place

Distribution strategy is concerned with getting the products to the right place at the right time and in the right quantity. Distribution should aim to make it as easy as possible for customers to buy the product – the more convenient the distribution is for customers, the more likely they are to buy.

Since distribution covers so many different possibilities in terms of routes to market, the strategic plan needs to consider the needs of channel members. Clearly a channel member might be extremely concerned if the company does something which might undermine the channel member's position in any way. Channel strategy is determined by the following:

1 Convenience for target customer groups.
2 Cost – which includes making an allowance for the profit margins of channel members.
3 Need for speed in getting products to market.
4 Need for reliability of distribution.

Note that there are trade-offs involved here: greater speed to market and/or greater reliability of distribution will involve extra costs.

Promotion

Developing an appropriate strategy for a product or company is likely to lead to a degree of integration of promotional tools. Planning a promotional campaign is a major undertaking in itself – there are many considerations to take into account, especially in terms of customer needs, likes and dislikes.

Promotion strategy is concerned with the following aspects:

1 The message platform, in other words the basic message to be conveyed.
2 Media choice.
3 Branding.
4 Choosing the correct promotional tools.
5 Deciding the degree of integration of the promotional mix.
6 Budgeting.

People

Employing, training and motivating the right people has strategic implications. If the company expects people to act on their initiative, for example, this implies hiring people who like to make their own decisions, training them to know what they can and cannot do, and ensuring that they do not become demotivated if their decisions are less than perfect.

People who are in the 'front line', i.e. those who meet customers on a regular basis, are obviously extremely important from a marketing viewpoint since (for the customers) they *are* the company. Having said that, other people in the firm will affect the customer experience – even people such as accounts department staff who prepare invoices. Everyone within the firm has some role in generating customer satisfaction, but in service-oriented businesses staff become even more important, since not only are they the company, they are often also the product.

Process

Especially in service industries, the process by which benefits are delivered to consumers is part of the overall package. From a strategic viewpoint, planners need to decide what the delivery process needs to be in order to meet customer needs most effectively. Process decisions revolve around the following:

1 Convenience for the customer.
2 Cost.
3 Reliability.
4 Corporate competencies – the degree to which the company is able to carry out a specific process.

As with all other strategic decisions, cost and overall effectiveness will come into play, as will competitive pressures. Often the process is what differentiates a company. McDonald's differentiated itself by the speed with which the food was delivered, until other fast-food companies developed similar systems.

Physical evidence

The tangible elements in the product mix can be the biggest differentiators. In the case of a physical product, this is clearly the case, but it can also be true of service products such as restaurants or hairdressing salons. Such businesses need to look clean, efficient and welcoming, and may well provide physical souvenirs of a visit – an appointment card for next time, or a gift to take home.

Planning for physical evidence may be constrained by the available premises and by customer expectations – clearly a business buyer would not expect a lollipop after making a purchase of wheel nuts.

Finally, marketing planning will also encompass the combination of the 7Ps to create an overall package – the marketing offering.

Summary

Strategic approaches to market segments involve choosing the segment, then choosing which of a range of possible strategies can be used to approach the segment. The choice of segment depends on a number of strategic issues, one of which is, of course, the ease with which the segment can be approached with a suitable marketing mix strategy.

The key points from this chapter are as follows:

→ The served market is the parts of the overall market that the company can realistically serve the needs of.

→ Segmentation operates at four levels: mass markets, segmented markets, niche markets and micromarketing.

→ People are prepared to pay more for a customised product.

→ The segmentation base is critical: one base for segmentation is unlikely to be sufficient.

→ Strategic potential for a segment may go well beyond its immediate tactical value.

→ Product strategy comprises new product development (NPD) and portfolio management.

→ Price has many strategic functions other than generating income.

→ The marketing mix needs to be seen as a strategic whole.

The company's overall strategy would be one of segmented marketing rather than mass marketing or niche marketing. The firm's resources could not possibly stretch to mass marketing, nor could the company produce mass-market products: its competencies clearly lay in producing innovative products for specialist segments.

The served market for Eden Garden Tools had clearly been the hobby gardener, but now the company was planning on moving into a new market with the pruning saw. Commercial growers and professional tree surgeons would need an entirely new approach – but the strategic fit, financial viability, technical feasibility and market opportunity all seemed to make this worthwhile. Strategically, the team felt that the new product might help reposition the firm in the commercial arena, as well as open up further opportunities to go global with a technically superior product.

The only real problem was a lack of marketing synergy for the new product – it would need to go through new channels, to a whole new customer base about which little was known. Meanwhile, the team was still no nearer to defining its market, since it had yet to make a clear segmentation.

Review questions

1 *What is the relationship between price and customisation?*
2 *Why is mass marketing unlikely to be a successful strategy?*
3 *Why might a company target an unprofitable segment?*
4 *What are the problems in using matrix models for portfolio management?*
5 *How might a company calculate the size of the served market?*

 ## Case study Boutique Caravans

Caravanning has been a part of the British holiday scene since the 1920s. The idea of towing a mobile home behind your car and heading out onto the open road is apparently as appealing now as it has ever been, despite legislation limiting caravan owners to licensed caravan sites.

However, there has been something of a shift in the market in recent years. Although there is still a market for the traditional lace-curtained caravan, many older people are selling their houses, selling off their possessions or giving the family heirlooms to their children and setting up home in a caravan instead. In some cases, people are buying caravans to travel, heading off around Europe or further afield to follow the sun and have a few adventures before making the inevitable trip to the care home, but in other cases downsizing to a static caravan on a caravan park frees up the equity in their houses so that they can have more spending power.

During 2009, as the pound weakened against foreign currencies and the recession began to bite, more and more people began to look at having their holidays in the UK rather than travelling abroad. This meant an increase in the number of people taking up caravanning, especially among 30- and 40-somethings, many of whom have young families.

Into this market has stepped Dick Shone, founder of Boutique Caravans. 'There are people of my generation, approaching 50, whose main asset is their house, who are thinking about downsizing to park homes for retirement. But when I looked at what was on offer, the aesthetic was rather old-fashioned,' says Shone, an art publisher. He set about rethinking the original concept of the caravan and came up with the Indy home. This is a caravan with a difference, more like the inside of a penthouse suite than a caravan. Its super-insulated wood and glass interior has full-size beds, state-of-the-art top-brand kitchens, power showers, underfloor heating and a sophisticated ventilation system. The Indy is intended as a static caravan, but can be used as an office, a home extension, or a summer house. Parking a caravan like the Indy does not usually require planning permission, and it can be delivered on a truck and be ready to move into in a single day. The caravans are not cheap, of course – from £40,000 for a very basic version, to more than £70,000 for the top-of-the-range version.

Shone is hoping to find a suitable piece of land to develop into an Indy park. This would be on the south coast of the UK, convenient for weekenders from London or for more permanent residents. The aim is to promote caravan holidays as being as luxurious as being at home – people no longer want to 'rough it' on holiday, especially if they are travelling with children. Old-fashioned caravans carry the image of being cold, noisy when it rains, inconvenient and uncomfortable; Dick Shone aims to break the mould.

Other companies are tapping into the 'new' caravanning market. T@B Caravans are touring caravans with a difference – smart, modernistic pods that are ultra-lightweight and can therefore be towed behind very small cars. The interiors still have king-size beds and enough space to seat five adults (although the caravan sleeps only two). T@B caravans even have an electric window so that the owners can sleep under the stars if they want to. The slightly larger versions can be fitted with a leather sofa, flat-screen TV, DVD player, gas fire, underfloor heating and a retro 'diner' area.

For years, caravanning has suffered from childhood memories of holidays spent sitting in a cold, damp, smelly caravan listening to the rain hammering on the roof and playing board games around a Formica table. Modern caravan producers are seeking to break the mould, attracting Generation X families to the new touring caravan and well-off Baby Boomers to the luxury static market. Boutique Caravans and T@B are at the sharp end of this new wave.

Questions

1 *How might Boutique Caravans define its served market?*

2 *How does the caravan market appear to segment?*

3 *At what level of segmentation is Boutique Caravans operating?*

4 *What is the role of price in the company's thinking?*

5 *Why would Shone want to develop a special park dedicated to Indy caravans?*

References

Abell, D.F. (1980): *Defining the Business: The Starting Point of Strategic Planning* (Englewood Cliffs, NJ: Prentice Hall).

Bardacki, A. and Whitelock, J. (2004): How ready are customers for mass customisation? An exploratory investigation. *European Journal of Marketing*, 38 (11/12) pp 1396–416.

Barksdale, H.C. and Harris, C.E. (1982): Portfolio analysis and the PLC. *Long Range Planning*, 15 (6) pp 74–83.

Calentone, R.J. and Cooper, R.G. (1981): New product scenarios: prospects for success. *American Journal of Marketing*, Spring (45) pp 48–60.

Carbonell-Foulquie, P., Munuera-Aleman, J.L. and Rodriguez-Escudero, A.I. (2004): Criteria employed for go/no-go decisions when developing successful highly-innovative products. *Industrial Marketing Management*, 33 (4) pp 307–16.

Jain, S.C. (2000): *Marketing Planning and Strategy* (Cincinnati, Ohio: South-Western College Publishing).

Srivastava, R.K., Leone, R.P. and Shocker, A.D. (1981): Market structure analysis: hierarchical clustering of products based on substitution-in-use. *Journal of Marketing*, 45 (Summer) pp 38–44.

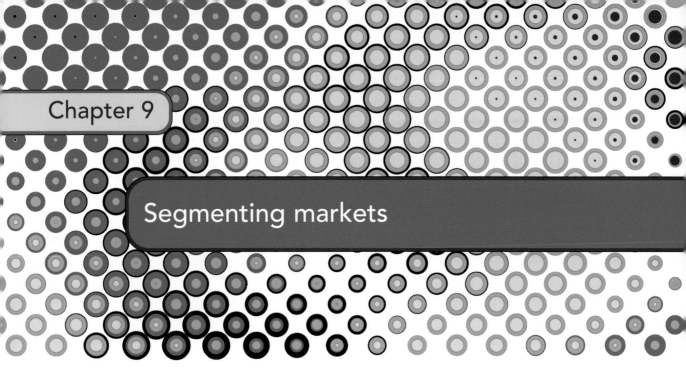

Chapter 9

Segmenting markets

Choosing the right segmentation strategy was one thing, choosing the right base or bases was something else again. Identifying groups of customers with similar needs was potentially a minefield, since the company had no market research of its own telling management what the existing customer base needed or did not need.

This meant that the senior management team had to rely on secondary data, and on looking at surrogates such as sales of other products with a similar potential market. Umar Sayeed was desperate to get some solid data on the current customer base, but there simply was not enough cash in the budget to carry out the necessary market research. All the company had to go on was an incomplete database of returned warranty cards, but since around two-thirds of consumers did not bother sending in the cards (especially if their purchase was a hand tool, where the cost is relatively low and the reliability relatively high), this was far from being an adequate basis for research.

The company was therefore shooting in the dark, relying on experience and hearsay rather than solid data. This was not a good place for Umar to be.

Objectives

After reading this chapter, you should be able to:

→ Describe the main bases for segmenting markets, and identify some sub-bases.

→ Explain the difference between *a priori* and *a posteriori* segmentation.

→ Explain why some segmentation bases are unreliable.

→ Explain the role of behaviour in segmentation.

→ Describe the nested approach to segmentation in business-to-business markets.

Introduction

Segmentation is the process of dividing up the market into groups of customers with similar needs. The purpose of the exercise is to channel the firm's resources into areas where they will do the most to generate competitive advantage. Segmentation is necessary because firms all have limited resources: it is not possible to please everybody, so managers have to decide which groups of customers will be the most beneficial (not always the most profitable) for the firm.

Choosing a base for segmenting the market is not as simple as it might appear at first.

Segmenting the market

Effective segmentation, like anything else in marketing, begins with developing a good understanding of customers' needs and wants. Sometimes this comes about from direct experience of dealing with people, sometimes it is the result of good market research. Either way, knowing which are the key issues that divide and unite people is essential. In practice, segmentation follows three stages:

1 **Develop an understanding of the various customers in the whole market**. It is rarely possible to have a perfect knowledge of everyone's needs, but the greater one's knowledge, the better the chances of finding a previously unidentified segment.

2 **Group customers according to their needs, behaviours and characteristics**. Identifying the most relevant characteristics is the difficult part of segmentation – whether people have red hair or not is unlikely to be a useful factor for a car manufacturer, but might be crucial for a hair cosmetics manufacturer.

3 **Select the groups to be targeted**. Rejecting some groups as being unprofitable or difficult to deal with is an important part of targeting – managers need to decide which groups of customers are undesirable, since this is a way of minimising the waste of resources that servicing such groups would entail. For example, a group might be geographically distant despite being desirable in other ways, or might simply be unlikely to pay the prices the company needs to charge.

There are many possible bases for segmenting markets, but in consumer markets they fall into three main categories: behavioural factors, psychographic factors and profile factors. These general groupings are not mutually exclusive, and in fact it is very likely that firms will use several different segmentation bases at once to refine their analysis of the market. Use of one base alone is likely to be too crude for the complex markets most companies face.

Figure 9.1 shows a possible segmentation of the market for motor vehicles, based on product type. The customer types are drawn somewhat crudely, however, and it would be better to begin by identifying a particular group of customers and deciding what type of vehicle they might find useful. For example, quad bikes were originally intended as a fun, sports vehicle; they are now frequently used by cattle ranchers in Australia and the United States instead of horses.

Figure 9.1 Segmentation of the motor vehicle market

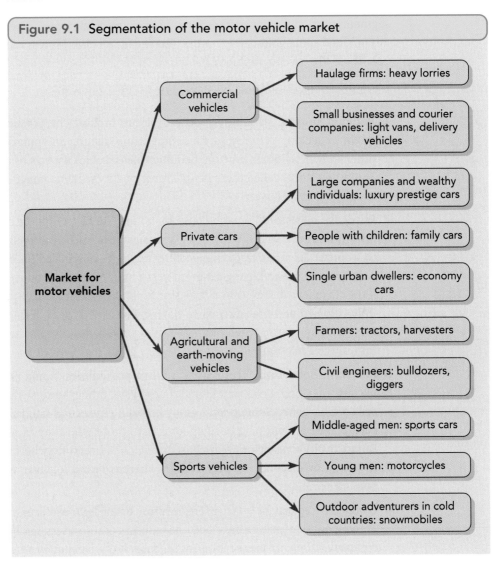

In industrial markets, segmentation bases fall into two main groupings: *a priori*, or before the fact, approaches which consider factors which can be identified through research, and *a posteriori*, or after the fact, approaches which identify factors which have become apparent only after starting to deal with the customers.

In the first instance, we will look at segmentation in consumer markets.

Behavioural segmentation

If we can segment a market according to people's behaviour we have (at first sight) a very straightforward base for decision making. A firm manufacturing golf clubs, for example, needs to know only that its customers play golf. Anyone who plays is a potential customer for the product, so (on the face of it) the company already has its segmentation and targeting strategy in place. In practice, though, the market segments further: some golfers are beginners, who may not want to spend a lot on a set of clubs, while others might be championship players, who are prepared to spend very highly indeed. Some golfers play frequently, some less often, some play on courses which tend to favour particular types of club, and so forth. So far these all fit within behavioural segmentation – but some golfers are influenced by celebrity endorsement while others are not, and some golfers rely on the advice of their club professional while others do not. These are psychographic variables.

The main behavioural bases for segmentation are as follows:

1 **Benefits sought**. In some cases, people are looking for practical benefits, some might be seeking the prestige that comes from owning an upmarket product, while others might be looking for the hedonic (pleasurable) aspects of using the product. Sampson (1992) called these people functionality seekers, image seekers and pleasure seekers respectively.

2 **Purchase occasion**. For some customers, the product might be a gift for someone else (it has been said that, in the UK at least, the bulk of after-shave lotion is sold to women). In other cases, the product might be purchased for own use. Purchase occasion may mean buying different versions of a similar product at different times – the traveller who stays in a four-star hotel on a business trip may prefer a traditional old bed-and-breakfast when having a weekend break at the seaside. A restaurant that one goes to when one is too tired to cook may not be the same one chosen for a special celebration.

3 **Purchase behaviour**. This covers a lot of possibilities. Some people shop online because they find it convenient and time saving, others because they find it easier to seek out bargains. Some people enjoy browsing in second-hand shops for bargains; such people are not necessarily poorer than those who shop in mainstream stores. Brand loyalty is also part of purchase behaviour – brand switchers simply pick up the cheapest, or the one on special offer, whereas brand loyalists will seek out their favourite brands.

4 **Usage**. People may be heavy users, medium users, light users, ex-users or non-users. Finding out why people have become ex-users or non-users can be very useful for a company. Often, ex-users represent the most lucrative market since they are already familiar with the product. In recent years, customer winback has become of increasing importance to firms. What many marketers try to do is target heavy users and lure them away from competing firms. This is problematical, however, because there will undoubtedly be resistance from the competitor. A better tactic might be to encourage light users up to being medium users, and medium users to heavy users, while re-recruiting ex-users.

5 **Buyer readiness stage**. All buyers go through a series of stages before reaching the final purchase decision. Some people may be unaware that the product exists, whereas others may be at the point of making a decision. Although the buyer readiness stage does not affect the product offering itself, it certainly does affect the type of communication the firm might need to use. For major capital purchases such as houses or cars, salespeople need to be aware of the buying stage – someone who is still information gathering will almost certainly be scared off by a full-blown sales pitch, whereas someone who is at the decision-making point will welcome the discussion.

6 **Attitude towards the product**. In some cases, non-users or ex-users may have formed such negative attitudes towards the product that they will never be persuaded to change their minds.

Behavioural segmentation can be misleading: sometimes people are loyal to a product because they have few, or no, other choices. Sometimes people behave irrationally, sometimes they feel coerced, sometimes they simply do not know that there is a better way of doing things. It would therefore be dangerous to rely entirely on behaviour as a base. Finding out why people behave as they do may also be important in the long run.

Geographic segmentation

Location affects consumption in many ways. Differences in climate, terrain and, of course, culture will have marked effects on what people buy. People in cold countries need warm clothes, warm housing, central heating and so forth; in hot countries people need air conditioning, sun screen, solar heating and cooler clothing.

However, geographical segmentation goes further than this. At the micro level, people living in particular areas of a city will have many things in common. They live in similar types of house, they have similar income levels, and they often have similar education levels. In many cases, they share an ethnic background: many cities in the UK have Chinese districts or Bangladeshi districts. Several systems exist for categorising areas in this way: ACORN and MOSAIC are two well-known ones, through which retailers can decide where to place stores and what to stock in them, insurance companies can calculate which areas are most likely to make claims, and home-improvement firms can estimate which areas are most likely to have houses which will need the product.

Geographic segmentation sometimes indicates behavioural differences which are not easily explained, such as food choices, but some less obvious purchase choices can have a geographical basis. For example, most washing machines in the United States and Australia are top-loading, whereas European washing machines are virtually all front-loading. The reason for this is that American and Australian homes are larger and there is therefore more room for top-loaders (which are easier to use and more reliable). Front-loaders fit conveniently under kitchen worktops, which saves space. Interestingly, people in hotter parts of Europe such as Spain, Greece and Italy often keep their washing machines outside anyway, so fitting under a worktop is not an issue.

Some problems with geographic segmentation are as follows:

1 It is often used for the firm's convenience, not for the customers. Salespeople are usually allocated geographical territories in order to minimise travel times, for example.

2 There is so much world travel and migration that boundaries become blurred. People come back from foreign travel with new ideas and needs, and migrants take their eating and clothing habits with them.

3 Sometimes people adopt food and clothing from other parts of the world as a way of identifying with them. For example, African Americans sometimes wear African-style clothing in order to identify with Africa, even though they have never been to Africa and are unlikely to go (deBerry-Spence and Izberk-Bilgin 2006).

Geographic segmentation can easily be confused with other segmentation bases. For example, a geographical region may have a specific dominant culture which influences consumption (e.g. a Muslim country will not be importing very much bacon), but this is actually a cultural issue rather than a geographic one; the country next door might be predominantly Christian and therefore would have no problem with pork products. This can even be the case within a single country – the Indian state of Goa is predominantly Christian and therefore is virtually the only place in India where pork curries are available.

Demographic segmentation

Demographics is concerned with the structure of the population in terms of age, wealth, income, gender, occupation, education level, and so forth. Demographic segmentation is extremely widely used, because it is relatively easy to identify the members of given segments and data is readily available from government and other sources. Consumption patterns often correlate well with demographic variables: people with large incomes tend to spend more money and also save more, but of course there are not many firm correlations with what they spend their money on. We cannot say for sure that wealthy people will always drive expensive cars, for instance, but we can say that poor people rarely do so.

Demographic segmentation can be misleading. It may, for example, appear that a product appeals to better educated people, whereas in fact it appeals to people with higher incomes. Since better educated people often have higher-than-average incomes, the two factors can easily be confused.

Age segmentation

Although demand for some products does change with age, for the majority of products age is irrelevant. Products such as pension plans and products to overcome physical changes such as wrinkles and grey hair will obviously become of greater interest as one grow older, but products such as cars, clothes, food, entertainment and holidays show very little relationship with age. The relationship between age and behaviour is far from linear (Simcock et al. 2006).

Age segmentation is also sometimes crudely applied, for example by carrying out research in which everyone aged over 65 is classified together. This implies that a 66-year-old woman has something in common with her 88-year-old father, which is plainly ridiculous. As the population ages, there may well be people over 65 with living grandparents – so researchers will need to have more boxes to tick in these older age groups.

For children, clothing is often sized according to age, but mothers quickly learn how to decide whether their child should be in an age larger or smaller. Children's toys tend to be age-specific, but even here age is a crude measure: a year is a long time in a child's life, and a six year old may well be able to play happily with toys intended for much older children. Gender is in fact a much better predictor of interest in toys, and in any case as children grow older they develop their own interests and attitudes so that other factors become much more important.

Age is an indicator of life experience: people in their 80s remember the Second World War, people in their 60s remember the Vietnam War protests, and people in their 30s grew up with the telecommunications revolution. These life experiences can be useful when designing communications, because marketers can use nostalgia to attract attention and evoke appropriate feelings. Music from one's teenage years is particularly powerful in this context.

Gender segmentation

Gender segmentation was, at one time, very clear. In recent years, gender roles have become much less prescriptive and consequently purchase behaviour is much less gender-specific. Research by Mintel shows that 28 per cent of men take the main responsibility for cooking, 20 per cent take responsibility for all the laundry, 40 per cent of men aged over 55 do at least half the grocery shopping. Men still take the bulk of the responsibility for household repairs and gardening, but women are gradually taking on more of these tasks.

Although many older couples still divide the housework along traditional gender lines, most young couples split the tasks more equally. Most younger women tend to have careers rather than the 'pin money' jobs their mothers' generation had, which means that household tasks must be divided more equally. Of course, women still take time out of their careers to care for small children at home, so may take on more of the household tasks, especially if the male half of the couple has to work longer hours to bring in money.

There are, of course, products which will always be gender-specific simply because of physical differences between men and women, and social mores also drive some purchases. It is still rare for men to wear facial make-up in Western societies, and few women take up contact sports such as boxing or wrestling.

Marketers have not been slow to notice these changes and act upon them. Advertising which shows men performing household tasks such as cooking and cleaning are common, especially when the advert is demonstrating something which makes the tasks easier or quicker (thus explaining the task to men who were not shown how to do it by their mothers), and flat-pack furniture instructions no longer assume that the customer studied woodwork in school.

Gender segmentation also includes sexual orientation. Homosexual people tend to be wealthier and better educated than average, and have fewer outgoings since they are less likely to have dependent children. In the UK, homosexuals' disposable income (called the Pink Pound) was estimated at over £6 billion a year as long ago as 1998 (BBC 1998). In the intervening decade the value has doubtless increased substantially. The same research showed that homosexuals earn (on average) 23 per cent more than the average, have twice as many credit cards as the general population, and spend more than the average on entertainment.

Estimates of the number of homosexuals in the population are difficult to make because there is still some reluctance to 'come out' and identify oneself as gay, since there is still a large degree of hostility towards gay people in some quarters.

Income segmentation

Segmentation by income is widely practised, although it is not a reliable base on its own. The reason is that someone may have a high income, but also have high out-goings. Someone earning £40,000 a year is earning almost double the UK average salary, but may be paying £1,000 a month for a mortgage and may have children to support, meaning he or she will have very little disposable income. Equally, someone with a pension of £15,000 a year may have paid off his or her mortgage, may have no dependent children now and may have a relatively high disposable income as a result.

Disposable income is therefore the key factor. Even then, disposable income tells us nothing about the individual's tastes and preferences, nor does it tell us about the degree to which the individual is prepared to spend rather than save. Rich people are often very careful about how they spend their money – not surprisingly, since this is probably how they became rich in the first place.

In some cases, companies have become successful by targeting people on low incomes. Discount retailers such as Lidl, Aldi and Netto site their stores in poorer areas, partly because this keeps costs low since rents are lower, and partly because it puts them close to their target market. However, during 2008 these stores reported a rise in turnover as the recession caused wealthier people to start looking for ways to cut their outgoings.

Religion, ethnicity and nationality

Nationality is a legal condition rather than a cultural condition, so it has relatively little effect on purchase. Its main effect is in global marketing, where companies often segment by nationality because of the legal restrictions which apply to products in different countries. Apart from flags, patriotic symbols and legal services, there are practically no products which are specific to nationality.

Ethnicity is a combination of factors which derive from culture and race. The cultural elements include eating habits, clothing, some entertainment products and some cere-monial products (for example the funeral money sold in Chinese grocery shops). Segmenting by ethnicity has become blurred in recent years because marketing activities and increased travel have caused culture swapping. People often eat food from other cultures and even adopt clothing from other cultures (Jamal 2003).

Race has some effect on purchasing, mainly in the area of cosmetics. Dark-skinned women need different cosmetics from light-skinned women, and the characteristics of hair differ between black, Asian and white people, which means that hair formulations need to be different – demand for different hairdressing treatments varies across racial groupings.

Religion affects many aspects of purchase, in particular food buying. Some foods are forbidden to the faithful of various religions: Jewish people should not eat shellfish, Jains and Parsees are strict vegetarians, Mormons do not drink tea, coffee or alcohol, and many Catholics still eat fish on Fridays even though this particular restriction was rescinded many years ago. Religion also affects some clothing purchases (burkas for Muslim women, yarmulkes for Jewish men) and of course affects purchase of religious artefacts such as crucifixes, rosaries, menoras and religious books. In Western industrial countries these religious influences are probably declining, but still have some importance.

Psychographic segmentation

Markets can be segmented according to lifestyle or personality characteristics. Lifestyle is the set of behaviours associated with a particular set of preferences, and therefore is both created by and dictates purchase choices. For example, someone who decides to live in an upmarket inner-city area probably enjoys what the city has to offer in terms of shops, entertainment, social life and so forth. Someone who chooses to live a self-sufficient lifestyle in the countryside would have very different purchasing patterns, but in each case these lifestyles are a product in themselves: the apartment the city-dweller buys, and the smallholding the country-dweller buys, are each statements in themselves.

Lifestyle segmentation has the big advantage that it relates directly to purchase behaviour. Segmenting consumers according to their chosen way of life is logical, considering that marketing is often said to deliver a lifestyle. One well-known lifestyle segmentation model is the VALS (values and lifestyles) structure. The model postulates nine basic lifestyle positions, as follows:

1 **Survivors**. These people have extremely limited income and wealth, and can barely manage to survive. They live in poverty and struggle to maintain any kind of lifestyle. They have very limited choices.
2 **Sustainers**. These people are slightly better off than survivors, but are still poor and have few choices available.
3 **Belongers**. These people can meet their basic needs comfortably and have enough spare resources to join with mainstream society. They are not excluded by reason of their poverty.

All three of these groups are driven by need and are concerned with security and belonging. The need to belong can be very powerful indeed – for example, members of a football fan club often resist buying anything from outside the group which might not confirm their membership of the group (Richardson and Turley 2006).

The next five groups are better off and divide into inner-directed groups (who tend to be independent thinkers who do not care what people think of them) and outer-directed groups (who are concerned with appearances and with good behaviour as judged by the society they live in). The following three groups are the inner-directed ones.

4 **I-am-me**. These people live their lives regardless of what others think, and sometimes with little regard for other people's comfort. They tend not to be heavy consumers, but often represent the more creative element in society. The artists, musicians and writers who make (and spend) very little money, but who produce cutting-edge work are often drawn from the I-am-me group.

5 **Experientals**. These people seek out new experiences, so are customers for travel, concerts, unusual foods, experiential gifts such as hot-air balloon flights or Formula One driving experiences, and adventurous pursuits such as climbing and windsurfing.

6 **Societally conscious**. This group tends to be cause-oriented, the kind of people who become activists of one kind or another and who become involved in charity work, pressure groups and political parties (Donnelly 1970).

Outer-directed groups are concerned with other people's opinions. They are as follows:

7 **Emulators**. These people take their cues from their neighbours and others. They are susceptible to suggestions from marketers and will typically follow fashion and be interested in what opinion leaders such as celebrities do and say.

8 **Achievers**. These people look for respect from other people and therefore are customers for prestige products such as upmarket cars, designer clothing and branded goods (Zhinkan and Shermohamad 1986).

The final group is usually the wealthiest and has adopted a balanced attitude to their lifestyle.

9 **Integrated**. The integrated group like to be respected and to respect others, but they do not let this drive their lives: they still like to act independently, to satisfy their internal drivers, but can equally be respectful of the feelings of others.

Personality characteristics

One of the advantages of segmenting by personality traits is that personality changes very slowly over time, if at all. This means that an individual is likely to stay in the segment for a long time. This is certainly not true of segmentation by age, and is often not true of segmentation by income.

The drawback is that it is extremely difficult to identify groups of people through their personality traits because it is virtually impossible to test large groups of people. For example, an insurance company might wish to target people who are afraid of being burgled because they would tend to have alarms fitted, have better locks on their houses, and take out bigger insurance policies. Unfortunately, there is no clear way to identify those people and no advertising medium which is aimed at them. The main way of approaching a segment defined by its personality is to use similar people in the advertising, an approach which has been used extremely successfully by Frizzell Insurance. Frizzell aims for a segment of public employees, and has been extremely successful using direct marketing approaches in the workplace. Public employees such as teachers, civil servants, local authority workers and the like have obviously chosen a safe lifestyle. However, Frizzell needed to expand its customer base, so it created advertising which used actors who appeared similar to the target market. The advertising was a runaway success, not least because it did not appeal to the customers Frizzell did not want.

A relatively recent concept in personality segmentation is that of the 'savvy' consumer. These are people who are marketing-literate and have wide knowledge of the available choices. They have the following characteristics (Macdonald and Uncles 2007):

1 They are competent in technology, especially communications technology.

2 They are competent in interpersonal networking.

3 They are good at online networking.

4 They are marketing-literate: they understand what marketers are doing to try to influence them.

5 They are empowered by their self-efficacy, in other words they know that they are competent consumers.

6 They are empowered by the expectation of firms, because they know how to manipulate marketers.

Savvy consumers pose a particular problem for marketers, because they know how to manipulate situations to their advantage. It is likely that savvy consumers will increase in number as time goes by – they are also prone to advise others on how to get the better of marketers.

Another emerging psychographic segmentation approach is the concept of interpretive communities, or groups of people who have similar ways of interpreting and responding to messages (Kates 2002). Interpretive communities are hard to identify except by the way they interpret messages, so the only way to reach them is by running an advert in a particular style and seeing who responds. For example, some people prefer to interpret messages visually, some are more open to tactile (kinaesthetic) interpretations, and some process information aurally. Each group will respond to advertising differently (Skinner and Stephens 2003).

TALKING POINT

So consumers are becoming more savvy. This is hardly surprising really – after all, so many people have studied marketing, and there is so much in the press and on TV about how marketers 'manipulate' people into buying things. There are really no secrets any more – no marketing technique remains unexplored by the average consumer, who by and large has conceived a deep mistrust of marketing and marketers.

So what does that mean for segmentation? How do we know whether somebody really belongs in a particular segment, or whether they are simply manipulating the marketers for their own advantage? Does it matter anyway – after all, if we are providing something that people need, at a price they can afford, why would someone who doesn't need the product and can't afford it try to manipulate the marketers?

Segmenting business markets

Segmentation of business-to-business markets differs somewhat from that for business-to-consumer markets, for the following reasons:

1 Consumer markets are characterised by customers who are the end users for the products, or at least are very close to the end users. Business buyers do not themselves use the products in most cases.

2 There are many more customers in consumer markets than is the case in business-to-business markets, so a greater degree of customisation is usually necessary.

3 Psychographic and demographic variables are almost always inappropriate because business buyers are (at least in theory) less influenced by personal factors.

Segmentation variables in business markets can be divided into two categories. The first, identifiers, are used by firms to establish segments *a priori* or before any direct data is collected (Day 1990). The data for these variables is relatively easy to obtain, either through observation of the buying situation or through published sources. These variables include operational factors, data on the product required and variables relating to the purchasing situation as well as the equivalent of demographic variables (size of firm, location, turnover, competitive situation, etc.).

The other group of segmentation variables is the response profile, or *a posteriori* group, which includes vendor product attributes, customer variables, application variables and the personal characteristics of the decision-making unit.

Identifier variables

Identifier variables are as follows:

1 **Demographics**. This includes industry classification, for example using the North American Industry Classification System (NAICS) which categorises firms according to what they produce. Firms might also be classified as original equipment manufacturer (OEM) firms which make end products to sell to consumers and others, as end users which use up the products entirely in the course of their business, or as aftermarket or maintenance, repair and operations (MRO) firms which provide services to companies and consumers. Demography would also include geographic location and financial status – credit rating, in other words.

2 **Operations**. This would include the type of technology used, the level of use of the products on offer (heavy, medium, light, etc.) and whether the firm has centralised or decentralised purchasing.

3 **Product required**. This is a question of whether the customer company would require a standardised product or a customised product.

4 **Purchasing situation**. This includes the buying situation (whether it is a new task, a repeat purchase, or a modified rebuy). It also includes the purchasing firm's attitude towards our firm and whether we have a good relationship with the decision-making unit.

For the most part, *a priori* variables can be estimated before making a sales pitch for a product.

Response profile variables

The response profile is about the way the vendor would respond to our sales pitch and would include the following variables:

1 **Vendor product attributes**. This encompasses the overall value of the product, its quality, the reputation of the vendor, the innovativeness of the product from the purchaser's viewpoint, the delivery reliability and the overall cost.

2 **Customer variables**. This would include the make-up of the decision-making unit at the purchasing company, the importance of the purchase, their attitude towards the product, and the corporate culture as it applies to buying new products (corporate innovativeness).

3 **Application**. This means the end use to which the product will be put and the importance of value-in-use (the money made or saved by using this product rather than another).

4 **Decision-making unit (DMU) personal characteristics**. This would include their risk tolerance, their loyalty to their current supplier, their age and experience, and their education level.

These variables are often *a posteriori*, i.e. they become apparent only after first contact with the customer.

The nested approach to segmentation

The nested approach uses multiple segmentation variables to refine the segment (Bonoma and Shapiro 1984). The nested approach is shown in Figure 9.2. Using this approach means that the selling firm can target the most likely customers more accurately. In business-to-business markets, the level of resources needed to make a sale is often much higher than that in consumer markets, and because there are fewer potential customers and the sales values are generally very much higher, the need to get the segmentation right is much greater.

The nested approach has been widely used in business-to-business markets, but in fact the method applies equally well in consumer markets. One segmentation method is rarely sufficient: several bases must be used to fine-tune the approach to an exact segment.

Global segmentation

There are many market segments which cross national boundaries, especially in business-to-business markets. For example, ICI Nobel Explosives offers mining

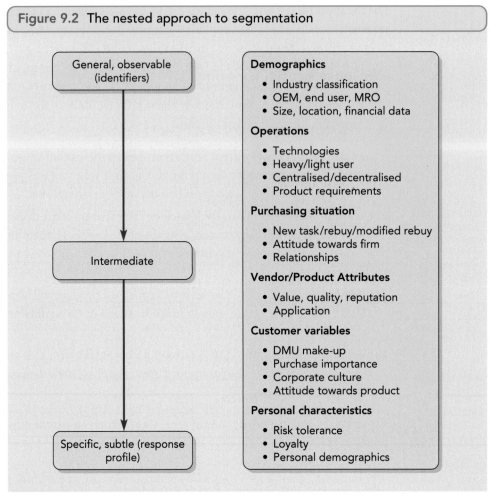

Figure 9.2 The nested approach to segmentation

Source: Adapted from Bonoma and Shapiro, 1984.

explosives across various countries to similar customer types, coordinating its activities in each country by segment and offering products and support activities accordingly (Gillespie et al. 2004). The main drawback is, of course, collecting data in different countries. Statistics are often collected differently, companies might be classified differently, and information may be missing entirely in some countries. Despite these difficulties, Schuster and Bodkin (1987) found that more than 40 per cent of firms they surveyed gathered substantial segmentation information on a global basis. More than 20 years have elapsed since then and globalisation has become much more important in the intervening period, so it might be safe to assume that firms gather a great deal more information now.

According to Yip (2003), customers can be segmented according to their degree of globalisation, as expressed through their purchasing behaviour. Global customers are willing to purchase from outside their home country, but control purchasing centrally from their headquarters. National global customers buy from all over the world, but use the products only in their home countries. Finally, multinational global customers buy from suppliers in many countries, but also use the products in many countries as well.

The main problem with global segmentation is differences in the purchasing decision process across borders. A study of purchasing decision processes in the US, Sweden, France and five South-East Asian countries found differences in the buying process and also in the structure of the DMUs (Mattson and Salehi-Sangari 1993). However, marketers need to look for commonalities in global markets rather than be daunted by the differences between countries: doing so will help generate economies of scale.

An alternative approach was suggested in 1999 by Keillor and Hult. Their NATID (national identity) approach comprised the following elements:

1 **National heritage.** This is the degree to which national history pervades the thinking of people from the culture.
2 **Cultural homogeneity.** This is the degree to which people within a given culture agree on its basic tenets.
3 **Belief system.** This is the shared set of beliefs people have about the way society should operate. These beliefs are the basic foundations of behaviour in any culture.
4 **Consumer ethnocentrism.** This is the degree to which people believe that their culture is 'right' and everyone else's culture is a poor imitation.

This framework was further developed by Phou and Chan (2003) to create a model in which five cells compare NATID scores with consumer ethnocentrism. Each of these cells has implications for segmentation.

The resulting five cells were:

1 **High NATID coupled with high ethnocentrism.** Customised products with high local content are most likely to succeed in these markets because these consumers share a strong belief in their history and culture, and believe foreign cultures are somehow inferior. Examples offered by Phou and Chan are Korea and Thailand.
2 **Low NATID with high ethnocentrism.** Standardised (i.e. global) products can succeed well, but the threat of imported products needs to be downplayed and the benefits to the nation as a whole need to be explained in any promotions. An example of this type of situation is Hong Kong, which has little national identity (as a former colony of Britain and a recent addition to China) but does have a strong belief that other cultures are inferior to its own.
3 **High NATID coupled with low consumer ethnocentrism.** Here the aim is to determine which of the key dimensions of national identity would be most helpful in segmenting the market. Standardised (global) products can compete extremely well when the marketing mix is adjusted correctly.
4 **Low NATID with low consumer ethnocentrism.** This combination means that standardised products can succeed well if the country is highly homogeneous, but if the market is heterogeneous the segmentation will need to focus on psychographic or other variables.
5 **Middle ground.** Finding a basis for differentiation is difficult in these circumstances, so marketers will probably have to fall back on traditional segmentation variables.

The difficulty with this type of segmentation is that the differences between individuals from a given culture frequently outweigh the average differences between the culture as a whole. This means that moving from the general to the particular is likely to prove disappointing – in other words, trying to guess how an individual from a given culture will behave, based on an overview of his or her culture, is unlikely to be very effective.

Summary

Splitting the potential market into manageable segments is a key function of marketing, but it can be effective only if the bases for segmentation are realistic. It is rare for one base to be sufficient to segment a market, and it is easy to make a mistake by confusing one set of data for another.

The key points from this chapter are as follows:

→ The main segmentation bases are behavioural, psychographic and profile. Within these general categories there are many sub-bases.

→ Segmentation can be *a priori* (carried out before any business is done with the customer group) or *a posteriori* (carried out after having some experience of dealing with the customers).

→ Segmentation by age is often unreliable, as is segmentation by gender.

→ Segmentation by ethnicity has become blurred in recent years.

→ Lifestyle segmentation relates directly to purchase behaviour, as do all behavioural segmentation approaches.

→ The nested approach to segmentation is essential in business-to-business markets, and extremely useful in business-to-consumer markets.

After some wrangling, in particular about definitions of who the customers are, the team settled down to segmenting the market. They saw the domestic, amateur gardening market as segmenting across the following bases:

1 Behavioural. People who spend time on gardening, versus those who do not.

2 Demographic. Able-bodied versus disabled, gender, age, wealth (wealthier people tend to have larger gardens, for example).

3 Psychographic. People who see the garden as another household chore, versus those who see gardening as a hobby.

Looking at the company's served market, the team realised that in fact they did not know a great deal about their end customers, the consumers. They had made a number of assumptions – that the Slick Mower mainly sold to wealthier people with unusual-shaped lawns or large, rambling gardens, and that the tools were sold to people who were committed to gardening as a hobby – but it could equally be the case that the mowers sold to people who had not got the time to create a smooth lawn, and the tools were sold to people who were simply looking for the easiest way to garden.

Finally, the directors agreed to find Umar some money to research consumers. He set up an online survey, mainly because the cost would be low, even though he knew the results might be problematic due to the tendency for online surveys to attract a particular type of person and exclude others. On balance, Umar thought this was better than nothing, though, so he went ahead. Sure enough, the study showed that most current customers for the hand tools were women, and of these the vast majority were hobby gardeners. The male respondents were largely reluctant gardeners, who saw gardening as a necessary chore rather than a pleasure. Umar was aware from his reading of the published market research that this view was common among younger men, since they had less time to spare from their careers than did older, retired men. The disabled market turned out to be smaller than anticipated, with few respondents. Whether that reflected a reluctance on the part of disabled people to participate in surveys, or whether they were in fact under-represented in the customer base, was impossible to say.

The consumer market therefore appeared to divide into segments, as follows:

1 Time-constrained younger men looking for a quick solution (behavioural, gender, age and situational factors involved).
2 Women with money to spend on their hobby (wealth, gender, behavioural and psychographic variables).
3 Well-off older people with large gardens (age, wealth, situational and behavioural factors).
4 Disabled and infirm gardeners (behavioural, psychographic and situational factors).

In the commercial arena, the way was somewhat clearer. Here, the market clearly segmented as follows:

1 Commercial growers according to size.
2 Tool hire companies.
3 Independent contractors (tree surgeons, etc.).

All these segments would need to be approached, but each would need a different strategy.

Review questions

1 *Why is a single segmentation base insufficient?*
2 *How can a priori segmentation be carried out?*
3 *Why is segmentation by age or by gender unreliable?*
4 *How might a company identify savvy consumers?*
5 *What are the main problems in segmenting global markets?*

Case study BMI

BMI, or British Midland International, is a UK-based airline which operates services throughout Europe, as well as to some long-haul destinations. BMI has its roots in the late 1930s. It began life as Air Schools Ltd, an independent flying school which specialised in training RAF pilots. During the Second World War the company grew dramatically as many more pilots were needed, so when the war ended the company's finances were in very good order, but of course demand for pilot training reduced dramatically.

In 1949, the company began trading as Derby Airways, eventually becoming British Midland Airways when it moved operations to the newly opened East Midlands Airport in 1964. In 1993, it became the first airline in Europe to offer a separate business-class cabin on short-haul flights. By this time the company was part-owned by Scandinavian Air Services (SAS). In 1999, Lufthansa bought part of SAS's share, so each foreign airline owned 20 per cent of the company, which became BMI in 2001.

In 2002, BMI launched BMI Baby, a low-cost subsidiary which operates entirely independently of BMI and has its own distinct branding. In the early part of the 21st century BMI expanded its long-haul routes, with flights to the US, India and the Middle East. The company bought out BMED in 2007 and thus acquired a number of new routes to Africa.

BMI Regional operates a fleet of Embraer commuter jets, which carry either 37 or 49 passengers depending on the type. These aircraft fly internal routes in the UK from 14 regional airports and act as feeders for long-haul flights. It is therefore possible for a passenger to travel from Aberdeen to Addis Ababa simply by changing aircraft at London Heathrow. Business-class passengers and frequent flyers (i.e. members of BMI's Diamond Club) have free access to the airport lounges at all airports on their itinerary.

BMI Baby operates at the other end of the spectrum from BMI's business class. As a low-cost airline, it offers no frills whatsoever: in-flight meals can be ordered and paid for, but they are of the sandwich-and-a-drink variety. Hold baggage is paid for, and hand baggage is strictly limited: the size and weight of cabin bags are checked, and any oversize or overweight bags are charged for. Check-in is online for those travelling with hand baggage only, and there is a charge for checking in at the airport. The fares are, of course, extremely low, provided one books far enough in advance – late booking, or booking for a popular route or time, will mean paying quite a lot for the ticket. Tickets are not issued – the passenger needs to print out the ticket, and the boarding pass if checking in online, before leaving home.

BMI Baby operates from regional airports such as Cardiff, East Midlands and eight others. There are some internal flights as well as those to European destinations. Cardiff has flights to Edinburgh, Glasgow and Jersey, for example. In the main, BMI Baby's flights to European destinations are the big sellers, though, especially those to holiday destinations in Spain, Switzerland and Portugal.

In overall size, BMI is not the largest airline in Britain, but it is a respectable size. It operates a total of 54 aircraft in the BMI fleet, plus 20 in the BMI Baby fleet. This compares with Aer Lingus (the Irish national airline), which has 44 aircraft plus 13 on order, or with the 234 aircraft operated by British Airways (with a further 51 ordered). BMI seeks to operate in all its possible markets, including hiring aircraft for private charter. Having separate branding for each element of its service is just one way of ensuring that its brands remain strong.

Questions

1 *How does the airline market segment?*

2 *What are the implications of operating BMI Baby as a separate brand?*

3 *Why offer a separate business class?*

4 *Why operate from so many regional airports?*

5 *What is the purpose of providing internal flights from both BMI Regional and BMI Baby?*

References

BBC (1998): BBC News, Friday 1 July.

Bonoma, T.V. and Shapiro, B.P. (1984): Evaluating market segmentation approaches. *Industrial Marketing Management*, 13 (4) pp 257–68.

Day, G.S. (1990): *Market-Driven Strategy: Process for Creating Value* (New York: The Free Press).

deBerry-Spence, B. and Izberk-Bilgin, E. (2006): Wearing identity: the symbolic uses of native African clothing by African Americans. *Advances in Consumer Research*, 33 (1) p 193.

Donnelly, J.H. (1970): Social character and acceptance of new products. *Journal of Marketing Research*, 7 (Feb) pp 111–13.

Gillespie, K., Jeannet, J.-P. and Hennessey, H.D. (2004): *Global Marketing: An Interactive Approach* (Boston, MA: Houghton Mifflin Company).

Jamal, A. (2003): Marketing in a multicultural world: the interplay of marketing, ethnicity and consumption. *European Journal of Marketing*, 37 (11) pp 1599–620.

Kates, S. (2002): Doing brand and subculture ethnographies: developing the interpretive community concept in consumer research. *Advances in Consumer Research*, 29 (1) p 43.

Keillor, B.C. and Hult, G.T.M. (1999): A five-country study of national identity: implications for international marketing research and practice. *International Marketing Review*, 16 pp 65–82.

Macdonald, E.K. and Uncles, M.D. (2007): Consumer savvy: conceptualisation and measurement. *Journal of Marketing Management*, 23 (5/6) pp 497–517.

Mattson, M.R. and Salehi-Sangari, E. (1993): Decision making in purchases of equipment and materials: a four-country comparison. *International Journal of Physical Distribution and Logistics Management*, 23 (8) pp 16–30.

Phou, I. and Chan, K.W. (2003): Targeting East Asian markets: a comparative study on national identity. *Journal of Targeting, Measurement and Analysis for Marketing*, 12 (2) 1 November pp 157–72.

Richardson, B. and Turley, D. (2006): Support your local team: resistance subculture and the desire for distinction. *Advances in Consumer Research*, 33 (1) pp 175–80.

Sampson, P. (1992): People are people the world over: the case for psychological market segmentation. *Marketing and Research Today* (November) pp 236–44.

Schuster, C.P. and Bodkin C.D. (1987): Market segmentation practices of exporting companies. *Industrial Marketing Management*, 16 (2) pp 95–102.

Simcock, P., Sudbury, L. and Wright, G. (2006): Age, perceived risk and satisfaction in consumer decision-making: a review and extension. *Journal of Marketing Management*, 22 (3/4) pp 355–77.

Skinner, H. and Stephens, P. (2003): Speaking the same language: the relevance of neuro-linguistic programming to effective marketing communications. *Journal of Marketing Communications*, 23 (3/4) pp 177–92.

Yip, G.S. (2003): *Total Global Strategy II* (Upper Saddle River, NJ: Prentice Hall).

Zhinkan, G.M. and Shermohamad, A. (1986): Is other-directedness on the increase? An empirical test of Reisman's theory of social character. *Journal of Consumer Research*, 13 (June) pp 127–30.

Chapter 10

Targeting

Deciding where to spend the company's very limited resources was the next problem for the management team. Umar quickly realised that he had made a fundamental error in segmenting the market – he had considered only Eden Garden Tools' existing customers for the consumer market, and not people who were not customers but might be in the future.

Secondary research sources showed that there was a growing trend for children to become involved in gardening, not least because parents who are keen gardeners want their children to enjoy the same pleasures. Parents were also coming to realise that a child who grows vegetables is likely to want to eat them – gardening was thus seen as a sneaky way of getting children to eat more healthily. Allotment holders were another growing market that Umar had not even considered – again, the kind of mistake a professional should be ashamed of, but Umar consoled himself with the thought that he was still not able to carry out any primary research.

Choosing which segments to target would be the next task facing the senior management team – and Umar would have to explain how it works.

Objectives

After reading this chapter, you should be able to:

→ Assess which segments are worth targeting.

→ Understand how risk can be assessed when selecting targets.

→ Explain how competition relates to assessing a target market.

→ Explain why firms need to target more than one segment.

→ Explain some of the problems of targeting more than one segment.

→ Describe the advantages and difficulties of targeting marginal segments.

Introduction

In Chapter 9 we examined the process of segmenting the market. This chapter considers how to choose which segments to approach. Selecting the right segments is not just a matter of estimating which will be most profitable; correct targeting can in itself generate competitive advantage by playing to the firm's strengths. In some cases, going for the most profitable segment merely invites competition.

Assessing segments

For a segment to be viable, it must have the following characteristics:

1 **It must be measurable, or definable.** If we cannot identify the members of a segment, we are not in any position to approach them with a product offer. Equally, if we cannot measure the size of the segment, we have no way of knowing whether there are enough potential customers in the segment to make targeting it worthwhile.

2 **It must be accessible.** This means there should be some way of contacting the members of the segment. If we cannot communicate effectively with them, we have no chance of promoting our brands. Accessibility also implies that we can deliver our products to the segment – if there is no way of doing this, business cannot result.

3 **It must be substantial.** The segment should be large enough to be worth targeting. Obviously this is a consideration that applies to different firms in different ways. A segment that is too small for one firm may be the right size for another; equally, a small firm with very limited resources will not be able to market effectively to a very large segment, tempting as it might be to try.

4 **It must be congruent.** Members of the segment must have needs similar enough that they can be targeted with a single product offering, or at least one which requires minimal adaptation.

5 **It must be stable.** The members of the segment should remain within it for a reasonable period of time. Equally, the basic needs of the members should remain stable over a reasonable period of time. Of course, what is reasonable in some cases may not be in others – no one expects a baby to stay in nappies for ever.

The three key criteria from the above are accessibility, substance and measurability, but of course it is important to look at the underlying reasons for people being members of the segment in the first place.

Freytag and Clarke (2001) have developed a model for segment selection, as shown in Figure 10.1. The first stage in the process is to consider the future attractiveness of the segment. This will include its current size and its potential growth: it may well be worthwhile to target a segment which is currently very small, if it is expected to grow. This would mean that the firm's brand would be established early on in the market and would (with luck) become the industry standard. Profitability is an issue in attractiveness, although it is not the only criterion. Sometimes a segment is worth approaching for strategic reasons, for example to lock out a competitor, even when the segment is not in itself profitable.

Figure 10.1 Segment selection

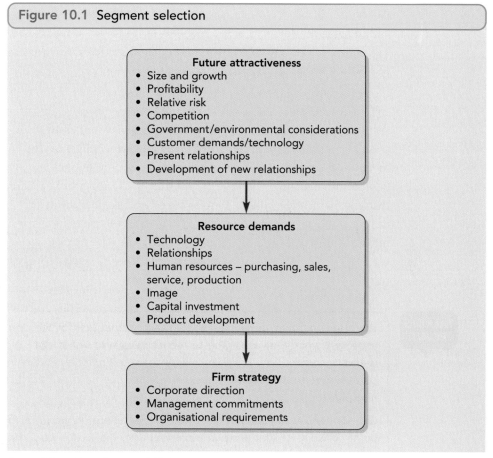

Source: Adapted from Freytag and Clarke, 2001.

The selection decision, according to Freytag and Clarke, is based on a combination of the future attractiveness of the segment, the resources available to the firm and the firm's strategy. As we saw in Chapter 3, firms cannot always simply follow what the market needs, because they have resource constraints which prevent this from happening. The future attractiveness of the segment is a more important consideration than its current attractiveness, because there will be a time lag between deciding to approach the segment and actually being able to target it effectively. Finally, whatever is decided must be decided within the context of the overall strategy of the firm, in other words its general direction and desired outcomes.

The relative risk of approaching one segment rather than another is an additional factor. For example, entering an overseas market when one has no experience of global trading is more risky than staying with one's home market, even if the foreign market is otherwise very attractive. Relative risk is difficult to assess, but one method is to multiply the potential loss by the percentage likelihood of loss. For example, if the company's downside loss could be £1.4 million, but the risk is only 10 per cent that it will happen, the risk can be assessed as £140,000. This might compare with a project wherein the loss is likely to be only a maximum of £700,000, but the risk is 50 per cent of the downside happening – this would value the risk at £350,000, a much worse proposition. The difficulty with this type of calculation is, of course, that it is subjective: estimating the percentage chance of the downside happening is a judgement call on the part of the manager, and very often the downside losses are also an estimate, since a failure may be damaging to the company's image and this may not be quantifiable.

The existence of competition is clearly a factor, but the company needs to look beyond the obvious. A great many managers think that there is no competition, whereas in fact there is *always* competition in any market. This is because people always have ways of solving their need problems, so there will be no competition only if there is no need for the product. For example, before there was television, there was radio, and before that people entertained themselves by conversing, playing games, playing musical instruments, and so forth. In order to assess competition, marketers need to consider how people are solving the need problem at the present time, rather than looking at firms in the same industry. A failure to recognise competition has been a classic error which has destroyed, or at least severely damaged, many established industries. The Swiss watchmaking industry, for example, did not recognise competition from electronic watches until it was too late, whereas Japanese watch makers such as Seiko embraced the new technology very quickly.

TALKING POINT

We often hear people say that there is no competition for their product – especially when they are trying to recruit people to sell it. Well, of course there is always competition, and even where there is a unique product we have to persuade people to buy it rather than spend their hard-earned cash on something else entirely.

OK, so that's established in our thinking, but where do we draw the line? At what point do we say, 'That product is competition, that one is not'? How can we measure the degree of competition we might expect from a similar product and the degree we might expect from something more distant?

Government and environmental considerations include more than just legislation and the ecology. The firm should look at the whole of the business environment, not just the immediate factors.

Customer demands and the technology needed to meet them are key factors in accessing a segment. If the firm lacks the appropriate technology to meet customer needs, the segment cannot be targeted, no matter how attractive it may be in other ways. For example, airlines are now expected to have online booking systems as a result of the incursions of low-cost airlines. An airline with a poorly performing website, or no website at all, will lose business to airlines with effective websites.

Present relationships with customers within the segment, or with distribution chain members which serve the segment, are clearly an advantage. For example, a firm may recognise a sub-segment within its main customer group and be able to target it with a specially adapted product – a firm which supplies baby products, for instance, may be able to supply other products to the baby's parents.

The potential for developing new relationships is often what makes small or unprofitable segments worth targeting. For example, major airlines offer low-cost flights to students on their gap year because they know that those students will, eventually, graduate and may well end up as business-class passengers in future.

The resource situation is one which often prevents a firm from targeting a segment at all. A lack of technology, lack of the appropriate relationships, lack of appropriate employees, having the wrong image, and lacking the resources to develop a product to meet customer need are as important as capital in terms of a firm's ability to target the segment.

Finally, the segment to be targeted must fit within the firm's overall strategy – going off at a tangent will not help the firm achieve its desired outcomes, so the target must fit with management commitments and organisational requirements. According to Bonoma and Shapiro (1984), the two major criteria for choosing a segment are customer conversion analysis and segment profitability analysis. There is some sense in looking at customer conversion analysis: after all, we cannot expect everyone in the target segment to adopt our product, so we will have to make an estimate of how much of the market we are likely to capture, and how quickly. However, profitability of the segment is only one of many possible criteria, as we have seen in the Freytag and Clarke model.

Targeting multiple segments

When considering targeting a segment, it is easy to forget that most firms actually need to satisfy the needs of several segments if they are to generate enough business to survive. Even small neighbourhood restaurants have to satisfy the differing needs of their lunchtime trade, their evening trade, vegetarians and children: each of these groups has differing needs and expectations, even when they have already made a fairly focused decision, (a) to eat out and (b) to choose a specific restaurant or type of cuisine.

In some cases, the company will have different brand names for the products aimed at each segment. A brewery might offer 'Lite' versions of its branded beers, or it may have a completely different brand name. An airline might have one brand name for its scheduled services and another for its charter flights, or it may have a low-cost subsidiary which has a completely different brand name.

As we saw in Chapter 9, producing an undifferentiated product for a mass market will usually result in competing on price alone, so most firms will try to target segmented markets. If the firm is targeting several segments, the key issue is the degree to which the brand values will be affected if the firm uses the same brand for all segments. Each segment will impinge on all the others if the same branding is used. Although some brands such as Richard Branson's Virgin seem to be infinitely extendable, most brands are not, and even Virgin suffered as a result of extending the brand to a railway service. If the firm believes that the brand might be damaged or at least altered by extending to a new segment, managers will need to decide either to target another segment or to launch a new brand. This is, of course, a more expensive option but might be worthwhile in the long run if it prevents an inadvertent repositioning of the firm's existing brand.

Examples of setting up a new brand to cover a different market segment include Iveco, the truck manufacturer. Iveco is a consortium of motor manufacturers including Fiat, Ford and Magirus-Deutz. The company shares its design and manufacturing capacity, and the brand is marketed as a subsidiary of each firm (Iveco Ford, Iveco Fiat, etc.). Another example is the Opodo online travel agency, which seeks to compete with other online agencies in targeting independent, bargain-seeking private travellers. Opodo is owned by nine major airlines, each of which has its own website and online booking system. Opodo is not limited to its owners' flights, of course – it will book passengers on any available airline – but since the nine majors have links with almost all the world's scheduled airlines it is fairly likely that the same flights could be booked directly with the one airline.

Companies have to make these decisions on the basis of the level of resources they are able to commit: a low-resource company cannot hope to approach a market characterised by large numbers of undifferentiated customers. Table 10.1 offers a decision matrix for illustrating this.

Table 10.1 Resourcing and degree of differentiation

High-resource company		
Type of market	Highly differentiated customers	Undifferentiated customers
Mass market	Differentiated product	Undifferentiated product
Specialist market	Differentiated product	Concentrated marketing
Low-resource company		
Type of market	Highly differentiated customers	Undifferentiated customers
Mass market	Concentrated marketing	Differentiated (perhaps geographically)
Specialist market	Concentrated marketing	Concentrated marketing

Targeting decisions

Choosing a target is a function of the segment size, the profit per unit sold and the level of competition in the market. The marketing strategy obviously needs to be built around the segment (see Chapter 8). This means that each of the 7Ps needs to be tailored to meet the needs of the segment. Accurate targeting cannot be achieved without a thorough understanding of the people in the target segment, and this is also true of business markets: knowing what buyers need, as well as what the companies they work for need, is as important in targeting as it is in segmentation.

Table 10.2 illustrates the relationship between the factors, and offers a decision rationale for each.

As with other decision matrices, this matrix can give a spurious impression of reliability. It is, in fact, fairly subjective: managers may have differing opinions as to whether a segment size is large, medium or small; they may have differing opinions about what constitutes a 'high' profit, and levels of competition are equally open to interpretation. This becomes even more acute a problem if the managers making the decisions have different experiences of other industries – competition which is regarded as cut-throat in one industry might be regarded as exceedingly gentlemanly in another.

Table 10.2 Targeting decisions

Segment size	Profit per unit sold	Level of competition	Strategic decision rationale
Large	High	High	Competitors will be attracted to a large, profitable market, so there is likely to be a price war as firms seek to maximise market share. This will lead to reduced profits and eventually to companies leaving the market.
Large	Low	High	This is a mature market, is probably stable, and will be difficult to enter.
Small	High	High	This market might be captured in its entirety by using a penetration pricing strategy, but this is dangerous since it will trigger a price war in which only the companies with the deepest pockets will win.
Large	High	Low	A large, profitable segment will attract competitors eventually. A price-skimming strategy is probably best, to cream off maximum profits before prices have to be dropped to match incoming competitors.
Large	Low	Low	This is a mature, low-risk market. Lack of competition makes capturing a share easy, and the low margins will discourage new competitors, but the margins may be too small to be worthwhile.
Small	Low	High	This market is dying. High levels of competition and low margins make it unattractive unless there is another strategic reason for entering.
Small	High	Low	This is a niche market, very suitable for a small firm: a tight targeting strategy could easily capture the whole market.
Small	Low	Low	This market is clearly not attractive unless there is a way of reducing costs for supplying the small number of customers (in which case it will become a niche market).

Making a decision to target a specific segment is not necessarily irreversible (see Chapter 11), but it can mean a large commitment of resources which might be wasted if the wrong target is chosen.

Targeting marginal segments

Sometimes there will be a wide range of segments, making it difficult to target precisely. In some cases, it may even be difficult (or prohibitively expensive) to identify individuals within the target segments, even though we might be aware that the segment exists. There are three generic approaches to this type of situation (Forsyth et al. 1999). The first is self-selection. This allows the customers to find the most appropriate product themselves (for example, the firm might offer three or four different pack sizes without needing to know who buys which size of pack, or why). Second, the company might use scoring models to put customers into specific categories when they contact the company. This is essentially what credit-card companies do when they are approached by a new applicant. Third, the firm might adopt dual-objective segmentation, in which customers who do not quite fit into existing segments are grouped into new segments. In some cases these customers will never be targeted; in other cases they may be sufficiently numerous to constitute a new segment.

Self-selection is a relatively straightforward approach for fast-moving consumer goods. The product is put on the shelves of appropriate retailers and consumers either buy it or not. The targeting issue comes into play when the firm is making distribution decisions, i.e. deciding which retailers to target for selling the product. At this level, the firm might still be able to use self-selection by placing the product in a cash-and-carry warehouse, where the retailers become the self-selecting customers. This has the advantage that retailers are closest to the end consumers, and presumably will be able to make a judgement as to what the customers will buy.

This may not always be appropriate, of course. In the case of financial services, banks and other lenders might credit-score customers, and have a cut-off point beyond which the institution will not lend. Part of the problem in the banking crisis of 2007 was that banks consistently pushed the boundary further out until they were lending to people who were unlikely to be able to repay the loans.

Grouping customers into new segments would mean identifying similarities among those customers. For example, Disneyland Paris found that there was a large number of people who would never visit the theme park because they had no children. In the United States, people who have no children are quite likely to visit Disneyland, but Europeans regard it as entirely an activity for children. Disneyland marketers decided to target the childless by offering a cut-rate evening ticket: people could enter the park after five in the evening, paying a reduced entrance fee. This opened up a whole new market, primarily among young Parisians going out on a date. After five in the evening, parents often take smaller children home (or to a hotel) because they need to sleep, so the park would tend to empty out. Disneyland's targeting of a marginal group kept the park filled all evening.

The purpose of targeting marginal segments is to pick up business at a relatively low cost from people who do not quite fit the main target markets. Often a marginal segment will prove to be profitable in the longer term, since the segment can now be assessed *a posteriori*, or after the event (see Chapter 9).

Generic targeting strategies

The five basic strategies of market coverage were outlined by Derek F. Abell in 1980. They are shown in Table 10.3.

Choosing the right market and then approaching it with the right marketing mix are probably the most important activities a marketer carries out. Choosing the wrong segment to target, or worse still not attempting to segment the market at all, leads to lost opportunities and wasted resources.

Accessing the target market is an issue which is likely to affect the viability of the segment. For a segment to be viable, it must be possible to communicate effectively with the people in it, usually through some readily identifiable communications medium. The segment may even be defined by the medium. Some segments comprise people who read a particular magazine or watch a particular TV station. For example, the UK men's magazine *Loaded* is aimed at a very specific group of young men. *Loaded* readers represent a group of 'laddish' men, usually with high disposable incomes and interests which involve expensive cars, gadgets, dating-game products and sport. These men represent a valuable market segment in their own right, but can probably be easily identified as a group only because they read *Loaded*.

Table 10.3 Market coverage strategies

Strategy	Explanation	Example
Product/market concentration	Niche marketing; the company takes over one small part of the market.	Tie Rack, Sock Shop.
Product specialisation	Firm produces a full line of a specific product type	Campbell's Soup.
Market specialisation	Firm produces everything that a specific group of consumers needs.	Titleist golf clubs, golf balls, tees, caddies.
Selective specialisation	Firm enters selective niches that are not closely related, but are profitable.	British Telecom sells telephone services to consumers and industry, but also owns satellite time which it sells to TV broadcasters and others.
Full coverage	Firm enters every possible segment of its potential market.	Renault, which manufactures every type of vehicle from compact cars through to giant articulated lorries.

Summary

Targeting is about choosing the right group of potential customers to help the company meet its strategic aims. The choice is not always straightforward, because of competition considerations and because of the time lags between deciding to aim for a specific group and actually gearing up the company's marketing thrust to reach the group.

Targeting also implies rejecting some groups, which (on the face of it) seems counterproductive. However, there are certainly some groups of customers which are not worth what it would cost the firm to target. These groups should be left alone.

The key points from this chapter are as follows:

→ Segments must be measurable, accessible, substantial, congruent and stable if they are to be worth targeting.

→ Risk needs to be assessed, possibly on a weighted basis.

→ If there is no competition, there is no need for the product.

→ Most firms need to target several segments.

→ There is a risk of losing brand focus if the firm targets several segments.

→ Targeting marginal segments can lead to the discovery of new main segments.

THE
**EDEN
GARDEN
TOOLS**
COMPANY LTD

As a relatively low-resource company, Eden Garden Tools would be forced into adopting a concentrated marketing stance. This would enable the firm to direct its resources into the most effective segments.

Since the company was trying to adopt a forward stance, Umar thought it would be best to think of the segments in terms of their potential, especially since garden tools and machines are relatively infrequent purchases. Looking at the consumer segments with the most potential, the obvious one is the children's market. Producing scaled-down versions of Eden Garden tools would encourage children to garden and would help parents in getting children interested. The tools might also make good gifts for children, especially with the modern emphasis on educational toys.

The resource demands for this segment would also be relatively small, since there would be no technical development for the products – some retooling in the factory would be required, but nothing else. The main problem would lie in protecting the idea – there would be absolutely nothing to stop competitors jumping on the bandwagon with 'me-too' products once the range was launched, so the Eden Garden Tools brand would be the only defence the company would have for its new market.

Another segment worth considering was the allotment holders. The problem with this segment would lie in accessing it effectively – there is no specific way of identifying and contacting allotment holders, since they come from many different walks of life, age groups and income levels. Without primary research, it would be difficult to identify specific needs that allotment gardeners have which are not the same as other gardeners. Perhaps the lack of electricity on site to run power tools might be a factor, perhaps the need either to transport tools to and from the allotment or to leave them there, with consequent risk of theft, or any number of other possibilities might need to be explored.

As far as the pruning saw was concerned, the biggest market undoubtedly would be the commercial growers, with tree surgeons coming a close second. The tool-hire market would develop once the product was established with professionals, and the professionals could be easily identified through sources such as *Yellow Pages*. It appeared, on the face of it, that taking a new product into a new market was going to be easier than sticking with the consumer markets.

Review questions

1 *What defines whether a segment is accessible or not?*
2 *Why is there no need for a product if there is no competition?*
3 *Why do firms need to target multiple segments?*
4 *What are the problems of extending the brand to new segments?*
5 *What are the dangers of targeting marginal segments?*

 ## Case study Balfour Beatty

Balfour Beatty is one of the UK's leading construction companies, specialising in major construction works such as social housing projects, railways and electrical engineering. The company was founded in 1909 by George Balfour, a mechanical engineer, and Andrew Beatty, a chartered accountant. The partners' first contract was to build a tramway system for the town of Dunfermline, in Fife, Scotland.

During the 1920s the UK economy suffered badly after the First World War, unemployment was high and business hard to come by. Balfour Beatty looked further afield to find work, building hydro-electric power systems in East Africa and water-supply systems in what was then Palestine (now Israel). By the 1930s Balfour Beatty was well established internationally, with offices in South America (Montevideo and Buenos Aires) and Malaya. George Balfour had become a Member of Parliament in 1918, and his contacts no doubt helped the company win contracts.

After the Second World War the company won a lot of new contracts for reconstruction, especially in rebuilding the bomb-damaged rail network and establishing the National Grid for electricity. The election of Labour in 1948 meant a lot of industries were nationalised, however, so Balfour Beatty began to look overseas again for work: the company won major contracts in Iraq and Canada.

During the 1950s Balfour Beatty found itself well placed to participate in the expansion of the London Underground. The unique combination of heavy construction experience, railway construction and electrical engineering meant the company was ideal for the task of building an electric underground railway. To this day, the majority of the world's underground railway systems have Balfour Beatty components in them.

Later, Balfour Beatty was the natural choice to lead the British consortium which built the Channel Tunnel: experience of underground railways was, of course, crucial to the project. The company also built the Cardiff Bay Barrage (in a joint venture with Costain) and the terminal building at Hong Kong's new airport.

Balfour Beatty is ranked 19th in size of all construction companies in the world, but is the largest railway contractor in the world. Recent railway projects include the Metro system in Oporto, Portugal, the Metropolitan Line upgrade in London, the 190 km Botnia line in Sweden and the Los Angeles Metro Eastside extension.

The company is now organised into four divisions: building, building management and service; civil and specialist engineering services; rail engineering and services; and investments. The company has expanded by acquisition, buying out such firms as GMH Military Housing, a US company which specialises in building accommodation for the defence forces.

Balfour Beatty has weathered many storms in its 100-year history. Two world wars, a dozen recessions, the Great Depression, nationalisation of its key customer (the UK rail network) and many other tribulations have been visited on the company. Despite everything, it has continued to grow and prosper, and bids fair to do so for at least another 100 years.

Questions

1 *Why has Balfour Beatty targeted the underground railway business?*
2 *What strengths does the company bring to construction of airports?*
3 *Why does the company not target house building?*
4 *What positives might there be for the company's railway-building business?*
5 *Why might the company seek to expand by acquisition rather than expand organically?*

References

Abell, D.F. (1980): *Defining the Business: The Starting Point of Strategic Planning* (Englewood Cliffs, NJ: Prentice Hall).

Bonoma, T.V. and Shapiro, B.P. (1984): Evaluating market segmentation approaches. *Industrial Marketing Management*, 13 (4) pp 257–68.

Forsyth, J., Gupta, S., Haldar, S., Kaul, A. and Kettle, K. (1999): A segmentation you can act on. *The McKinsey Quarterly*, 3 pp 6, 10.

Freytag, P.V. and Clarke, A.H. (2001): Business to business market segmentation. *Industrial Marketing Management*, 30 (6) pp 473–86.

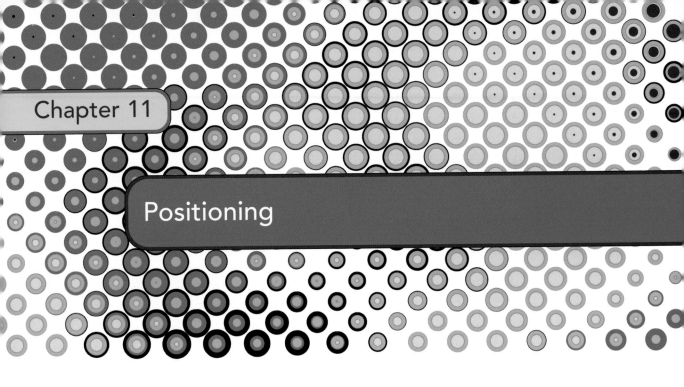

Chapter 11

Positioning

THE EDEN GARDEN TOOLS COMPANY LTD

After Umar Sayeed presented his thinking to Mike and Hugh, the three decided that adding the children's market segment to their existing segments would make sense in the short run. Although Umar was reluctant to admit his error in failing to segment the market properly, he did say that the company should, in the longer run, commission some qualitative market research to complete its understanding of the market as a whole, not just its existing customers.

Having decided on the segments Eden Garden Tools would be tackling, the three then turned to considering the position the brand currently had in the minds of consumers, and (perhaps more importantly) the position they thought it should have, relative to competitors. This would be a crucial piece of information once the company started planning its communications campaign and if the company were to compete successfully against other firms in the garden tools business.

Objectives

After reading this chapter, you should be able to:

→ Explain the elements of perception.

→ Describe what is meant by positioning.

→ Explain the eight generic factors that determine position.

→ Describe the basic positioning strategies.

→ Understand the role of direct experience as opposed to promotion in developing a position.

→ Explain the rationale behind repositioning.

Introduction

Positioning is the process of creating a perception of a brand relative to competing brands. In effect, positioning refers to the place the product occupies in consumers' minds: high or low quality, high or low price, reliable or unreliable, and so forth across several dimensions.

Positioning is very much the domain of marketing communications. Company-generated communications will help to promote aspects of the product and create an overall image. The image needs to correspond closely with the customer's subsequent experience of the product, of course.

Perception and positioning

Perception is the means by which people make sense of the world. All of us carry in our heads a model of how the world works, based on our experiences and on our analysis of what we experience. This mental view of the world is in fact our reality. Although people tend to talk about perception as if it differs from reality in some way, this is not the case – what we have in our heads is the only reality we know.

Perception is both analytic and synthetic. We cannot possibly take in all the information that surrounds us in the course of a day, so we analyse our surroundings and pay attention only to what appears important. This means that each of us takes in a different view of the world, and it also means that there are big gaps in our world view. The result is that our subconscious minds fill in the gaps, or synthesise part of the world view.

Thus each of us carries around a slightly different view of the world. Fortunately, our world views are generally close enough that we are able to function with each other, and we can easily function at the level of knowing how to open doors, how taps work, how to drive, and so forth. The differences in world view are what make conversation interesting, of course.

From a marketer's viewpoint, marketing communications are aimed at shifting perceptions. What we are trying to do is create a collective perception among our target audience such that they are more likely to want to do business with us.

The world view, or perceptual map, that people carry around with them contains information about the brands and products that people buy, consider buying, or would never buy. Positioning is about placing the product at the appropriate point in people's perceptual maps, relative to competing products.

Figure 11.1 shows a simple perceptual map for a group of products. This map has only two dimensions: price and quality. In the real world, perceptual maps are multidimensional, but this is somewhat difficult to show in a book.

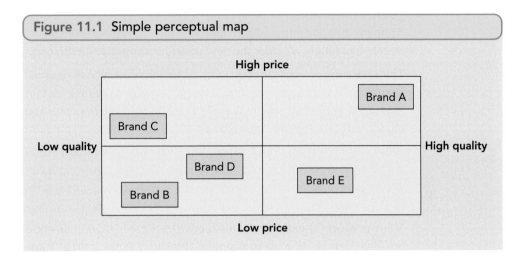

Figure 11.1 Simple perceptual map

Product A is perceived as having a high quality, coupled with a high cost. This is definitely the upmarket brand and will be bought by people who are looking for the best in the category. Product B is perceived as being a low-quality, low-cost product and will be bought by people who have less money and are prepared to accept a lower-quality product as a result. Product C has a problem: it is perceived as being poor quality but is medium-priced, which means it will be seen as poor value for money and will probably not sell well. Product D offers a slightly downmarket but reasonably priced product and will probably sell well. Finally, Product E is perceived as a good-quality, reasonably priced version and is probably the market leader. Of course, offering good quality at a low price is likely to cut profit margins – being market leader comes at a price.

Given that positioning is a multidimensional construct, companies are not limited to the price/quality trade-off. A brand can be positioned as the 'friendly' brand, or the 'safe' brand. Many companies seek to provide themselves with a differential advantage in this way – sometimes with greater success than at other times.

Factors in positioning brands

Positioning the brand against its competitors is a matter of positioning it in the minds of the consumers. It means developing a theme which provides a 'meaningful distinction for customers' (Day 1990) so that the product stands out from the others around it. This is intended to produce a differential advantage, i.e. a perceived advantage over the other products in its category. Obviously this will not necessarily be a perceived advantage for every customer (since everyone has a different world view), but the aim of good marketing communications is to create a position in the majority of the target audience's minds.

Developing a new position is somewhat like the new product development process, and begins with identifying alternative positioning themes. There are, of course, many possibilities and the various themes need to relate to competitors. Having come up with a set of possible alternatives, managers should screen each alternative according to whether it is meaningful to customers, feasible for the company (in terms of its competencies and customer perception of the firm as it is), whether it is superior to the competition's position and provides a unique advantage which is difficult for them to match, and finally whether the new position is congruent with corporate objectives.

This screening process may still offer several feasible alternatives. If this is the case, the company should choose the alternative that arouses the most enthusiasm and commitment among the staff who will have to implement the new position. Finally, the company needs to design the programmes which will be needed to achieve the new position.

Although this process appears straightforward, there are many subjective factors which will affect the outcomes: for example, someone who has spent a great deal of time and effort on developing a new product might well be disappointed if the company decides that it should be positioned as a downmarket, cheap brand.

Many products already have a distinctive position in the minds of customers, and these positions can be difficult to dislodge (Ries and Trout 2001). There are eight generic factors which determine a brand's position, as follows (Blankson and Kalafatis 2004):

1 **Top of the range**. Products in this position are regarded as being of the highest quality and probably also as the most expensive. Being the most expensive is not necessarily a drawback – plenty of people like to buy the top of the range, whether it is a consumer buying a prestige gift for a friend, or a business buyer choosing a new computer system. 'Nobody ever got fired for buying IBM' is a well-known adage in business-to-business marketing, for example.

2 **Service**. The service element of any brand is often a key differentiator. Offering a top-class service will certainly be a factor in positioning the brand.

3 **Value for money**. This does not necessarily mean being the cheapest. Value for money is the relationship between quality and price, so a cheap but poorly performing brand is not going to represent value for money in the same way as a well-made, medium-priced brand will.

4 **Reliability**. Some brands have a reputation for reliability which makes them stand out from all others. Volkswagen is one example: the cars are regarded as extremely reliable, to the extent that a Volkswagen Sharan is regarded as a better car than a Seat Alhambra, even though they are in fact identical and the engines for both cars are made by Volkswagen.

5 **Attractiveness**. The attractiveness of a brand may be a factor in some markets more than in others, but in any market where appearance counts, attractiveness will be a factor in positioning.

6 **Country of origin**. The country where a product is made will affect its brand values. Germany has a reputation for good engineering, Italy has a reputation for stylish design, and China has a reputation for cheapness. There are undoubtedly

German brands which are poorly engineered, ugly Italian products, and very expensive Chinese products, but the perceptions still stand. Country of origin may have less effect in consumer markets. A study conducted in Canada found that 93 per cent of consumers did not know the country of origin of goods they had just purchased, and of the ones who did know, only 2 per cent thought that the knowledge might have affected their decision to purchase (Liefeld 2004).

7 **Brand name.** Having a good brand name helps 'pigeonhole' the product in people's minds. For example, Cif cleaning products convey virtually nothing as a brand name, whereas Mr Muscle carries an image of strength and energy.

8 **Selectivity**. People are selective in the information they take in and consequently may not position a product in the place the company would like them to. Positioning is largely about perception, and perception is, by its nature, both selective and synthetic. In other words, people select limited information from their surrounding environment and then use their imagination to fill in the gaps. There is more on this in the next section of this chapter.

According to Ries and Trout (2001), there are three generic strategies in positioning. First, the company can strengthen its position by reinforcing the factors that gave it that position in the first place. Second, the company can find a new position by seeking out gaps in the consumer's mind. Third, it can attempt to deposition or reposition the competition. This strategy can be dangerous, since it usually means saying something about the competitors, which of course means putting their name forward in consumers' minds. The most successful example of this approach comes from the car-hire business. When Avis wanted to assail Hertz's dominant position in the market, it came up with the concept 'We're Number Two, so we try harder'. This immediately characterised Hertz as being complacent, without ever mentioning the company's name. In fact, Avis was no bigger than any of the other companies jockeying for second place after Hertz, but it immediately established itself in the second position in the market.

TALKING POINT

Are we really this easily manipulated? Do we really develop a whole new perspective on a company, simply because of a brand name?

Shakespeare's Juliet asked, 'What's in a name? That which we call a rose by any other name would smell as sweet.' Yet if a rose was called 'stinkweed' or 'cabbage flower', we might well feel differently about it. How many of us, as children, have made fun of another child's name? Or said to somebody we've just met, 'That's a nice name!'

Maybe we really are that shallow!

In the case of companies with multiple brands, people tend to look at the overall, umbrella brand first before considering the position of the sub-brands. Thus people have a perception of Virgin and use this to interpret the sub-brands (the airline, the record company, the railway, the finance company, the TV cable company, etc.). Sometimes the perception of the sub-brands will affect perception of the overall brand, but the fact that people tend to consider the parent brand first is what allows brand extensions to work so effectively.

Positioning and the marketing mix

It could be argued that the entire marketing mix is aimed at obtaining the right position. Clearly communication has a strong part to play in perception, but communication alone will not overcome direct experience – actually using a product or service is what counts the most in people's perceptions. The following section looks at the effect each element of the 7Ps has on positioning.

Product

The product itself will have some (probably several) features that distinguish it from its competitors. Some of these may simply be about appearance, others will be about ease of use of the product, still others will be about its quality or reliability. Direct experience of the product, either by buying it or by borrowing it, will put the product firmly into the individual's perceptual map.

Price

Price not only provides income for the firm, it also signals quality. People tend to assume that a higher-priced product is also of a higher quality. Obviously, if direct experience of the product contradicts this, the customer will be disappointed and a complaint of some sort is likely to result. Price is one of the most important tools in positioning. Interestingly, people will tend to buy the mid-priced product (in the absence of other information), so it is frequently the case that a low-priced competitor actually helps the sales of a higher-priced product.

Place

The location where the exchange takes place will affect perception of the product. If the product is offered only through exclusive, upmarket outlets it will be positioned as an exclusive, upmarket product. In the case of services, the location of, say, a restaurant will immediately position it in the minds of its customers – being in a posh part of the city centre provides a very different perception from being in a run-down suburb or slum area.

Promotion

In the absence of other cues, marketing promotion is used as a temporary indication of an appropriate position. Once an individual has direct experience of a product, the promotional message tends to be ignored in favour of direct knowledge. Promotion is therefore important in the early stages of developing a position, but once the product is established in people's minds it becomes hard to shift. Some elements of the promotional mix have specific risks and benefits – over-use of sales promotions can easily damage the brand and make its position worse, whereas effective salespeople can move a brand up in people's estimation.

People

The individuals who have direct contact with customers are crucial in establishing a position for the overall parent brand. In the case of services, of course, these people often are the product anyway: hairdressers, chefs, waiters, accountants and motor mechanics are selling their time and skills. Even salespeople actually are the company as far as the buyers are concerned. Rude or careless staff will undoubtedly position the brand badly in the minds of the people they annoy, and helpful staff will put the brand in a good position. Since most firms employ a lot of people, and people have good or bad days, perception of the brand (especially in service industries where the people element is strongest) can vary greatly.

Process

Process has a bearing on quality. The process of buying a hamburger in McDonald's is very different from buying a hamburger at the Hard Rock Cafe, and the positioning of the restaurants is therefore very different. McDonald's is perceived as a place to grab something fast to eat, or to take children, whereas Hard Rock is regarded as an upmarket, interesting restaurant. A hamburger served in a five-star restaurant will be called a Vienna steak, but the process will position the restaurant as somewhere for a special occasion.

Physical evidence

Physical evidence includes paperwork, decor, souvenirs, and indeed anything that can be touched. In positioning, it provides a tangible part of the overall experience, which reinforces the position the brand holds. Physical evidence can be used to create impressions of quality, of reliability, of consistency, even of solid respectability (this used to be the main consideration when designing banks). Physical evidence is, of course, important in any market, but comes to the fore in services markets, where it acts as a reminder that the service has taken place at all.

Positioning multiple brands

As we saw earlier, companies with multiple brands will often have an 'umbrella' brand which covers all of the sub-brands in the set. When new products are introduced, they should be positioned carefully to avoid cannibalism of existing products as far as possible. Obviously there will always be some cannibalism – if the company launches a new product it is quite likely to take sales from existing products, but this is not necessarily a bad thing. If the new product meets customers' needs better than does the old product, it is clearly better that the company should be meeting those needs rather than that a competitor do so.

Cannibalism rates will vary according to cost structure, degree of market maturity and the appeal of competitors' offerings. If a current brand is vulnerable to competitors, then sooner or later they will enter the market, so it is clearly a good idea to introduce a new product into such a (presumed) gap in the market even if it does result in some cannibalism.

There may be other effects on the positioning of the company's other brands. For example, the launch of a more upmarket sub-brand might cause existing brands to be perceived as higher quality. It is certainly the case that the reverse is true. Bic was successful in marketing disposable pens, then disposable razors and disposable cigarette lighters, but disposable underwear failed completely.

Often firms end up going the multiple-brand route because they find that competitors are attacking their lead position. A firm which markets a single brand (these are few in number) may well find its lead being eroded by competitors with differentiated products, in such a way that the firm finds it necessary to produce its own 'specialist' versions of the product in order to avoid losing ground.

Repositioning

Moving an existing brand from one position to another can be difficult because it is necessary to remove people's existing view of the product first. There are four main reasons for repositioning:

1 A competitor produces something which is positioned head-on against the company's brand and appears to be taking substantial market share.
2 Consumer preferences change. This happened to Heinz Salad Cream in the UK. Consumers moved towards mayonnaise over a period of years, until eventually salad cream was repositioned as an ingredient rather than as a salad dressing.
3 New customer preferences are identified, such that they might be met with the existing product. For example, Lucozade was originally marketed as a drink for invalids, helping people to recover from illnesses. During the 1980s it was repositioned as an energy drink for athletes.
4 A mistake is made in the original positioning. The breakfast cereal Ready Brek was originally launched in the UK as an instant porridge, aimed at people who liked porridge but did not like the messy saucepans it created. Unfortunately, real porridge fans did not take to the product – some did not like the flavour, others said it was not 'real' porridge because it was too easy to make. Eventually Ready Brek was repositioned as a children's breakfast, using the strap line 'Central heating for kids'.

Repositioning is risky. The promotion needed to move the product in people's perception might alienate existing users without attracting sufficient new users. Equally, the new position might turn out to be less attractive than the former position – not a good outcome either. Finally, repositioning can be carried out only occasionally: continually trying to shift the brand around in people's perceptions will simply create confusion.

Repositioning has three main sub-divisions: repositioning for existing customers, repositioning for new users and repositioning for new uses.

1 Repositioning for existing customers. One of the safer ways of repositioning a product for existing customers is to suggest alternative uses for it. This can be useful in moving the product from being a standard, regularly purchased commodity to being a product which is keeping up with new ideas.

2 Repositioning for new customers. Repositioning for new users means trying to establish a new image among people who do not currently buy the product. They may not buy it because they have an unfavourable opinion of it, which of course makes it difficult to persuade them, or it may simply be that they are unaware of all the features and benefits of the product and therefore have an inappropriate opinion of it.

3 Repositioning for new uses. Often, consumers discover new uses for products. Astute manufacturers will discover these new uses and use them in their promotions. For example, some women use powdered gelatine to strengthen their fingernails, so gelatine manufacturers could promote this as a new use for the product. Other uses for products may be less attractive from the producer's viewpoint, of course – some gardeners use beer as a bait for slugs, for example.

All repositioning carries a degree of risk. Provided the product is selling reasonably well in its existing market, it may be better to leave well alone, but if the product is losing ground, repositioning may be the best option.

Summary

Positioning the product in consumers' minds relative to competitors is a major function of marketing communications. The purpose of positioning is to ensure that people have a clear idea of what they are buying – and what it will represent in terms of value for money. Clearly, though, marketing communications is no substitute for direct experience of the product, and in practice all the elements of the marketing mix have an effect on positioning.

The key points from this chapter are as follows:

→ Perception is both analytic and synthetic.

→ Position has many dimensions.

→ There are eight generic factors which determine a brand's position: top of the range, services, value for money, reliability, attractiveness, country of origin, brand name and selectivity.

→ There are three generic positioning strategies: reinforce the existing position, reposition, or deposition competitors.

→ Promotion is important in positioning, but cannot substitute for experience of the product.

→ There are four reasons to reposition: responding to competitors, a change in consumer preference, the discovery of new consumer preferences, and a mistake in the original positioning.

According to Umar's discussions with staff, the company appeared to be positioned as being old fashioned and reliable. The 'reliable' part of this seemed fine, but the 'old fashioned' part had come as a shock to Mike and Hugh, who thought the company was go-ahead and innovative. At present the senior management team had no real idea whether the staff view of the company was close to the customers' view or not.

Having said all that, the company would still need to reinforce its position as an innovative company – the situation was not that it needed repositioning, it needed to be positioned firmly in the first place. This would be especially true in the new markets (children's tools, pruning saw) where currently the firm had no presence.

Given the very ready availability of cheap garden tools made in the Far East, Eden Garden Tools would hardly be able to compete on price. Mike knew that UK manufacturing costs meant high prices if the firm was to be profitable, and although John Peters (as a salesman) would tend to prefer prices to be cut to the bone, he also knew that positioning Eden Garden Tools in the 'cheap and cheerful' category would be a disaster. There were other aspects to consider apart from the price/quality relationship too. Another perceptual dimension was innovativeness, and yet another was the 'fun' aspects which could be played on for the children's market. The Eden Garden Tools brand conveyed a sense of fun, but also an old-fashioned, kitsch image. The team wondered whether it was time to rebrand altogether as a simpler alternative, but the cost could be high and rebranding is always risky since it is easy to lose the brand equity one already has without gaining any new advantages.

Finally, the team narrowed down their decisions. Innovativeness, solid reliability and practicality would be the position adopted for the pruning saw, which would place the tool at the high end of the medium price range. For the children's market, the team decided that they should try to come up with a fun sub-brand for the tools, retaining a clear link with Eden Garden Tools. Various suggestions were made, but by this time the team members were running out of energy, so they agreed to meet once more to discuss possibilities. Again, there would be an emphasis on innovativeness and solid quality: the children's tools would be real tools, not just toys, and they would help create a genuine love of gardening. The design of the tools would rely on Mike's expertise, but the team felt very positive about the new project.

Review questions

1 *What are the dangers of repositioning a product?*

2 *How might a company reinforce the position of its brands?*

3 *What is the strategic importance of positioning?*

4 *How might a firm provide experience of a product?*

5 *What are the potential dangers of depositioning a competitor?*

Case study Bulmer's Cider

Bulmer's Cider has been around a long time. The traditional British summer drink, especially in rural areas, cider was first made commercially by Henry Percy Bulmer and his brother Fred, the sons of Reverend Bulmer, a keen amateur cider maker who proposed commercial production as a way of using up surplus apples in years when the harvest was especially good. The Bulmer brothers worked hard to get the business off the ground, but in 1893, just seven years after starting up, they were producing between 3,000 and 4,000 gallons of cider per day.

Some of the company's best-known brands were launched early in the company's history. Woodpecker was launched in 1896, and Pomagne was launched in 1906 after Fred visited Germany on a fact-finding tour. Woodpecker proved to be somewhat sweet for customers in the 20th century, so Bulmer's launched Strongbow in 1960 as a direct competitor for beer. Strongbow is a strong, dry cider and has always been positioned as a 'macho' drink, using the imagery of two arrows being fired into a bar top.

The company also manufactured perry (made from fermented pears), but in recent years has rebranded this as pear cider. This is because younger audiences did not understand what perry was, so to save lengthy explanations, the company simply called the drink pear cider. This also helped to distance the product from Babycham, the perry which was popular in the 1960s and 1970s, and which was positioned as a girls' drink. Babycham had lost popularity with the advent of ready mixed drinks, and had become the butt of a great deal of humour. Several attempts to relaunch the brand have met with mixed, or even poor, results. The pear cider tactic has certainly worked in terms of providing a more macho image for perry.

In 1934, a Tipperary man by the name of Magner began producing cider from local apples. In 1937, he agreed a joint marketing arrangement with Bulmer's of the UK and began marketing his cider as Bulmer's, taking advantage of the UK brand's popularity. In 1949, the companies went their separate ways, but Magner retained the Bulmer's name within Ireland (effectively being prevented from exporting the cider). Unable to expand beyond Ireland, the Bulmer's brand saturated the Irish market.

Within Ireland cider acquired a bad reputation in the 1980s for being the drink of choice of hooligans. So-called 'cider parties' became a synonym for groups of hooligans getting as drunk as possible as cheaply as possible: strong, cheap cider was reputed to fuel their behaviour. Bulmer's in Ireland brought in Grayling, a PR agency, to reposition cider generally and Bulmer's in particular. Grayling began by establishing the Cider Industry Council, an organisation managed by Grayling to act as a focal point for queries from the press and the judiciary. The Cider Industry Council issued press releases and sponsored various events in the sport, music and comedy arenas. The aim of the campaign was to place the cider where people might not expect to see it: in golf clubs, at race meetings, and so forth.

At the same time, the company reduced the alcohol content of the cider from 6 per cent to 4.5 per cent and abolished the 2 litre flagons it had been sold in. These changes reduced the perception of cider as being a high-alcohol, cheap drink. Bulmer's ad agency, Young RSCG, developed a campaign which emphasised the traditional heritage of the drink. The agency avoided the slick, jokey approach of most beer ads and concentrated on showing Irish orchards, focusing on the natural qualities of the product.

➡

The theme carried over into the UK market, where the Irish company now exports the cider under the brand name Magner's. This has led to the bizarre situation in which Irish Bulmer's is competing with UK Bulmer's using a different brand name. Magner's in the UK uses the same basic advertising platform as that used in Ireland and has made considerable inroads into the UK market.

Positioning cider and perry as sophisticated drinks has a long history; Babycham, Woodpecker, Bulmer's Original and Magner's have all gone that route. Whether the success story will continue, or whether further repositioning will be needed, remains to be seen.

Questions

1 *How might Babycham be repositioned?*

2 *What were the key features in repositioning Bulmer's in Ireland?*

3 *What are the key factors in Magner's success in the UK, in terms of its positioning?*

4 *How might Bulmer's in the UK counteract the threat from Magner's?*

5 *What positions currently appear to be available in the cider market?*

References

Blankson, C. and Kalafatis, S.P. (2004): The development and validation of a scale measuring consumer/customer derived generic typology of positioning strategies. *Journal of Marketing Management*, February, 20 (1) pp 5–43.

Day, G.S. (1990): *Market-Driven Strategy: Process for Creating Value* (New York: The Free Press).

Liefeld, J.P. (2004): Consumer knowledge and use of country-of-origin information at the point of purchase. *Journal of Consumer Behaviour*, 4 (2) pp 85–96.

Ries, A. and Trout, J. (2001): *Positioning: The Battle For Your Mind* (New York: McGraw-Hill).

Part 4

MARKETING PLANNING IN CONTEXT

The final section of the book examines the contexts in which marketing planning operates. For plans to work, they must be implemented. This is by no means as easy as it sounds, since competitors do not stand still or quietly give up their share of the market without a fight, and in many cases vested interests within the firm itself might resist, or even sabotage, plans.

Chapter 12 considers some of these issues, while Chapter 13 examines the ways in which marketing planning has to be prepared to adjust to events as stakeholders respond to the company's initiatives.

Implementing marketing plans

THE EDEN GARDEN TOOLS COMPANY LTD

When the team met again to discuss brand names for the children's tools range they decided to pool their ideas, without criticism, and decide as objectively as possible. The suggestions were:

Little Green Fingers
Little Gardener
Play Farm
Garden Elves
Growing Up
Play Planters.

The general feeling was that anything to do with 'play' should be dropped: these were not toys, they were serious gardening tools. Garden Elves was a popular name, but there was some doubt as to whether it would play well to boys. 'Little' seemed condescending, especially for older children.

In the end the team decided to run the names past some children of around the age of the target market. Asking round the office and factory, they found several employees with children of about the right age, and asked for their help in choosing. The result of this exercise was a victory for Garden Elves. The slightly mischievous aura of 'elves' may have helped, of course.

Promoting the brand would rest on two factors. First, the new line would be sold into major retailers and garden centres, placing an emphasis on personal selling. John Peters would be looking to recruit some people to form part of a national sales team in order to gain much better coverage. He would handle key accounts himself, possibly with help from Hugh, who already had established relationships with many major buyers. The second element of the promotional campaign would be a national gardening competition aimed at children. Details would need to be worked out, but the team envisaged a vegetable-growing theme rather than a flower-growing theme, thus tapping into the 'healthy eating' campaign. With luck, children's TV programming might be persuaded to come on board and promote the competition – shows such as *Blue Peter*, the long-running BBC children's show, might well be prepared to give air time to the competition, or could participate in some way.

The objective would be for 20 per cent of the children in the country to have at least some Garden Elves tools within five years. This would amount to 1.2 million children approximately, with total sales of around 2 million tools.

The pruning saw presented another problem, since the Eden Garden Tools brand was regarded as purely a domestic, hobby brand. Estimating sales was problematic, since the business-to-business market was new to everyone, and global marketing even more so. The export house the company had been using for the Eden Garden Tools range would be unlikely to have the expertise to handle the saw, and none of the team had much experience of dealing abroad. The best way forward seemed to be to find a company already in the garden products market worldwide, and try to piggyback the product with them. The team set an objective of achieving an expression of interest within three months, and a completed deal within a year of obtaining the funding from the venture capital company.

This rough outline of objectives would need to be refined considerably, and sub-objectives developed as the plan crystallised, but the team began to feel they were getting somewhere.

Objectives

After reading this chapter, you should be able to:

→ Explain how creativity can be managed.

→ Describe the bases for marketing measures.

→ Explain the role of feedback.

→ Explain the role of control systems and describe the main systems in use.

→ Recognise the problems of applying feedback systems which have been designed for machines rather than for people.

→ Describe the basic control methods used in organisations.

Introduction

Translating strategy into tactics, and then carrying out the tactical tasks, is the final stage of the planning process. The strategy itself cannot be set in stone, because circumstances change. Therefore managers need to monitor the implementation of the strategy to ensure that the firm remains on course.

This chapter is about the challenges involved in implementing plans: managing change, budgeting, developing suitable feedback systems which will inform the strategic planning process, and which will also help in flagging up key issues for the staff who have the task of implementing the strategy and converting it to a set of tactical outcomes.

Implementing the plan

It is one thing to formulate an effective marketing plan, but quite another to implement a strategy. Unless the strategy is implemented effectively, nothing will change, and it is not unusual for strategic plans to be shelved and forgotten about. Piercy (1997) called this phenomenon SPOTS (Strategic Plan On The Shelf). In some cases this happens as the planners have only produced a strategic plan because their bankers or shareholders required one; in other cases, implementation fails because of resistance to change within the organisation; in still other cases, the planning process was so time consuming that the plan was obsolete by the time it was completed – business carries on while planners finalise their strategies.

Planning therefore cannot be divorced from implementation. The questions which need to be asked are as follows:

1 Is the structure of the organisation capable of implementing the strategy?
2 Are resources deployed effectively, and if not, can the necessary changes be made?
3 Are managers suitably empowered to implement changes?
4 Do organisational policies support the strategies?
5 Will staff members be affected by the strategy in such a way that they might try to sabotage its implementation?

Even when planners believe they know the answers to these questions, subsequent experience can prove them wrong. Effective monitoring and control systems need to be in place because responsibility for operations is delegated. The structure of the monitoring systems is dictated by the strategy, but the problems raised when the system goes into operation are likely to lead to changes in the interpretation of the strategy.

For example, if managers decide on a strategic objective of increasing sales to a particular group of customers, a system may be put in place to compare sales to this group with sales overall. The system may be designed to give extra rewards to salespeople who sell a higher proportion of the business to the special group of customers, but the result may be that salespeople concentrate almost exclusively on the special group, neglecting their existing customers in the process. A shift in the proportion of sales to the new group may then occur simply because sales to anybody else fall off due to this neglect. In other words, what gets measured is what gets done – what is not measured suffers as a result.

The relationship between strategy and systems structure is therefore iterative. Strategy dictates system, which in turn dictates strategy, and so forth.

Translating strategy into tactics

The dividing line between strategy and tactics is often blurred. Network-level tactics (tactics which occur between companies) become strategies at the corporate level, and tactics at the corporate level become strategies at the functional level. In most firms, marketing operates at a functional level, the level at which the 4Ps (or 7Ps) are handled. Strategies are formulated and handed down to managers to achieve, and in turn these managers need to organise resources (including staff) to carry out the strategic plan.

One of the key identifying features of tactics (as opposed to strategy) is that tactical decisions are relatively easier to reverse. This means that tactics can more easily be changed in unstable environmental conditions.

For a strategy to be converted to tactics, the following four elements need to be put in place:

1 **A specific action** (what is to be done).
2 **An accountability** (who is to do it).
3 **A deadline** (when it should be done by).
4 **A budget** (what it will cost to do it).

Usually a set of tactics will be developed to implement the strategy, and these tactics will need to be coordinated. An example in marketing is the development of integrated marketing communications. For example, a biscuit manufacturer might decide that it is worth running a TV ad campaign only once at least 50 per cent of the retailers in the area stock the product. The tactical approach to this will involve the salesforce pushing the product and working to a strict timetable – one of the key elements in the sales pitch will be that a TV campaign is planned. The salespeople will need to be fairly specific about the timescales involved, and the advertising agency will have to produce the advertisements and book the media space appropriately. If the processes do not happen at the right times, the whole campaign will be adversely affected: if the salespeople do not deliver, the product will not be available when the campaign begins, and likewise if the campaign does not materialise on time the firm's credibility with the retailers will be lost. Furthermore, market research will need to be carried out in the area on a regular basis to ensure that the product is on the shelves and people are aware of it. Within the framework described, a failure to reach 50 per cent penetration within the specified time frame will result in a shift in tactics – the market research should, if it is conducted properly, reveal better ways of achieving the ultimate strategic goal. Note that the strategy remains unaltered by the tactical changes.

Strategy and organisational structure

The structure of an organisation is intended to define the roles, tasks and work to be carried out, breaking it down into components which might define the boundaries of the various departments or business units which have to carry out the work.

It is not always clear whether strategy dictates structure, or structure dictates strategy. Although the former view appears more logical (because the strategy dictates most things), the latter view also has its merits. The existing organisation structure will be a factor in deciding which strategies are appropriate, and a lack of an appropriate structure might preclude some strategies from consideration. A different kind of structure, however, might well help create a different type of competitive advantage. For example, a small organisation with a flexible structure might be able to develop competitive advantage by being quicker to respond to customer needs. A small engineering company might be able to respond much more quickly to customer needs simply because it is small and has a more organismic structure which is able to adapt to change more quickly.

Equally, a hierarchical, inflexible structure does not lend itself to rapid changes and the strategy needs to take account of this. A strategy which involves maintaining the status quo is appropriate for such organisations, and works well in firms which are large enough to have some degree of control over their environment – for example, major oil companies. A large firm such as BP has considerable control over the environments in which it operates and can therefore operate well with a fairly hierarchical structure.

Managers need to ask the following questions:

1 Is the structure capable of implementing the ideas?

2 Are resources deployed effectively within the organisation?

3 Are managers suitably empowered?

If any of the answers to these questions is No, then either the structure of the organisation is wrong or the strategy is wrong. Either one can be changed, but obviously the decision will rest on which is the easier (or safer) to change in order to ensure the organisation's survival in the longer term.

Implementation and change

Any new strategy will involve change for the members of the organisation. Difficulties arise because change may mean that some people lose out. Resistance to change is common, and in particular change is likely to be resisted in hierarchical, mechanistic organisations where the individual's status might be adversely affected by any changes.

Changes brought about by implementation may be direct or indirect. Indirect changes are often the most desirable, but direct changes are often the easiest to dictate. Equally, direct changes are the most likely to provoke attempts at sabotage, and indirect changes are more likely to pass unchallenged. Aspects which can be changed directly are shown in Table 12.1.

When strategic plans are implemented, some changes will occur indirectly. These are as follows (Thompson 1997):

1 **Communication systems**. Formal information flows are effected directly by management, but a large part of the communication system within any organisation is carried out informally. Any changes to this system are indirect (for example, if staff are moved to a different location), and it is not usually possible for management to make direct changes.

Table 12.1 Directly changeable aspects of implementation	
Aspect	Explanation and examples
Organisation structure	The hierarchy of the organisation can be redrawn with new posts created or old ones removed. The informal structure will remain intact, insofar as the individual staff remain employed under the new structure.
Management systems	Information systems, feedback systems and control mechanisms (for example, rewards and sanctions offered to staff) will need to be changed carefully, and with consultation.
Policies and procedures	Procedures are often the easiest aspects to change and therefore are often the first aspects which the less competent manager will address.
Action plans and short-term budgets	Action plans outline the tactics to be used to achieve the strategy. Tactics are relatively easy to change. Short-term budgets can also be altered with relatively little difficulty.
Management information systems	The methods by which management is fed information affect the type of information that is supplied. Managers cannot be aware of everything that is going on within the organisation; therefore they are, to some extent, at the mercy of the staff below them, who supply the information on which decisions are based. Changes in the information system will inevitably impact on future strategic decision making.

2 **Managing and developing quality and excellence.** Much of the quality and excellence in the organisation's work comes from the attitude of staff and their willingness to pay attention to detail. This cannot be dictated by management, although it can be fostered by appropriate policies.

3 **Manifested values and the organisational culture.** The organisational culture is the product of the people who work within it. Again, this cannot be directly changed by management, even though changes can be fostered. If staff are not prepared to accede to management plans to change the culture, they will not go along with it.

4 **The fostering of innovation.** Creativity and innovation cannot be ordered. In Edison's words, creativity is 2 per cent inspiration and 98 per cent perspiration, and there is really no way that managers can demand that people be inventive. It is, of course, possible to reward creativity and create the right conditions under which it can flourish, but this alone will not force it to happen.

There are four basic problem areas associated with strategy implementation (Owen 1982):

1 Strategy and structure need to be matched so that they support each other, but at the same time each product in the organisation's portfolio needs to match closely with its target market. This inevitably creates conflicts.

2 Communications and feedback systems may not be adapted to the new regime, so that the managers have difficulty in assessing whether the strategy is running into trouble or is proceeding smoothly.

3 Any strategic change involves risk and uncertainty. This creates problems for staff, who may therefore agree to changes when in meetings but will not implement the changes later.

4 Other management systems such as staff development schemes, pay structures and communications systems have been developed to meet the previous strategic structure of the company. Constant modification is difficult or impossible, so these historical schemes may stand in the way of implementing the new strategy.

Problems can arise if managers do not take full account of the amount of time that implementation will take, fail to forecast correctly the bases on which the strategy was formulated and do not recognise the obstacles that may appear (Alexander 1985). Second, there are many other distractions which divert attention away from making strategic changes – the day-to-day problems which arise in any organisation can force attention away from long-term projects. Third, because strategy implementation is necessarily time consuming, the reasons for making the changes might disappear or at least change in nature in the meantime.

Overcoming these problems is never likely to be totally effective, but some precautions might help. Owen (1982) suggests the following:

1 Clear responsibility should be allocated for the outcomes of strategic change.

2 The number of changes being implemented at any one time should be limited. The ability of staff to cope with change is often a key determinant of strategy.

3 Necessary actions to implement strategy should be identified, and responsibilities allocated.

4 Progress measurement points should be established, so that the strategy implementation can be mapped against expectations.

5 Performance measures should be established, along with suitable monitoring and control mechanisms.

In the 21st-century environment, change is a constant factor. It is no longer feasible in most industries to consider change as a series of discrete events, but rather to see it as a continuous flow.

TALKING POINT

We hear a great deal about the rapid change that is characteristic of 21st-century business life. But is change really more rapid than it was 100 years ago? Where is the evidence?

In 1903 the Wright Brothers carried out the first powered flight. Within the following decade, airmail services had been established, war aircraft had been designed and built, and the first passenger services were beginning. Within 20 years of the first flight, air travel had become regular, with scheduled services between London and Paris. Within 50 years, jet transport was available, intercontinental passenger services were established, and the sound barrier had been broken – not to mention that the first space flights were well under way.

Compare with the Internet, which has its beginnings in the 1960s. Forty years later, most people in the world still do not have access to it, most companies using it for commercial purposes have lost money at it, and it is beset by software problems, from viruses to simple overload of the system. So is change really moving faster? Or is this just a perception of the stressed-out, overloaded 21st-century mind?

These practical problems may mean that it is easier to change the strategy, and some managers will certainly take this option. Yet a change in the strategy might prove fatal to the organisation, and therefore the strategy which is correct for the organisation might be forced through over the objections of the staff.

This is clearly problematical. If staff do not support the changes, feel threatened by them and feel that their status or job security is threatened, they are likely to sabotage the changes. This may happen officially, through industrial action or union representation, or it may happen covertly through non-cooperation with the changes. Managements in hierarchical organisations can easily acquire the reputation of being bullies, and it is common for firms in trouble to bring in 'hatchet men', who use force of personality to push changes through, often with little regard for casualties.

The tactics outlined in Table 12.2 might be useful in reducing the problems outlined above.

Table 12.2 Tactics for improving the acceptance of structural changes

Problem	Tactical alternatives
Career paths become unclear	New career opportunities under the new regime will exist and these should be pointed out early on the process – for example, a document which begins, 'Due to our ongoing commitment to improving the organisation, a restructuring will be implemented. This will mean that the following posts will be created, and priority will be given to existing staff in making appointments to these posts.' This positive approach is more likely to be supported than an approach which says that posts will disappear.
Networks with colleagues will disappear	Time spent in building networks is never wasted. People who are well networked should be identified, as they are often the best drivers for the new structure since they are usually influential in the organisation.
New roles take time to learn	Before the new structure is implemented, an audit should be taken of staff to find out who already has the necessary skills for the new structure. These people should be given status and preferably also the task of teaching others whenever this is possible. Obviously managers should be tolerant of mistakes at this early learning stage.
More mistakes will be made	Tolerance of mistakes is of course essential, but managers need to be extra vigilant during transition periods. Training is only partly effective: often people will do well in the training sessions, but apply the learning correctly only once they have started trying to do the job they have trained for.
Staff may feel that this is an opportune moment to leave	Change is always disruptive, even when it is beneficial. Staff who can see that the change will be beneficial to themselves are more likely to accept the changes. Emphasising the career benefits and medium-term improvements that the changes will bring will certainly help. Emphasising the ways in which the firm will benefit is likely to be counter-productive, since it signals that the management are more concerned with the shareholders than with the staff. Although this might be obvious to staff anyway, it is tactless to make it explicit.
The most talented people will find it easiest to leave	Any strategic changes should (ideally) benefit the most talented staff most directly. These people need to be brought into the confidence of senior management – in fact, if possible, everybody in the organisation should be kept as fully informed as is reasonable.
Some people will lose status	Ideally, this should not happen, but if it does, then such people should either be compensated in some way or should be offered the chance to take redundancy payments. They would almost certainly be entitled to this anyway, as a reduction in status would be regarded as a constructive dismissal by an employment tribunal. Perhaps surprisingly, however, some people may be prepared to downshift in status if this also means a quieter life.

Sometimes replacement of staff is unavoidable. Some skills become obsolete, others become essential and are unavailable from within.

Strategic changes will be easier to implement if managers (and indeed staff) feel that they own the mission and corporate strategy. Suitably empowered managers and staff will be able to be more innovative, more flexible and more able to take risks in order to improve the outcomes of environmental threats and opportunities.

Budgeting

Budgets are clearly extremely important in terms of resource allocation. Table 12.3 illustrates some methods for setting marketing budgets.

Table 12.3 Promotional budgeting methods

Method	Explanation	Advantages	Disadvantages
Objective and task method	Identify the objective to be achieved, then determine the costs and effort required to achieve those objectives.	This is logical and links to the firm's strategic goals.	The marketing research needed for this method is expensive and outcomes are hard to predict.
Percent of sales method	The planner simply allows a fixed percentage of the company's sales to be used for promotion. This is a common method of budgeting.	This is simple to calculate and also ensures that, if sales drop off, costs also drop.	This is based on the false premise that sales cause promotion, rather than promotion causing sales. It would be more logical to increase expenditure if sales fall.
Competition matching method	The marketer matches expenditure to that of competitors. Thus the firm does not lose ground if a competing firm increases its budget.	This method should maintain the firm's position relative to competitors, reducing wasted expenditure.	The method is not customer-oriented, and also means that competitors are setting the firm's budgets.
Marginal approach	Marketer spends only up to the point where any further spending would not generate enough extra business to justify the outlay.	This method should maximise profits since no excess spending would result.	Given the changing nature of markets, this method is almost impossible to calculate.
All-you-can-afford method	The marketer spends whatever money can be spared from other activities. Often used by small businesses when starting out.	Company cannot become over-committed or run into trouble by relying on sales which do not, in the end, materialise.	This means that expenditure bears no relationship to the state of the marketplace. Also, it means that marketers have to fight for budgets with colleagues within the firm, which causes resentment and also means that the size of budget depends on office politics, not on the needs of the company and its customers.

In the real world, marketers usually adopt a combination strategy, using several of the above methods (see Figure 12.1). Even an objective-and-task approach might begin by looking at what the competition are spending (comparative parity approach) if only to determine what the likely spend would have to be to overcome clutter. Likewise, a marketer may be part-way through a campaign and be told by the finance department that no more money is available (or perhaps be told that more than anticipated is available) and will switch to an all-you-can-spend policy.

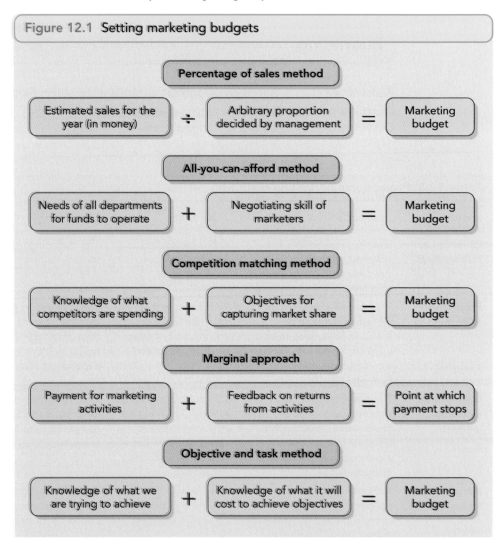

Figure 12.1 Setting marketing budgets

Percentage of sales method

Estimated sales for the year (in money) ÷ Arbitrary proportion decided by management = Marketing budget

All-you-can-afford method

Needs of all departments for funds to operate + Negotiating skill of marketers = Marketing budget

Competition matching method

Knowledge of what competitors are spending + Objectives for capturing market share = Marketing budget

Marginal approach

Payment for marketing activities + Feedback on returns from activities = Point at which payment stops

Objective and task method

Knowledge of what we are trying to achieve + Knowledge of what it will cost to achieve objectives = Marketing budget

TALKING POINT

Budgeting seems to be somewhat hit and miss. After all, we can't be rigid about how much money will be available – the customers and investors have control over that. We might not be as good at bargaining as are our colleagues – if we are negotiating against the managing director's blue-eyed boy, we won't have much chance of success.

Maybe marketers need to develop the kind of rigid systems that accountants have, where everything is calculated to the last decimal place (at least, that's what they tell us) and there is no argument. Maybe marketing hasn't reached that level of sophistication – but isn't it time it did so?

Monitoring and evaluating marketing performance

Feedback is essential for monitoring performance and in an ideal world no marketing activity should be undertaken without having a monitoring and evaluation system in place beforehand.

There are two basic groups of approaches for performance analysis: sales analysis and marketing cost analysis. Sales analysis looks at the income generated by the firm's activities, whereas marketing cost analysis looks at the costs of generating the income. Table 12.4 illustrates some sales analysis measures.

The collection of the amount of information needed for this type of analysis may involve the firm in substantial market research expenditure, since market research is the cornerstone of monitoring and evaluation.

Table 12.4 Methods of sales analysis

Analysis method	Explanation
Comparison with forecast sales	The firm compares the actual sales achieved against what was forecast for the period. Discrepancies may mean that the forecast was wrong, or that something has gone wrong with the marketing tactics.
Comparison with competitors' sales	Provided the information is available, the firm can estimate the extent to which marketing activities have made inroads into competitors' business. The problem here is proving that the difference has been caused by the high quality of the firm's marketing activities rather than by the ineptness of the competitor.
Comparison with industry sales	Examination of the firm's performance in terms of market share. This is commonly used in industries where a relatively small number of firms control the market – for example, the car industry.
Cash volume sales analysis	Comparison of sales in terms of cash generated. This has the advantage that currency is common to both sales and costs. It has the disadvantage that price rises may cause the company to think it has done better than it has.
Unit sales analysis	Comparison of sales in terms of the number of units sold, or sometimes the number of sales transactions. This is a useful measure of salesforce activities, but should not be taken in isolation – sometimes the figures can be distorted by increased sales of cheaper models.
Sales by geographic unit	Sales are broken down regionally so that the firm can tell whether one or two regions are accounting for most of the sales, and whether some less productive regions are not worth what they cost to service.
Sales by product group or brand	This is particularly important for judging the product portfolio (see the BCG Matrix in Chapter 8). This serves two purposes: it is possible to identify products which should be dropped from the range, and it is also possible to identify products which are moving into the decline phase of the product life cycle and should therefore be revived.
Sales by type of customer	This analysis can reveal, for example, that too much effort is being expended on a group of customers which makes relatively few purchases. This is not a problem if the customers have potential, but it is a problem if they will continue to be rare purchasers.

An alternative approach to monitoring is to assess the cost of achieving the goals which have been specified. Marketing cost analysis is a set of techniques for breaking down the costs of the firm's activities and associating them with specific marketing objectives. Costs can be broken down (broadly) into direct costs, such as salespersons' salaries, which can be directly attributable to a given activity, traceable common costs, such as costs of advertising, which can be traced back to specific products, and non-traceable common costs, such as the cost of PR or corporate advertising, which cannot be allocated to any particular product range or brand.

The main problem with marketing cost analysis is that the firm's accounting systems may not be organised in a way that easily permits analysis. For example, payroll records may not be easily broken down by job function. In a small firm, it may be difficult to find out how much time each person spends on marketing-related tasks, and it may even be difficult to find out what the pay bill is for the salesforce if salespeople have other duties such as delivery, servicing or collecting debts. Likewise, defining which jobs constitute marketing jobs and which do not also presents problems, especially in firms which are strongly customer-oriented.

For the market-oriented firm these answers are obvious, since all the activities of the firm are regarded as marketing activities. In other firms, not all managers agree with the basic premises on which marketing is based, and may find it difficult to gear the organisation's activities towards a consumer orientation.

A problem with all of the above evaluation approaches is that they are financially based and predicated on the assumption that marketing is about making sales rather than about achieving strategic marketing objectives. For example, a firm may have a legitimate marketing objective to improve customer loyalty. While this may increase sales in the long run, the appropriate measure of success would be the degree to which customers make repeat purchases, which in the short term may actually lead to a reduction in sales as the firm shifts the emphasis away from recruiting new customers towards retaining existing ones.

Balanced scorecards

The balanced scorecard approach was suggested by Kaplan and Norton (1992). The authors suggest that the organisation should measure performance using a limited, specific set of measures derived from the success factors which are most important to the stakeholder groups.

The measures to be used can be grouped in the following categories:

1 **Financial measures**. These would include return on capital employed, cash flow, growth in share value, and so forth.

2 **Customers**. These measures would include perceived value for money (not necessarily cheapness), competitive benefits package, and so forth.

3 **Internal processes**. These might be enquiry response time, or conversion rate from enquiry to order.

4 Growth and improvement. This would include the number of new products on offer, the extent of employee involvement and empowerment, employee attitudes to the firm, and so forth.

The balanced scorecard is an attempt to integrate all the factors which would impact on the organisation's long-term success so that the strategy does not become unbalanced. To be most effective, managers need to apply some weighting to each of the factors in order to ensure that attention is paid to those areas which are most closely allied to the corporate mission or vision.

Feedback systems

Discrepancies will almost always appear between the plan and the real world, in which case the marketing manager will need to take action. This will usually take the following sequence:

- Determine the reason for the discrepancy. Was the original plan reasonable? Have the firm's competitors seized the initiative in some way, so that the situation has changed? Is someone at fault?
- Feed back these findings to the staff concerned. This can be in the form of a meeting to discuss the situation, or can be less formal – an e-mail or a report.
- Develop a plan for correcting the situation. This will probably involve the cooperation of all the staff concerned.

Feedback should be both frequent and concise, and any criticisms should be constructive. Managers should never, for example, go to a sales meeting and offer only criticism since this sends the salesforce out with negative feelings about themselves and the company.

Marketing strategy and planning is much like any other planning exercise – it relies on good information, a clear idea of where the organisation is going, and regular examination of both outcomes and methods to ensure that the plan is still on target.

Control systems

The purpose of any strategic control system is to decide whether the current strategy is correct and should therefore be retained, or whether circumstances have altered in such a way that the strategy should be scrapped and a new one formulated.

Most control seeks out variances in performance and applies a correction to redress the variance. Negative feedback acts against the trend of the variance in order to reduce it. Positive feedback tends to increase the variance and is generally considered to be counter-productive since it creates a situation where the system runs entirely in one direction. Positive feedback can happen if there is a temporary change in performance which is over-compensated so that variance increases rather than decreases. This comes about because of time delays in the feedback systems.

> *Feeding back into the system seems to be fraught with risks. Too early a feedback increases the problem, too late a feedback seems to be wasted effort. If we look at the most important fluctuation of all, the economic cycle, we must wonder whether it's worth bothering at all.*
>
> *Since the 1930s, governments have sought to control the boom-and-bust cycle, taking the credit when the economy booms and passing the buck when the economy crashes. Yet all the feedback, government initiatives, job-creation schemes and rhetoric seem to have done nothing whatsoever to cure the problem.*
>
> *Maybe there is no problem. Maybe fluctuations are just a natural part of life: the process of sleeping and waking, applied to business. In which case, why are we bothering with feedback at all?*

Some fluctuation is inevitable; minor deviations from the plan will always occur sooner or later. The difficulty for managers lies in judging the extent to which such deviations are permissible before action must be taken.

Difficulties with control systems

The type of thinking that applies to engineering problems is not necessarily applicable to human problems. Each has its own set of assumptions which may not hold true for the other; certainly many of the assumptions made by managers prove to be false when attempts are made to put them into practice. Finlay (2000) says that there are four assumptions borrowed from engineering which do not transfer to management. These are shown in Table 12.5.

Table 12.5 Assumptions underlying control systems

Assumption	Problems with this view
Objectives can be devised and can be stated precisely	Most organisations do not have clear objectives, but rather have broad goals. For example, it is almost impossible to set objectives for a personnel department or a legal department, and in many cases it is difficult to do so for a marketing department. Companies led by visionaries neither have nor need objectives – the vision is sufficient.
Achievement can be measured and a measure of variance can be calculated	Without measurable objectives, achievement cannot be measured. Even if there is a measurable objective, the reason for the variance may be difficult to calculate – a fall in sales may be due to a great many factors, some of which are beyond the marketer's control.
Variance information can be fed back	Unstructured activities involve judgement and are often unique, so feedback for one activity is unlikely to be directly applicable to another. Indirect feedback is about accumulating knowledge and extrapolating from it, not about applying a set, known correction.
The feedback is sufficient to maintain control	The system will work only if the applied feedback is bigger than the environmental shift. For example, a company selling over-the-counter cold medicines might decide that a fall-off in sales should be followed by an advertising campaign to boost customer interest. This will not work if someone finds a permanent cure for the common cold.

Because of these problems, firms need to use adaptive controls. While much of the control system can be automatic, managers need to use human judgement to override the system when necessary, otherwise long-term change is unlikely to happen. Two methods of control exist: first, to change the organisation's behaviour in some way to overcome the difficulty and reach the objective, or second, to change objectives and aim for something that is achievable rather than something that is not.

Controls come in hierarchies, and levels of control are exercised at different levels of the organisation. Three generic ways of controlling the course of events in the business are available: first, changing the inputs to the system; second, the process itself can be controlled; third, the objective of the organisation can be changed.

Tactics of control

There are three basic types of control, as shown in Table 12.6 (Johnson and Gill 1993).

Administrative control is often exercised through planning systems, which control the allocation of resources and monitor the utilisation of resources against the plan. Planning systems might be top-down, centralised systems in which the standardisation of work procedures is paramount. Even in service industries the routinisation of working practices has been achieved – McDonald's hamburgers are produced in a routinised way which would have been thought impossible in the restaurant businesses of 100 years ago.

Such centrally planned systems often use a formula approach, for example setting budgets as fixed percentages of turnover or allocating resources on the basis of numbers of customers dealt with. This tends to place an emphasis on bargaining within the organisation to vary the formula in some way.

Control through direct supervision is common in small organisations, where one person is able to control resources effectively. In large organisations it is really possible only in conditions of stability, or during times of crisis (for example if the survival of the organisation is threatened). Autocratic direct control by one person might be the only way the necessary changes can be forced through – although, of necessity, this is a route which is likely to lead to considerable resentment among lower-grade staff who are displaced or undermined.

Table 12.6 Types of control

Type of control	Explanation and examples
Administrative control	Based on systems, rules and procedures, administrative control is typical in hierarchical organisations which often have large numbers of rules and regulations.
Social control	The control exercised by workmates and the organisational culture. This is common in organismic organisations and smaller organisations.
Self-control	Control exercised by individuals on themselves, based on their own interpretation of correct behaviour. This is common in organisations composed of professional people, who may be working to a professional code of ethics rather than a set of rules laid down by the employer.

Control through performance targets became popular during the 1990s, especially as a way of controlling the newly privatised natural monopolies of power supply, railways, telephone systems, and so forth. Setting the correct performance indicators is far from easy – indicators often give only a partial view of the overall situation, and it is usually the case that activities which are measured are the ones that get done, regardless of the real-life situations faced by the staff and managers in the organisation.

Responsibility for marketing is likely to be devolved to the divisions, since marketing (in a customer-oriented firm) pervades all the activities of the organisation. An organisation given to using financial controls is likely to establish such divisions as profit centres, which rather complicates the issue for the divisions since they will be working towards marketing-based objectives, but will be judged on a finance-based objective. Strategic planning-based organisations will be more likely to use cost or revenue centres, with marketing planning being carried out at the centre.

Social and cultural control comes from the corporate culture. In organisations with a strong culture, people behave in the way they do because it is the right way to behave, not because of administrative controls and procedures. In the 21st-century organisation, this type of control is likely to become much more prevalent – people are becoming more individualistic and more idealistic, and less inclined to obey orders blindly. Also, social controls are much more effective in organisations which are facing chaotic situations or circumstances of rapid environmental change, in which it is impossible to lay down fixed procedures for dealing with every possible eventuality.

Social controls can sometimes hinder senior management because cultural norms are difficult to change, and people who regard themselves as professionals are likely to prove difficult if asked to do something which they feel impinges on their professional prerogatives.

In some respects, the 21st-century workplace is likely to be less about controls and more about influences. Managers may not be able to impose fixed procedures on workers, partly because such procedures will be difficult to formulate and partly because a well-educated, independent-minded workforce is unlikely to be as prepared to accept management by diktat as workers were 50 or 100 years ago. Influence can come from many sources, but the greatest influences are likely to be social ones, created by and in turn creating obligations between the staff. This implies that managers will need to be charismatic rather than autocratic, and will need to lead rather than drive the workforce.

Summary

Feedback and control are essential if the strategy is to be kept on course, even if the company is in a changing environment. For firms in stable environments, formalised systems of feedback with clear parameters for working will be effective; in a rapidly changing environment, the strategic vision is maintained by social and cultural controls rather than by formal regulations.

The key points from this chapter are as follows:

→ Creativity can be encouraged, but cannot necessarily be ordered.

→ Marketing measures are usually based either on sales or on costs.

→ Feedback is about identifying divergence from pre-set targets.

→ Control is reactive: it responds to divergences identified by the feedback system.

→ Human beings are not machines. Feedback systems based on engineering theory will need to include the possibility of being overridden by human managers.

→ Administrative controls work best in stable environments; socio-cultural controls work best in conditions of change; self-controls work best in professional organisations.

Forecasting the sales for the pruning saw would naturally prove extremely problematic, since this was entirely new territory for the firm. By the same token, monitoring outcomes would be equally difficult. The obvious solution, and one which appealed to Umar Sayeed, would be to measure tactics on the basis of marketing outcomes.

If this approach was adopted, the company would measure the success of its personal selling by the number of retailers stocking the Garden Elves tools. The success of the pruning saw would be judged on the company's success in finding a partner, and subsequently on brand awareness in overseas markets. Success of the gardening competition promotion would be gauged by the number of entrants and the level of press coverage gained, and so forth.

Bringing the employees on board presented another set of problems. Hugh thought it would be good to have some special events to celebrate the product launches – office parties or similar – and this was generally thought to be a good idea, but at the same time Mike thought a more formal explanation of what the new strategy consisted of would be more effective. Eventually the team compromised – the firm would have an 'away day' during working hours, closing the factory and offices for one day and taking the staff to a conference centre. During the morning the new plan would be outlined, then the afternoon would be given over to a barbecue at a local beauty spot. Umar and Mike were to work out the morning programme, while Hugh and John took charge of organising the 'fun' part of the day. In the run-up to the away day, Umar and Mike would draw up a detailed plan of what needed to be done, and would identify individuals within the organisation who would be most effective in implementing the plan. These new roles and responsibilities would be announced at the away day, once the individuals concerned had accepted their new roles.

Already both Hugh and Mike could envisage problems with some staff members. Some of the factory-floor workers were known for being conservative, putting it kindly, and at least one of the company's administrators was known to be difficult about questions of status. These people would certainly need careful handling.

Review questions

1 *A common method of obtaining feedback in service industries is the use of customer response forms. How might you ensure that every customer completes one of these forms?*

2 *If control is reactive, how might you ensure that managers are able to vary the responses to match actual circumstances?*

3 *Socio-cultural controls exist in the minds of staff. How might this affect an induction programme?*

4 *What are the problems associated with giving feedback in circumstances of rapid environmental change?*

5 *How might administrative controls be helpful in an organismic organisation?*

 Case study Organising Honda

Honda's annual report contains the following statement:

By following a corporate policy that stresses originality, innovation, and efficiency in every facet of its operation – from product development and manufacturing to marketing – Honda has striven to attain its goal of satisfying its customers.

Nowhere is this emphasis on originality and innovation more apparent than in Honda's internal management systems. For most managers in most companies, management problems appear as a series of trade-offs: individualism versus group needs, quality versus cheapness, cost savings versus differentiation, and so forth. Japanese business practices have tended to reject these trade-offs and replace them with something wholly new – getting the quality right first time, for example, actually saves money in wasted materials and time over the previous system of testing at the end of the production line.

Honda has applied this type of thinking to the conflicts inherent in organisational structure and management. To this end, the company has virtually done away with the hierarchical management structure. Although there are still clear vertical lines of control, the company cuts past these on a regular basis. Senior executives meet regularly with shop-floor supervisors, for example, and manufacturing managers share viewpoints with sales personnel. The career paths of individuals do not necessarily follow a hierarchical path, either – it is quite feasible for technical staff to be promoted several times without ever having to manage people. Staff are often promoted diagonally – in the late 1980s one of Honda's senior marketing people was promoted to oversee the expansion of one of its US factories.

Furthermore, Honda is a company which places an emphasis on praising individuals in the firm. Quality circles operate company-wide; individuals are rewarded for innovation, and remain closely associated with the products and processes for which they have become responsible. However, individualism is not stressed above cooperation – each has its place in the organisation.

Honda's decision-making process is characterised by collectivism. The company's top executives do not have separate offices, but instead share one large, open-plan office in which there are spaces for them to sit together and talk, as well as their individual desks. Executives are allowed to have individual offices if they so wish, yet most do not do so, preferring the collective system and easy communication of the open-plan room.

Honda has undergone some fairly dramatic changes of direction in the past 25 years. Again, these are seen as positive by the management: each change of tack moves the company a little further forward, building on the progress made in previous years. No doubt the firm will change direction again many times in the next 25 years, but for Honda this is just part of being a flexible and responsive company.

Questions

1 *What problems might arise for Honda in carrying out an internal audit, given the fluidity of its structures?*

2 *How might Honda's senior management reconcile the problem of creating career paths for the staff?*

3 *What type of organisation structure does Honda appear to tend towards?*

4 *What would be the problems for Honda in setting up a decision-support system?*

5 *How might Honda respond to a technological breakthrough, for example a new type of motive power for cars?*

References

Alexander, L.D. (1985): Successfully implementing strategic decisions. *Long Range Planning*, 18 (3).

Dermer, J. (1977): *Management Planning and Control Systems: Advanced Concepts and Cases* (New York: Irwin).

Finlay, P. (2000): *Strategic Management* (Harlow: Financial Times Prentice Hall).

Hofstede, G. (1978): The poverty of management control philosophy. *Academy of Management Review*, 3 (3) July pp 450–61.

Johnson, P. and Gill, J. (1993): *Management Control and Organisational Behaviour* (London: Paul Chapman Publishing).

Kaplan, R.S. and Norton, D.P. (1992): The balanced scorecard – measures that drive performance. *Harvard Business Review*, January–February.

Owen, A.A. (1982): How to implement strategy. *Management Today*, July.

Piercy, N. (1997): *Market-led Strategic Change: Transforming the Process of Going to Market* (Oxford: Butterworth-Heinemann).

Thompson, J.L. (1997): *Strategic Management: Awareness and Change,* 3rd edition (London: International Thomson Business Press).

Chapter 13

Adapting marketing planning to context

THE EDEN GARDEN TOOLS COMPANY LTD

The plan was certainly coming to fruition now, even though there were still some gaps to fill (not least of which was the finance needed to implement the plan). The final piece of the jigsaw was to consider the effects of the plan within the different contexts in which the firm operates, or rather was intending to operate.

The key arenas in which the firm was entering new territory were the business-to-business arena, the global arena and the consumer arena, at least as far as the children's tools were concerned. Given the current discrepancy between the staff view of the company and the directors' view, there would also need to be some internal marketing in place.

Objectives After reading this chapter, you should be able to:

→ Explain how planning might be different for firms in business-to-business markets as compared with business-to-consumer markets.

→ Describe some of the key elements in planning for global markets.

→ Explain the specific problems faced by charities in terms of planning.

→ Identify the differences between services marketing and physical product marketing in terms of planning and strategy.

→ Explain the different strategic paradigms as they affect small-to-medium businesses.

Introduction

As with every other activity, planning relies on its context. Marketing operates in many contexts, and although the examples usually given in marketing textbooks tend to assume a manufacturing company with a portfolio of physical products which it sells to consumers, this is not the scenario most practitioners are faced with.

Planning in business-to-business markets

Business-to-business markets differ from business-to-consumer markets in the following ways:

1 There are relatively fewer customers.

2 Order values are much bigger.

3 Business buyers are buying on behalf of an organisation, not for their own use.

4 Businesses may not consume the products themselves – they might simply sell them on.

Business customers can be classified as follows:

1 **Business and commercial organisations**. These organisations buy goods and services for two purposes. Some of what they buy is consumed in the course of running the organisation (for example, copier paper used in the offices, or legal services). Some of what they buy is incorporated into their own products (raw materials, components, servicing agreements for end users). The things supplied might be foundation goods and services (which are used to make other products), facilitating goods and services (which help the organisation achieve its objectives), or entering goods and services (which form part of another product after being processed by the organisation).

2 **Reseller organisations**. These are wholesalers and retailers who buy goods simply to sell them on, unchanged.

3 Government organisations. Governments buy everything from paperclips to warships through their various departments. Because they operate under very specific rules, special planning is needed to approach such organisations.

4 Institutional organisations. These include charities, educational establishments, hospitals, and so forth. Usually they have needs which greatly exceed their resources, so special tactics may be needed (for example, finding creative ways for them to pay for the goods and services they need).

Business-to-business markets tend to be less volatile, and it is easier to develop long-term relationships, so planning is easier in many ways. Relationship marketing is more successful in a business context as opposed to a consumer context because businesses are slower to change their needs than are people – for example, BMW continues to need electrical wiring, oil, nuts and bolts, and windscreen glass just as it has done for more than 100 years. Few human beings would retain the same needs for that length of time.

Planning in business-to-business markets is therefore likely to be much more detailed and careful (since there are fewer customers, it is dangerous to lose even one) and is likely to focus on establishing long-term relationships. Salespeople and key-account managers become much more important in this context.

Globalisation strategy

In the global context, competitive advantage can be achieved in different ways for each market the firm operates in. A company which is the cost leader in its domestic market might very well find itself to be a differentiator in a foreign market, perhaps because its products are unknown there. Firms will find it more difficult to achieve customer intimacy in a foreign market, especially when they first enter the market – establishing a rapport with customers requires a deep understanding of the local culture, and this can take some time to reconcile with the existing corporate culture.

Firms which succeed in establishing themselves globally usually develop international competitive strengths that are not available to purely domestic firms. They will also view the market globally, looking for opportunities and threats on a worldwide basis. This does not, of course, preclude the firm from having a national strategic orientation in its local markets.

There are four main strategic options open to the globalising company (Grosse and Kujawa 1992):

1 Aim for a high share of a global market.
2 Aim for a niche in a global market.
3 Aim for a high share of a national market.
4 Aim for a niche in a national market.

The firms seeking a high share of a global market will look for high-volume segments which exist globally, in other words segments which cross national boundaries.

Examples are the global car business and the global airline business. In most cases firms will need to produce a wide range of products to meet the needs of that market segment or those market segments. Because global niche marketers can capture big enough markets by targeting people with very specific needs, the global high-share company must seek those benefits which come from being able to supply a wide range of products. These include inbound logistics advantages such as being able to use the same raw materials to produce many products and the ability to offer customers a wider range of choice.

Global niche strategists target a single industry or a single type of problem. For example, Microbiological Systems Ltd supplies biologically based environmental pollution-detection systems to the chemical industry. The firm is at the cutting edge of research in the area and is able to supply systems which are cheaper, more sensitive and more reliable than anyone else's. Such firms protect their market niche by holding the key patents on the processes they use and by spending large amounts on R&D in order to stay ahead of the competition.

Global nichers usually avoid competing directly with major firms, because they do not have the resources for an extended battle. A niche policy works best for firms which have a global advantage (i.e. an advantage over all other firms in the industry wherever they are located) and where the product does not need to be adapted much (or at all) to meet local conditions.

National high-share strategists target countries where they think they can obtain a high share of the market. This may come about because of tariff barriers which prevent other foreign firms from entering the market (as in the case of a customs union or common market), or it may be that local firms are unable to supply the demand for the products. In some cases the production facilities for a firm may be located in a country where the raw materials are easily available. For example, Rio Tinto produces aluminium in Australia and New Zealand, copper in Papua New Guinea, and uranium in Namibia. In each case the company is well placed to supply local or regional demand for the end product as well as to supply export markets. National governments will often help such firms to establish production facilities rather than simply export raw materials because adding value in the host country provides employment and increases revenues.

Selecting one country rather than another is difficult when there are so many to choose from. A number of researchers have proposed using an adaptation of the well-known GE matrix. This market choice matrix is shown in Figure 13.1.

The market choice matrix compares the firm's specific competencies with a particular market's attractiveness. On the vertical axis, the firm's product or business strengths relate to the specific competencies of the firm. Some possible factors for this axis include:

- Business size
- Financial strength
- Technology superiority
- Brand perceptions
- Personnel.

Figure 13.1 Market choice matrix

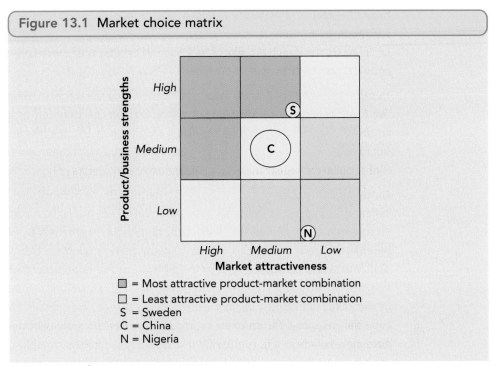

Adapted from: GE Strategic Planning Grid

The horizontal axis, market attractiveness, would include factors such as:

- Trade barriers
- Competition
- Cultural acceptance
- Technological readiness
- Previous corporate establishment
- Availability of distribution.

Each of the factors for product/business and market attractiveness should be given a weight and then each sub-factor rated. When the weights and ratings are summarised, an overall number can be developed. From this number, the placement on the country market portfolio grid would be determined. The relative size of the market can be shown by varying the size of the circles representing each country market.

Figure 13.1 shows a firm whose business strengths are only around the medium level for competing in China. China also is only medium attractive as a market, but the country is represented by a large circle since it has a very high market potential due to its size. Sweden is represented as a market where the firm's competencies would be high compared with competitors, but the attractiveness is again only medium due to high levels of competition. The size of the Swedish market is shown with a smaller circle, because it is a much smaller market overall. Finally, Nigeria is shown as a medium-sized circle in the lower right-hand corner because the firm has little strength and the market attractiveness is low. The overall market size in Nigeria is about the same as that of Sweden, because Nigeria is a relatively poor country. This firm would be unlikely to target Nigeria, and planners would need to make an executive decision whether to go for the large Chinese market where they have relatively low competitive advantage, or to go for the much smaller Swedish market where the company should be able to compete successfully.

In some cases national high-share strategists allow the national government a share in the firm. This type of joint venture is favoured in Sweden and in many Third World countries, where the governments find it a useful way to raise revenue without increasing taxation. From the firm's viewpoint, having the government as a shareholder means that legislation will often favour the firm over some of its competitors.

National niche strategists specialise on a national basis because this helps defend their segments against local and international rivals. This works best where global product strategies are not compatible with local demands, especially where products have to be adapted from country to country. Competitive advantage derives from the firm's ability to adapt to local needs. For example, a car manufacturer may need to adapt the vehicles to suit local climatic, geographic and infrastructure differences. The quality of the roads is likely to make a difference to suspension specifications, mountainous countries require different gear ratios, countries with extensive motorway, freeway or autobahn networks will require overdrive top gears, and so forth.

Garten (2000), in reviewing the requirements for global strategy, advises the following:

- Rethink everything about the strategy – even what the strategy means in a fast and brutally competitive environment.
- The best strategies are developed by organisations which can gather and process massive amounts of information.
- Companies that succeed globally are constantly innovating.
- To succeed globally, firms need to create a culture which allows for extensive internal and external collaboration.
- Global change offers unprecedented opportunities to capture markets.

In general, globalisation generates economies of scale and allows firms to spread their risk across a number of countries. The downside is that it creates problems of adaptation of strategy to meet local conditions in the target markets.

Non-profit marketing

Not all marketing activities take place in a profit context. Defining marketing solely as profit-led is misleading, since many activities which we would normally define as marketing take place within a non-profit context. Charitable organisations spend large sums on advertising in order to persuade people to donate, or to change their behaviour in ways which fulfil the aims of the organisation.

Non-profit marketing falls into two main categories: charitable donations and cause-related marketing. Charities may simply be seeking donations to fund their work, or may be seeking to change public attitudes concerning an issue. For example, Oxfam frequently runs TV advertising asking for donations so that it can build wells or provide food aid in emergencies, both of which are expensive things to do. The National Society for the Prevention of Cruelty to Children (NSPCC) runs campaigns encouraging people to report cases of child abuse, and the Samaritans runs advertising encouraging depressed or suicidal people to call the Samaritans for help. Between 1999 and March 2003 the NSPCC's Full Stop campaign raised £120.7 million in the biggest-ever campaign by a charity, breaking new ground in its sector (Pegram et al. 2003). Non-profit organisations are often more brand-oriented than are commercial, profit-making organisations (Napoli 2006).

In non-profit marketing, it may be difficult to define what the exchange is, in other words what the contributors to charities gain from their donation. In the case of government advertising (for example, encouraging people to give up smoking) it is hard to see what people gain from responding (apart from a healthier life, but there can be few smokers who are not aware of this already).

In the case of charities, the donors obtain a sense of having done the right thing by giving (see Figure 13.2). In the case of contributions from businesses, socially responsible behaviour on the part of corporations boosts sales. Also, charities supported by a corporation with a previous poor record of social responsibility often receive higher donations from the public at large (Lichtenstein et al. 2004).

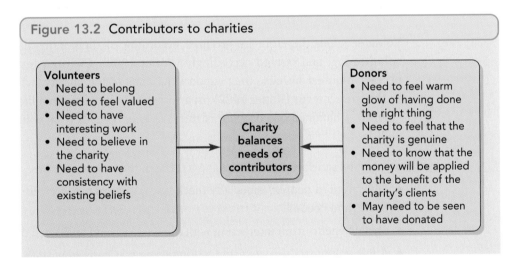

Figure 13.2 **Contributors to charities**

In one study of high-earning young professionals in the City of London, researchers found that these people tended to support charities with well-established reputations, and also liked to be rewarded with 'social' events such as invitations to gala benefit dinners. 'Planned giving', where the donors receive tax breaks, were not highly regarded by this group, which evidently enjoys the high-profile aspects of being seen to support the charity (Kottasz 2004).

In recent years, not-for-profit marketers have been prepared to take bigger risks with advertising, making it more hard-hitting than in previous years. Their remit does not fit the same paradigms as profit-based organisations, so they can afford to take greater risks (West and Sargeant 2004).

The exchange is not always made in financial terms. Charities frequently use volunteers, whose needs must also be met – they give up their time in order to help the charity and need to feel compensated in some way. Sometimes volunteers feel rewarded through social contact, since many of them are either retired or unemployed and enjoy the company of other people in a work environment, while at the same time remaining in control of the hours they work and the degree of commitment they give. Women tend to volunteer much more often than do men (Rohrs 1986), although this trend may be reducing as more women have careers outside the home. Although some researchers have found that volunteers are motivated by the desire to help others, such self-reports may not be reliable; other authors suggest that all volunteers are actually motivated by self-interest. In fact, the truth is likely to lie somewhere in between – as might be expected, different volunteers act for different reasons (Wymer 2003).

If people volunteer to help a charity only because there is something in it for themselves, is this really volunteering at all? Shouldn't we be helping out simply because it's the right thing to do – not expecting a ticket of admission to the Kingdom of Heaven for our efforts?

Or perhaps we should give people credit for being the kind of person who derives pleasure from helping others – in contrast to some people who apparently derive pleasure from harming others!

Volunteers can therefore be grouped according to their individual motivation for volunteering, and treated accordingly (Kotler 1982). Charities tend to assume that people volunteer because they support the aims of the charity, which may well not be the correct focus (Kotler 1982). In a survey of volunteers for a literacy programme, volunteers obtained one or more of the following benefits from volunteering (Wymer 2003):

- Personal satisfaction from making a difference to someone's life.
- Older retired people, especially teachers and librarians, derived a sense of feeling useful and needed.
- Social benefits from interacting with the students and with each other.
- A few volunteers reported that volunteering was consistent with their Christian or other religious beliefs.

In terms of demography, this study found that volunteers tended to come from wealthier households with small families. Gender, age and income were all significant, but personality traits such as self-esteem and empathy do not appear to affect whether someone volunteers or not. Clearly, there is scope for much more research on this topic. Presumably it would be more realistic to consider how volunteers differ from each other and to try to meet the needs of a group of volunteers who have similar needs (Yavas and Reicken 1985).

The other aspect of non-profit marketing is that of changing people's attitudes and behaviour. This is especially interesting for political parties. A view is emerging that political parties have concentrated too much on 'spin' (the manipulation of the news media to create a favourable impression) and not enough on marketing (meeting the needs of their constituents). In particular, information needs of voters are not being met (Mortimore 2003).

From a planning viewpoint, the large number of stakeholders involved in a non-profit scenario creates a series of conflicts in trying to balance the needs of many different people, all with different agendas. This is especially difficult when the charity uses volunteer workers, who (since they are unpaid) feel that they can come and go as they please, and not necessarily put a great deal of effort into what they are doing. Charities therefore have little control over their internal environment, but may have more control over at least some of their external environment since they are, essentially, giving away goods and services. They also have the moral high ground when it comes to dealing with outside organisations such as government officials and the news media.

Internal marketing

Internal marketing is aimed at using marketing techniques to mould the corporate culture. Organisations are composed of people who will develop a corporate culture without any outside help – such cultures have their own language, customs, hierarchy and traditions. Within the organisation sub-groups and individuals will have their own agendas and aspirations, alliances will form within groups, and pressure groups will form. The organisation will have its own rules and regulations, some of which will be the unwritten rules by which organisation members live and work. These rules operate alongside official company rules.

From the viewpoint of marketing, the members of the organisation are participating in an exchange process. This goes beyond exchanging their time for the organisation's money: employees contribute a varying amount of commitment to the firm and their colleagues. This is called emotional labour. People think about their work, talk about it at home, sometimes work extra hours without pay, and otherwise go beyond the strict letter of the contract. In general, people do it because they feel a degree of responsibility towards their colleagues and also feel the need to do a good job. Praise or approval from management is part of the reward that staff can reasonably expect from an employer in exchange for emotional labour.

Using the categories outlined in Maslow's famous hierarchy of needs, Table 13.1 shows examples of work-related need fulfilment.

Since marketing focuses on meeting needs in exchange for value, it seems reasonable to suppose that any request for extra effort from staff should be accompanied by some statement showing how such efforts will result in staff's personal needs being met more closely. Sales managers tend to be adept at this (perhaps because of being marketing-oriented) and can often obtain remarkable effort from salespeople, simply by being attuned to the individual needs of the employees they manage.

Table 13.1 Work-related need fulfilment

Need	Example
Physiological needs	Fair salary, comfortable working environment, suitable working facilities and equipment.
Safety needs	Secure employment prospects, safe working environment, medical insurance, pension plan.
Love needs	Respect of management, deserved praise, group membership and feeling of belonging.
Esteem needs	Achievement and recognition of achievement, opportunity to acquire a good reputation, feeling of working for a well-respected organisation.
Aesthetic needs	Pleasant working environment, well-designed working spaces, opportunities to participate in creative activities.
Self-actualisation needs	Opportunity to go on training courses, opportunities for promotion, opportunities to participate in the running of the organisation through participative decision making.

Services marketing

Much marketing theory has been developed around the marketing of physical products, but in fact the majority of day-to-day marketing is concerned with services. Marketing academics are divided on the issue of whether services marketing is actually a separate set of problems or whether the principles of marketing remain the same whether dealing with a service or a physical product. The key reason for this thinking is that, conceptually, every product provides a service outcome. Someone who buys a drill is actually buying a hole-boring service, for example.

Even under traditional thinking, virtually all products are a mixture of service elements and physical product elements. In other words, products are on a continuum, with services at one end and physical products at the other. For example, a life insurance policy has virtually no physical existence, apart from the document, whereas a bag of builder's sand has a physical presence but almost no service aspects apart from delivery. At the extreme end of the spectrum, service products have the following characteristics:

1 **Intangibility**. The product cannot be touched, which means that it is difficult to evaluate in advance of purchase. It also has no second-hand value, so in a sense cannot be owned. For example, a haircut cannot be tried out before purchase, nor can it be sold to a friend, unlike a guitar or a car.

2 **Inseparability of production and consumption**. In most cases, the production of a service and its consumption happen at the same time. A concert happens as it is being heard and although the effects may last for some time afterwards in the memories of the audience, the main benefits are consumed at the time.

3 **Variability**. Because services are produced on an individual basis, they are often variable in nature. In some respects this is a benefit for the customer – being able to ask the chef to cook one's steak rare rather than medium is useful, but the chef might

be having a bad day and may overcook the vegetables. Things go wrong with services because they are difficult to standardise.

4 **Perishability**. Services cannot be stockpiled for later use. An airline seat is available only for a specific flight on a specific day – once the aircraft takes off, the seat cannot be sold.

From a planning perspective, services marketing usually involves a large input from employees. In effect, a service company such as a restaurant or hairdressing business is buying staff time wholesale and selling it retail. Since time is extremely perishable, planning needs to consider the loading element of demand, and demand will need to be managed in some way. Low-cost airlines do this by having flexible pricing: the aim is for every aircraft to take off full, even if some passengers have paid only a low fare, because even a small amount of money is better than nothing at all. Other service businesses have discounts for students or senior citizens during quiet times, or have 'happy hour' discounts, or promote in other ways to fill quiet periods.

Planning in SMEs

Small businesses have specific problems and advantages in terms of planning. In most cases, small firms have few resources to devote to the level of research and planning time that a full-blown marketing plan would require. Nevertheless, small firms are often run by a single entrepreneur or a small team of partners who are able to respond rapidly to changes in the market.

For most small firms, a business plan is simply something that a bank manager requires if the firm needs to borrow money. The plan is unlikely to be followed rigidly, since circumstances can change rapidly for small firms – a key employee leaving might well be a major setback, whereas a larger firm would have enough people on hand to take up the slack.

Richard Whittington (2001) questions the 'toolbox' approach of most strategic management texts. Whittington examines four generic approaches to strategy, which are outlined in Table 13.2.

Each approach offers a different set of answers for what strategy is. Classicists say that strategy is rational and consists of a set of deliberate calculations aimed at achieving a market position and maintaining it in the face of opposition. It implies rationality, long-range focus, responses to environmental shifts in a calculated manner, and so forth.

Evolutionists believe that the environment is too unpredictable for long-range planning to have any reasonable chance of success. For the evolutionists, it is the market, not the managers, that make the important choices, and firms are almost certainly unable to adapt quickly enough to make much difference to their survival chances (Hannan and Freeman 1988; Williamson 1991). Thus successful strategies emerge only as a result of ruthless natural selection, in which the firms with inappropriate strategies go broke and the ones which happen to have hit on a strategy which meets the needs of the market go on to succeed.

Table 13.2   Generic approaches to strategy

Approach	Explanation
Classical	Relies on rational planning methods, using environmental analysis as the basis for decision making and planning for the long term.
Evolutionary	Assumes that only the fittest will survive: correct strategies will result from adapting to the environment and ad-hoc solutions are used in response to environmental pressures. Evolutionary strategic thought is about accommodating to the law of the jungle: long-term planning is therefore not feasible.
Processualist	Strategy accommodates to the fallible processes of both organisations and markets. Strategy is therefore a bottom-up process, coming from the exigencies of the situations the firm faces.
Systemic	The ends and means of strategy are linked to the cultures and powers of the local social systems in which it takes place. Companies therefore follow policies which are dictated by their local social constraints rather than by strict business considerations.

For processualists, the processes of organisations and markets are rarely perfect. This means that the market is not as implacable as the evolutionists believe, nor is the firm able to plan as thoroughly as the classicists would like. People are unable to be so precise and unvarying as to be able to carry through a detailed plan, particularly in the face of the difficulties and unforeseen circumstances which are bound to arise in an imperfect world. Therefore, firms develop strategy (or have it forced upon them) via a series of bodgings, ad-hoc decisions, compromises with reality, and learning by mistakes rather than by long-range planning and rationality (Mintzberg 1994). For the processualist, failure to carry out the perfect marketing strategy is unlikely to prove fatal (although there may be some loss of ground).

Systemic theorists believe that people are capable of carrying out rational plans of action and are also confident that it is possible to define strategies in the face of environmental forces. However, their view is that the objectives and practices of strategy are embedded in the social system to which they belong. This means, for example, that profit maximisation is not necessarily a strong factor in strategic planning. This argument carries considerable weight in a world in which the non-profit organisation and the 'fair trade' corporation are in the ascendant.

The systemic perspective also finds support in the fact that firms within different social systems have differing strategic perspectives. German and Japanese businesses were restructured after the Second World War to engender close cooperation between banks and enterprises, and to operate within a paternalistic state structure which encouraged worker participation and universal social security. The Anglo–American business structure, meanwhile, operated in an environment of hostile takeovers, impatient lenders, adversarial labour relations and (frequently) governments committed to giving capitalism free rein.

In fact, all the generic philosophies of strategy have some facets which are evidenced in the real world. The business world is sufficiently complex to allow for a wide range of experiences and models. For example, some industries change very little over time: light-bulb manufacture has changed relatively little since the 19th century, as has house building, even though the technology has shifted somewhat. This means that it is reasonable to develop long-term strategies for these industries, to take account of fairly predictable economic or environmental shifts. In other industries, such as the restaurant trade, conditions can change rapidly and unpredictably, so an evolutionary paradigm prevails. Processualists find support for their arguments in those industries which are dominated by small firms, and in industries such as the computer software industry where technological breakthroughs happen on an almost daily basis.

The differences between the generic strategies do matter, because they offer radically different recommendations for managers. For every manager, the strategy-formulation process always begins with a decision as to which theoretical picture of the world best fits with his or her own experiences and attitudes. If the manager's view is that the world is orderly, with sufficient information and capacity to analyse, and sufficient availability of organisational control, then the classical paradigm would be most likely to be adopted. If, however, the manager believes that the environment is cut-throat and unpredictable, the evolutionist paradigm will prevail.

Some of the different contexts under which each strategic paradigm will succeed are shown in Figure 13.3.

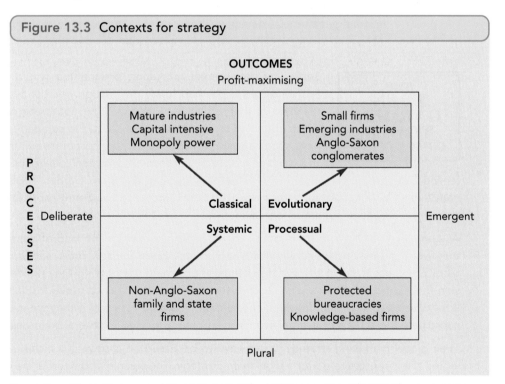

Figure 13.3 Contexts for strategy

Source: From 'What is Strategy – and Does it Matter?', Richard Whittington, Copyright 2001, Thomson Learning (EMEA) Ltd. Reproduced by permission of Cengage Learning.

From this model, it is clear that small firms are likely to be profit-maximising and emergent, and therefore strategy will evolve rather than be planned. In the context of what small firms do, this is a crucial observation: such firms are not in a position to plan effectively because they can be affected too easily by competition from larger firms and are in effect at the mercy of their external environment. This does not mean that they have no strategy – it simply means that it changes from day to day as circumstances dictate. Because such firms operate under an evolutionary paradigm, however, only the fittest will survive.

Summary

Marketing planning does not happen in a vacuum. The planning process and outcomes will be affected or even negated by the context in which they occur. This chapter has examined some of the contexts in which planning happens and has discussed some of the issues which arise for planners.

The key points from this chapter are as follows:

→ Business-to-business markets have fewer customers, bigger order values, professional buyers, and are not end users for most of what they buy. This has profound effects on planning.

→ Global firms can aim for niche markets or for mass markets, but the customer needs must be universal if the market is to cross borders.

→ Charities have a large number of stakeholders, most of which are not under the control of the organisation.

→ The perishability of services means that loading is a key factor in planning.

→ Small businesses usually operate in an evolutionary environment and therefore strategy emerges from circumstances rather than from formal planning.

Setting up an internal marketing programme would need to go further than the planned 'away day'. Hugh was handed the task of planning further activities to improve the corporate culture, a job which appealed to his nature. At present, the company did not even have a staff newsletter, and the existing corporate culture had simply grown up as a result of interactions between colleagues. The general feeling among the team was that staff enjoyed working for Eden Garden Tools – the company's relatively low staff turnover evidenced this – but there was clearly room for developing a much greater commitment among staff.

As a small firm, there was some doubt expressed as to whether the kind of detailed planning they were undertaking was really necessary. In fact, Eden Garden Tools' senior management team knew that they would have no chance of obtaining the funding they needed for expansion if they did not have a plan, and in any case the idea was to move from being a small firm to being a large firm, in which case a plan would be essential if they were to be able to coordinate the actions of a larger workforce, possibly located in several countries.

Their global marketing strategy would have to be based on capturing a niche, since the firm lacked the resources to go for a high-share strategy. They would also need to be very cautious about the markets they entered – each country would have to be entered separately, unless the prospective 'piggy-back' partner thought otherwise.

For the business-to-business aspect of marketing the pruning saw, Eden Garden Tools felt confident of being able to capture a strong share of the market. The saw would be a big time saver, and in business time is money since staff are usually the biggest overhead.

Overall, the team now felt very confident that they were in a position to write the marketing plan – and in turn, to win the funding the company needed.

Review questions

1 *What are the differences in planning for business-to-business markets as opposed to consumer markets?*

2 *What specific issues arise when planning for global markets?*

3 *How might a charity balance the needs of its stakeholders?*

4 *Why is it difficult for small businesses to plan effectively?*

5 *What problems might affect a small service business such as a hairdressing business?*

 ## Case study The Real Seed Catalogue

Throughout the UK there has been a revival in the idea of growing one's own food. Everywhere there are waiting lists for allotments as people move away from buying supermarket vegetables and processed food – the level of interest in home-grown, mainly organic crops is at its highest since the Second World War.

Into this burgeoning market has come the Real Seed Catalogue. The founders of the catalogue, Ben and Kate, are certainly engaged in a labour of love rather than a commercial enterprise – passionate believers in saving the ecosystem, they grow their seeds on a smallholding in Wales. They are not certified organic, because in their own words 'we'd rather be out growing vegetables than filling in forms, to be honest', and they are reluctant to pay the necessary fees for certification. That said, their seeds almost certainly exceed the criteria for organic certification. They grow all their own food for personal consumption, and their house and office are solar-powered, heated from wood-burning stoves which burn renewable, coppiced wood, and they rarely use a car and never fly anywhere.

The couple separate, sort and package the seeds themselves, and if they sell out of a particular variety they simply flag up on their website that the seeds have been sold. They do not buy in seeds from commercial suppliers, although they have about 15 sympathetic friends throughout the country who will grow seeds for them, and they will occasionally source seeds from known organic seed companies in order to grow new varieties. As far as possible the Real Seed Catalogue contains heritage varieties – there are no hybrid seeds, so those who buy the seeds can grow their own for next year. Ben and Kate actively encourage their customers to do just that – which may seem bizarre, since it would apparently hurt sales to do so, but in practice it simply means that people come back again next year for more seeds for different varieties. The Real Seed Catalogue is simply a company that people trust: Kate and Ben are so obviously transparently honest and passionate about helping people to grow their own.

Of course, the business has to make money, or it cannot stay in the game. The seeds are not unreasonably priced, but equally they are not usually the cheapest available. However, they tend to grow a lot better than commercially produced hybrids, which are treated with fungicide and are in any case intended for growing in controlled, fertilised, pesticide-treated conditions. Most of the Real Seed Catalogue's seeds are heritage varieties, i.e. plants which used to be widely cultivated but which (for one reason or another) are not suitable for large-scale industrial farming. The Real Seed Catalogue has an efficient website on which people can order their seeds: payment by cheque, cash, credit card, euros, and US dollars are all acceptable. Seeds are dispatched by post, and there is a replacement guarantee if the seeds disappoint for any reason whatsoever (even incompetent growing). Seeds can also be ordered by post, using a form from the website or a simple letter. The company does not promote itself in any other way, relying almost entirely on word of mouth to attract new customers.

The Real Seed Catalogue almost isn't a business at all: rather, it is a crusade to bring real food back into people's lives. Ben and Kate make no secret of the fact that they are trying to convert people to the cause – but it is a worthy cause, and one which has a resonance with the mood of the age.

Questions

1 *To what extent do Kate and Ben fit the model of the opportunistic entrepreneur?*

2 *Which of the four generic strategic approaches does the Real Seed Catalogue most closely resemble?*

3 *To what extent would you expect the Real Seed Catalogue to engage in formal planning?*

4 *Who are the main stakeholders for the firm?*

5 *How does Maslow's Hierarchy of Needs relate to the Real Seed Catalogue?*

References

Garten, J.E. (2000): *World View: Global Strategies for the New Economy* (Harvard Business School Publishing) pp xiii–xiv.

Grosse, R. and Kujawa, D. (1992): *International Business* (Homewood, IL: Irwin).

Hannan, M.T. and Freeman, J. (1988): *Organisational Ecology* (Cambridge, MA: Harvard University Press).

Jayawardene, C. (2004): Management of service quality in Internet banking: the development of an instrument. *Journal of Marketing*, 20 (1) pp 185–207.

Kotler, P. (1982): *Marketing for Non-profit Organisations* (Englewood Cliffs, NJ: Prentice Hall).

Kottasz, R. (2004): How should charitable organisations motivate young professionals to give philanthropically? *International Journal of Nonprofit and Voluntary Sector Marketing*, 9 (1) pp 9–28.

Lichtenstein, D.R., Drumright, M.E. and Braig, B.M. (2004): The effects of corporate social responsibility on customer donations to corporate-supported non-profits. *Journal of Marketing*, 68 (4) pp 16–32.

Mintzberg, H. (1994): *The Rise and Fall of Strategic Planning* (New York: Free Press).

Mortimore, R. (2003): Why politics needs marketing. *International Journal of Nonprofit and Voluntary Sector Marketing*, 8 (2) pp 107–21.

Napoli, J. (2006): The impact of non-profit brand orientation on organisational performance. *Journal of Marketing Management*, 22 (7/8) pp 673–94.

Pegram, G., Booth, N. and McBurney, C. (2003): Full stop: an extraordinary appeal for an extraordinary aspiration – putting leadership theory into practice. *International Journal of Nonprofit and Voluntary Sector Marketing*, 8 (3) pp 207–12.

Rohrs, F.R. (1986): Social background, personality and attitudinal factors influencing the decision to volunteer and level of involvement among adult 4-H leaders. *Journal of Voluntary Action Research*, 15 (1) pp 87–99.

Whittington, R. (2001): *What is Strategy – And Does It Matter?* (London: Thomson).

Williamson, O.E. (1991): Strategising, economising and economic organisation. *Strategic Management Journal*, 12 pp 75–94.

Wymer, W.W. (2003): Differentiating literacy volunteers: a segmentation analysis for target marketing. *International Journal of Nonprofit and Voluntary Sector Marketing*, 8 (3) pp 267–85.

Yavas, U. and Reicken, G. (1985): Can volunteers be targeted? *Journal of the Academy of Marketing Science*, 13 (2) pp 218–28.

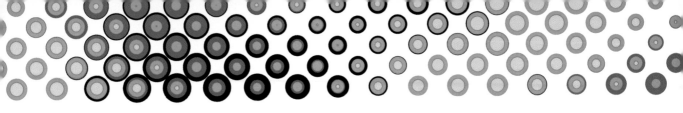

Marketing plan for The Eden Garden Tools Company Ltd: 2010–2014

The outline marketing plan presented here is an illustrative example based upon a hypothetical company, The Eden Garden Tools Company Ltd, which manufactures specialist gardening products and markets them to amateur gardeners both in the UK and in the European Union.

The context of the plan is that of the recent recession and how a small private limited company (essentially a family business) can face up to difficult market and competitive conditions through undertaking marketing planning and producing and implementing a marketing plan. The scenario for development involves sales growth from both new products and new customers as a basis for attracting external finance from venture capitalists. The plan has been produced for a five-year period, which provides an alternative step towards setting out a successful future for the business without having to go the whole way and provide a plan for a 5–7-year exit strategy as the new investors originally required. The main issue underlying the plan is the lack of marketing understanding of the current management and the need to adopt a more customer-focused basis for the company's future success. The current deficiencies of planning and focus need to be remedied if the business is going to face up to the challenge of emerging from the recession and going forward on a successful footing.

The sample outline plan constructed for Eden Garden Tools is in very broad terms based on the structure presented in Chapter 1 of the text. However, it is important to understand that this is by no means the only framework that can be adopted and that balance of marketing plan structure and content (including appendices) should reflect the circumstances of the organisation involved.

BACKGROUND

With a retail turnover of over £5 billion a year, the UK gardening industry is a buoyant and growing market. The market has enjoyed good growth over the last 10–15 years, not least as a result of changes in lifestyle and disposable incomes. Socio-economic conditions have worked in favour of the gardening industry with an increase in home ownership, higher disposable incomes and an ageing population. What's more, consumers are becoming better informed gardeners and are more demanding, requiring better service and value. Gardening is even – dare we say it – becoming increasingly fashionable. The popularity of the grow-your-own movement is testament to the public's increased interest in their environment, the garden as a refuge and a greater desire to connect with the earth.

Horticultural Trades Association, 2009

Eden Garden Tools is a small player in an industry which is becoming increasingly polarised, with large multinational manufacturers dominating mass-market, branded sales together with a proliferation of cheaper non-branded and retailer-branded low-cost alternatives manufactured in the Far East. The firm requires a strategy to come out of the recession which will give it a platform for growth and development. It produces specialised equipment that differentiates its offer from the mainstream, and regards itself as the most innovative player in the industry. It already has a good export presence, which will need to be extended, as will the range of products that the company produces. It also needs to identify and enter alternative markets to those that it currently serves at home.

Having recognised its marketing shortcomings in recent years Eden Garden Tools has appointed a marketing manager, Umar Sayeed, and tasked him with producing an outline marketing plan to be presented to the venture capitalists. However, he has only a limited amount of resources and time to do this, so the shape and content of the plan will reflect this, as indicated below. Once the outline plan has been presented to the potential investors, Umar and the other senior managers will need to provide a much more detailed assessment of what marketing they have planned over the coming years so that they have a blueprint for the future of Eden Garden Tools.

1 EXECUTIVE SUMMARY

The Eden Garden Tools Company Ltd is a small garden tools and equipment producer based in the UK. It has been operating for 15 years and has developed steadily over this period through the manufacture and supply of innovative products targeted at specific customer groups with particular requirements. This includes ergonomically designed tools for those who find gardening difficult and the Slick Mower, which is designed to deal with uneven lawns. Although the company has been reasonably successful in UK and international markets as a result of the trend towards greater participation in gardening, growth has slowed in recent times due to the onset of the credit crunch and the economic recession.

The owners of the business have identified that they need to undertake business development. They have recruited some key personnel to do this and have put together an outline plan to be presented to potential investors in three weeks' time. The plan provides a background to the situation, the business, the industry and its main drivers. The strengths and weaknesses of Eden Garden Tools are identified, together with market opportunities and threats.

A strategy for development is presented based upon the company differentiating its offer and brand in terms of innovation and carefully targeted segmentation strategies, which provide a platform for significantly increasing its global presence. The business has integrated a new commercial product into its planned portfolio in addition to launching a revitalised range of hand tools and a separate sub-brand targeted at children.

A broad set of marketing-mix activities has been proposed over a five-year timescale to achieve the marketing objectives set out in the plan. Implementation factors associated with funding the plan and the necessary structures, responsibilities, and monitoring and control approaches are considered in the context of the planning process for Eden Garden Tools.

2 ORGANISATIONAL STRATEGIC POSITION

Eden Garden Tools' mission is to deliver innovative gardening products to a range of customers and to create a love of gardening amongst its user base, whatever their age or personal circumstances. In so doing it will be a profitable business that will provide long-term value to its shareholders and sustain this through growing its market share both at home and internationally.

The company will strategically differentiate its offer from its competitors by meeting the needs of specific target customer groups through providing them with benefit-based gardening solutions. It will achieve this through building the brand and its sub-brands and expand its focus from the UK and Europe into a wider international sphere.

The values of the company are to positively support gardening as a worthwhile pastime and form of exercise for all individuals and to support the horticultural and agricultural industry in general as important contributors to local, regional, national and international economies. Eden Garden Tools therefore has a stance that is supportive of environmental sustainability and will always endeavour to behave in an ethical way with regard to its customers, employees and the wider community.

The company recognises that customers are key to its success and that satisfying their needs will be achieved only through harnessing the skills of its valued employees. On this basis the company has the following vision as the focus of its future development:

'The Eden Garden Tools Company Ltd will be the leading company in horticultural innovation in the UK. This will be achieved by a policy of continuous innovation, coupled with sound engineering and a focus on customer need, whether for the amateur gardener or the professional grower.'

From its current position the company intends to achieve these general corporate objectives:

- Reduce its debt/equity ratio by 5 per cent per annum over the next five years.
- Increase total sales turnover by 40 per cent in two years.
- Achieve a break-even position on UK and European business by mid-2011 and a 20 per cent profit margin on sales in these markets by end 2012.
- Generate 10 per cent of sales from non-UK and European markets by end 2012 and increase this to 20 per cent in five years.
- Over five years achieve 90 per cent brand awareness of Eden Garden Tools in its consumer household segments in the UK and Europe, and 60 per cent in its business-to-business and professional markets.
- Actively promote through its brand position the sustainability and health advantages of gardening to the wider community and emphasise the inclusive nature of gardening as a pastime for anyone.
- Stress the importance of horticulture and agriculture industries to the economy and promote Eden Garden Tools as a supporter of their success through its innovative business solutions.

3 SITUATION ANALYSIS: EXTERNAL AND INTERNAL MARKETING AUDITS

3.1 External analysis

The market for Eden Garden Tools' products can be broadly defined in terms of garden tools and equipment and includes lawnmowers, other powered tools, hand tools and watering products (hosepipes, etc.).

3.1.1 Market analysis

Domestic market

According to Key Note (2009), consumer spending on garden equipment and tools in the UK was approximately £851 million in 2008, which had risen from around £753 million in 2004. All categories of the market grew over this period at a rate of 3.5 per cent per annum, although there was a slowdown in 2008. The more expensive items including lawnmowers and power tools were worst affected as the market growth rate started to level off.

Of the total market sales in 2008, lawnmowers contributed £378 million (44 per cent), power tools £326 million (38 per cent), hand tools £86 million (10 per cent) and watering products £61 million (8 per cent).

The lawnmower market has three main product categories: hand-propelled mowers, petrol-driven mowers, including ride-on mowers, and electrically powered mowers. Electric mowers are the most popular type, outselling petrol-driven models by around two to one; 90 per cent of sales in the electric category are made up by hover mowers. The sector is highly fragmented, with more than 30 manufacturer brands, plus retailer own brands. Weather is a crucial influence on lawnmower sales, with good weather in the spring and early summer leading to greater demand.

Power tools follow a similar pattern of demand and can be broadly categorised into three main types: tidy-up machines including blowers and shredders, etc., cutting and edging products, such as strimmers, shears and saws, and lawn-care products such as electric lawn rakes and scarifiers. The market is again fragmented, with a large number of suppliers, but it is dominated by major players Black & Decker and Bosch.

The hand tools sector is made up of low-technology items that have long life cycles. Market penetration is high – most households have at least one product such as a trowel or a fork – and the market is mature, with a large number of suppliers producing a range of items. Previously well-known brands have lost their share of the market to retailers' branded and non-branded, low-cost imports. A recent development has been the introduction of ergonomically designed products that can reduce strain on the back.

Water equipment includes hoses and related items. Hozelock is the market leader, but Asian non-branded, low-cost manufacturers are increasing their share of the market. Growth of this market has been hampered by high rainfall in recent years and the UK climate precludes significant growth compared with other countries with warmer climates and lower rainfall (e.g. the US and southern Europe).

Customer analysis

The TGI (2008)[1] report on ownership of gardens and allotments shows that 85 per cent of adults in the UK have gardens and 2.5 per cent have allotments, so the potential market is large. More older people have gardens, with 55–64 year olds being the main target group in terms of size, although 88 per cent of all adults aged over 35 have gardens. Social grade is not an important consideration in garden ownership, with all groups having at least 75 per cent, yet ABs tend to be over 90 per cent. Allotment ownership is higher in the C2s and lower in the E social grade group. London-based consumers are the lowest in terms of garden ownership.

With regard to specific product ownership, around 60 per cent of adults own a lawnmower, with a greater number among older people. There is a relationship between the younger first-time buyer 25–34 age group and those buying a new lawnmower, although older customers clearly buy replacement mowers and these are more prevalent in the higher social grades. London has the lowest penetration of lawnmower ownership.

---

[1] Target Group Index (TGI) (2008), survey on ownership of gardens and allotments (Ealing, London: BMRB International).

Garden tools are owned by over 54 per cent of adults. Strimmers and hedge trimmers have more than 25 per cent ownership penetration, but there is low penetration of other products, which suggests there is potential for market penetration and development in this area.

In terms of spending, most people spend less than £100 on a lawnmower and less than £50 on other garden equipment items, which indicates that there is potential to sell higher-priced items particularly to better-off consumers and those seeking added value from the product in terms of benefit.

Analysis of buying by children under 15 is not available, although it can be assumed that this is undertaken on their behalf by parents or relatives buying as gifts.

The HTA Gardening Continuum profiles the UK population by gardening interest and likelihood to buy or do some form of gardening. The Continuum identifies the following five broad types of gardener:

Category of gardener	Description	Proportion of the UK population
Very keen gardeners	Those who positively enjoy gardening, are interested and knowledgeable and spend time pursuing what is really an established hobby.	13 per cent
Quite keen gardeners	Those who claim to be quite interested and who make a positive claim about enjoyment. Although they actively work in their own gardens, they do not express a desire to increase the amount of gardening that they currently do.	11 per cent
Marginal gardeners	Those who do some gardening, are not hostile to gardening and express a willingness to do more.	30 per cent
Not keen gardeners	Those who do some gardening, but do not wish to do more, coupled with negative attitudinal responses indicating that the gardening undertaken is not because it interests them. Largely those who see gardening as a chore.	27 per cent
Definitely hostile	Those with a place to grow outdoor plants who do very little or no gardening and who have totally negative attitudes to or interest and enjoyment in gardening, with low knowledge and absolutely no wish to do more.	16 per cent
Unavailable	This group do not lack interest in gardening nor do they lack knowledge. However, they do little or no gardening, possibly due to insurmountable obstacles such as health or domestic responsibilities.	3 per cent

Source: The Horticultural Trades Association's Garden Industry Monitor.

Overseas market

UK consumers spend more per head on gardening than consumers in other countries. In the EU, the French spent around £6 billion on garden products in 2008, while the Germans spent around £9 billion. The total retail market for garden supplies in the EU is estimated to be worth around £50 billion (Key Note 2009). However, the US is the largest single market in the world, with sales of garden products worth around £55 billion. Many of the trends seen in the UK are also evident in other markets. These include the impact of recession, the influence of garden reality programmes and increasing interest in growing fruit and vegetables.

International trade statistics do not distinguish between products destined for retail sale to individual gardeners and those that are acquired for commercial use, such as on golf courses or recreation grounds, or for use in agriculture and horticulture. Yet the data identify a general trend and show that the penetration of imports is increasing, particularly from low-cost producing countries which are not faced with technological barriers to trade in this market.

3.1.2 Market drivers

The main drivers of the market in the UK include the following:

- *The media.* TV and radio programmes, magazines and newspaper sections have for many years supported the growth in popularity of gardening and this has been boosted by garden makeover TV programmes over the past 20 years or so. The market for garden products has been spurred on by this increasing popularity.

- *Grow-your-own activity.* Growing fruit and vegetables has become more popular for various reasons, including the onset of economic hardship leading to more demand for allotments and the growth in vegetable seeds. Growing food has also become popular as it is seen to be sustainable, healthy and better for you. Gardening is also seen as a cheap and productive form of leisure activity.

- *Effects of the weather.* The weather is an important factor in driving the demand for garden equipment. Recent poor weather in the spring and early summer has had a negative effect on garden equipment sales.

- *Impacts of the economic and housing market downturn.* Expensive gardening equipment is sensitive to both the economic climate and the state of the housing market. Poor performance on both these counts has led to a decline in the sales of gardening equipment. People are not buying new equipment but are keeping their old machines and tools longer. However, they are investing in equipment to enhance the sale of their property or to maintain their new gardens, particularly in the case of first-time buyers.

3.1.3 Competitors and intermediaries

The garden products industry is highly concentrated and dominated by a number of important established brands with good consumer awareness, particularly at the top end of the market. There has also been recent significant growth in the provision of low-cost imports from the Far East and some of the major manufacturers have shifted their production to low-cost overseas bases.

Estimating the number of manufacturers of garden equipment is difficult as the market is highly polarised and fragmented. The Garden Industry Manufacturers Association lists 7 suppliers of garden machinery, 19 suppliers of garden tools and gloves, 30 suppliers of garden equipment and 12 suppliers of watering equipment. The Agricultural Engineers Association also lists 25 lawn and garden equipment manufacturers.

A further branch of the industry covers horticulture. The Commercial Horticultural Association represents manufacturers and distributors of items to commercial horticultural growers throughout the world. The Horticultural Trades Association represents 1,600 businesses and 2,700 outlets whose members comprise retailers, growers, landscapers, service providers, manufacturers and distributors of garden materials. Retail membership includes specialist retail nurseries, the vast majority of independent garden centres, garden-centre chains and some DIY and high-street multiples.

The main manufacturers of garden tools and equipment include:

- Black & Decker (manufacturer of powered gardening products)
  - lawnmowers, lawnrakers, shredders, blower-vacs, strimmers and hedge trimmers
- Bosch (manufacturer of powered gardening products)
  - hedgecutters, shredders, chainsaws, line trimmers, pressure washers (Bosch), lawnmowers (Atco & Qualcast)
- Fiskars (manufacturer of garden-cutting tools)
  - shears, secateurs, hedge trimmers and lawn-care products (also Wilkinson Sword brand)
- Hayter (manufacturer of grass-cutting equipment)
  - lawnmowers and hedge trimmers; commercial-sector products
- Husqvarna (manufacturer of powered garden tools)
  - lawnmowers, hedge cutters, chainsaws
- Spear & Jackson (garden tools manufacturer)
  - hand tools and other equipment
- Wolf (manufacturer of garden tools)
  - hand tools, lawnmowers, hedge trimmers and scarifiers.

Distribution channels

Distribution of garden equipment is extremely concentrated through multiple retail DIY outlet businesses (60 per cent). Garden-centre chains and smaller independent garden centres (20 per cent) also play an important role as distributors in local and regional markets. There is a good proportion of trade that goes through mail-order and catalogue distributors (12 per cent) and other outlets including hardware stores and garden-machinery specialists (8 per cent).

3.2 Internal analysis

The company's internal situation is difficult to assess in detail in the short period of time available so a basic structure was adopted.

3.2.1 Products

The current product portfolio comprises the Slick Mower and a range of tools produced for use in specialist markets. The Slick Mower is starting to see a levelling off of sales and is approaching the peak of its product life cycle, so is in need of a significant upgrade if it is to continue to generate revenues for Eden Garden Tools to invest in other areas. The rest of the portfolio has many products starting to approach maturity, but no emerging products which are going to generate good future cash flows. There is an urgent need to look at developing new products. The perceived innovativeness of the business is not upheld by the reality of the new product development that has been undertaken in recent years.

3.2.2 Human resources

Staff are skilled and loyal to the business and many of them have worked for the company since its inception in 1994. Yet they are somewhat conservative in their perspective of the business and what it does and may find change difficult, especially if it involves some restructuring of roles and responsibilities. The management's expertise is in engineering and industry knowledge, and they had always seen themselves as an innovative company that was able to provide products to meet market needs. However, there is a clear limitation in marketing knowledge, particularly in terms of customer and competitor understanding, and a distinct lack of market orientation. To counter this, a marketing manager with relevant experience in the garden tools sector has been appointed, as has a sales manager with experience in markets that are related to future growth areas. The lack of innovation is something that has been recognised by the staff, which they sum up in identifying Eden Garden Tools as 'old fashioned'.

3.2.3 Finance

The finances of the business are not strong, although this is more of an issue of cash flow rather than the balance sheet. Indeed, the fixed asset position of the business is good and the order book is quite strong. However, there is increasing debt, which needs to be serviced, and no cash reserves, which have been run down in the recession. This makes financing a turnaround through innovative new product development and targeting new markets difficult and hence there was a need to seek external investment based on a plan for the future.

3.2.4 Marketing

The overall level of market orientation is low, with a particular weakness in broad market knowledge. Marketing information and research are poor, which makes planning difficult. The appointment of a marketing manager with good general market knowledge has been a positive move to resolve this and there is now some awareness of key market and business drivers: innovation, social responsibility, sustainability, globalisation and stakeholder relations.

Understanding of the customer base is weak and more detailed specification of target markets is required, although some insights can be gleaned from the analysis of records and industry customer classification types. The brand positioning is unclear and needs strengthening and refinement, particularly if new markets are to be considered beyond the existing range of customers. In the international arena there is only limited recognition of the potential threat of overseas competitors entering the UK market. In addition, the use of export houses in international markets hinders strategic development, especially that linked to new products in new markets.

3.3 SWOT analysis summary and imperatives

Growth opportunities may exist for Eden Garden Tools from the overall increased demand in gardening and the consequent requirement for tools and equipment. This is being driven by a range of social, demographic, economic, technological and other factors, which has seen a long-term trend emerge for greater leisure activity throughout the developing world, especially in Eastern Europe and the Far East.

The company needs to raise its game from a marketing perspective generally if it is to take advantage of these opportunities in an ever more competitive environment. Competition is fierce in all areas of the market, so a clear strategy and plan of action are essential to secure the company's success. This should be based on understanding the various needs of different components of the market in both consumer and business constituencies throughout the world.

3.3.1 Strengths

- *Innovative offer.* Well established in UK and overseas markets with current range of differentiated products: technically and ergonomically.

- *Recognition as key player in certain market segments.* Specific needs of women, elderly and disabled customers are well addressed. Company franchise with consumers in these groups in terms of meeting particular requirements, which can be extended into other niche markets, e.g. children. Also a reputation for producing equipment that caters well for difficult jobs, e.g. mowing uneven lawns.

- *Established as a supplier with intermediaries.* Has a presence with all the major UK retailers and wholesalers (DIY and garden centres). Knows how they trade and do business.

- *Loyal skilled workforce.* Capable of producing high-quality goods, although may need to be more flexible in future.

3.3.2 Weaknesses

- *Limited knowledge and understanding of customer base.* Records are incomplete and market research data are sparse, which makes planning relating to current products and markets difficult.

- *Unclear market positioning.* Uncertain what key platform for success should be based on business and marketing strengths including the brand.

- *Lack of competitor awareness.* Limited recognition of the threat of overseas competition in domestic markets.

- *Product portfolio unbalanced.* No succession of new products flowing through to provide future income streams. Other products reaching maturity and potentially the decline stage of the product life cycle.

- *Marketing function underdeveloped.* Despite new appointments there is a lack of market orientation and supporting aspects of the marketing process, particularly planning.

- *Cash flow problem.* Limited funds for development and investment in marketing.

3.3.3 Opportunities

- *Long-term growth in potential gardening market.* Social and economic factors positively influencing market growth throughout the world but especially Eastern Europe and the Far East.

- *More elderly consumers.* Demographic trends in favour of niche expertise of Eden Garden Tools.

- *Increasing popularity of gardening and vegetable growing.* Possible new markets among the young driven by interest in nature, food and sustainability.

- *Drive for greater efficiency and reduced business costs.* Horticultural sector becoming more competitive and requiring greater efficiency savings through innovative production methods.

3.3.4 Threats

- *Short-term demand deficiencies.* Recession still influencing overall market demand, which makes tool replacement less important, hence hindering market growth.

- *Domestic market entry from overseas competitors.* Low-cost producers threaten hand tools in particular.

- *Pressure on price points.* Range of forces driving down prices generally, including retailer margin requirements, competitors, greater value expectations of customers.

- *Technological development by competitors.* More advanced and sophisticated solutions being developed by rivals taking away market from Eden Garden Tools.

4 MARKETING OBJECTIVES

The main marketing objectives of Eden Garden Tools are as follows:

- To establish a clear, differentiated brand positioning based on innovation, reliability, practicality and inclusiveness by mid-2010.
- To successfully launch the new Slick Mower by end 2010, Garden Elves range by beginning 2011 and tree trimmer by mid-2011.
- To achieve increase in sales revenue from existing products of 70 per cent by end 2013.
- To achieve 25 per cent of total sales revenue from new products in consumer markets by end 2012, and 50 per cent by end 2014.
- To grow market share to 2 per cent in UK, 0.15 per cent in Europe and 0.05 per cent in ROW by end 2014.
- To establish 20 per cent of sales online by end 2012, and 35 per cent by end 2014.
- To have 75 per cent presence in UK and European distribution channels and 30 per cent in ROW by end 2014.
- To develop international business in excess of £20 million, representing 75 per cent of total sales by end 2014.
- To build 90 per cent brand awareness in consumer markets and 60 per cent in commercial markets in UK and Europe by end 2014, and 25 per cent and 10 per cent in ROW markets in same timescale.

Complementary financial and non-financial objectives are stated in the organisational strategic position statement.

5 MARKETING STRATEGY

5.1 Target markets

5.1.1 Consumer markets

Sub-dividing the total consumer market for targeting purposes can be undertaken at a number of levels for household consumers. The objectives of the company to grow business outside its domestic markets require targeting at three levels, UK, Europe and ROW, but within each of these the target customer groups will remain the same.

Existing products

The main targets for the existing hand-tool products and Slick Mower remain the 'better off' customer that mainly reside in the very keen gardeners (VKGs) and quite keen gardeners (QKGs) categories, although marginal gardeners (MGs) will be specifically targeted in countries where the market is well developed, such as the UK. In locations where the gardening market is less well developed, the emphasis will be on VKGs and then QKGs. Within these broad parameters the emphasis is on women, the elderly and the disabled, who derive specific benefits from the Eden Garden Tools ergonomic design and particular innovative features of the product range, especially the Slick Mower (which will be relaunched by end 2010). Allotment owners will be a secondary target.

The sales figures for this product group in the different geographical areas are outlined opposite.

Existing product sales		Sales units (000s)	Sales revenue (£)
UK	2010	100,000	1,200,000
	2011	110,000	1,500,000
	2012	125,000	1,625,000
	2013	140,000	2,100,000
	2014	150,000	2,700,000
Europe	2010	50,000	750,000
	2011	60,000	1,080,000
	2012	70,000	1,400,000
	2013	90,000	2,250,000
	2014	100,000	2,750,000
ROW	2010	30,000	1,200,000
	2011	45,000	1,840,000
	2012	55,000	1,625,000
	2013	65,000	2,370,000
	2014	80,000	3,200,000

New products

The main new product drive in consumer markets will be in developing the Garden Elves range for children and the sales of the electric tree-pruning saw to households. The children's line will be targeted at children generally through appropriate channels but will focus on those related to VKGs and QKGs (typically grandparents or parents, who will be buying for the children to use or as gifts). The MGs will be a secondary target as these may include professional parents who are time poor but are inclined towards greater gardening participation, and will wish to spend their leisure time with their children undertaking the same activities.

The other new product opportunity in the consumer sector will be the tree saw, which may have a limited sales potential in the VKG segment, or people with large gardens in need of the tool to care for their trees.

New product sales		Sales units (£)	Sales revenue (000s)
UK	2011	75,000	750,000
	2012	100,000	1,100,000
	2013	200,000	1,850,000
	2014	250,000	2,300,000
Europe	2011	200,000	1,875,000
	2012	250,000	2,225,000
	2013	300,000	2,400,000
	2014	350,000	2,850,000
ROW	2011	200,000	1,500,000
	2012	250,000	1,750,000
	2013	300,000	2,850,000
	2014	350,000	3,500,000

5.1.2 Commercial markets

The commercial sector will be targeted with the new product opportunity of the tree saw, and any secondary sales that may arise of existing tools and equipment that Eden Garden Tools will be able to supply into its new B2B customer base, either directly or through distributors. The target organisations are tree surgeons, professional gardening businesses, horticulturalists, smallholders and farms, commercial growers, plantation and orchard owners, and tool-hire centres. The target group would be prioritised according to the part of the world that was being focused on.

New per cent existing product sales		Sales units (£)	Sales revenue (000s)
UK	2011	1,000	120,000
	2012	1,500	187,500
	2013	2,000	260,000
	2014	2,500	340,000
Europe	2011	7,500	750,000
	2012	10,000	1,100,000
	2013	12,000	1,440,000
	2014	15,000	1,950,000
ROW	2011	-	-
	2012	10,000	1,000,000
	2013	15,000	1,800,000
	2014	20,000	2,500,000

5.2 Competitive advantage and positioning

The advantage of Eden Garden Tools lies in its innovative, reliable, practical and inclusive offerings to particular user groups with specific requirements. The added value provided to its target customers enables the company to charge medium- to high-end prices and sets it apart from the low-cost alternatives available in the markets that it operates in. Additionally, Eden Garden Tools is seeking to expand its overseas operations significantly with both its existing and new products, and therefore needs to be viewed as an international player with a well-developed brand image that is recognised in its key markets throughout the world.

5.3 Strategy specification

The competitive nature of the markets for Eden Garden Tools' current and future products requires that the brand and sub-brands of the company are clearly differentiated from all competitors in terms of their ability to deliver innovative and highly targeted solutions to gardeners and commercial users. In consumer markets the platform is further supported by the benefits derived by users with particular needs, therefore extending the inclusivity principle of gardening to those at the margins (i.e. those who find it more difficult to participate). For commercial users the solutions relate to adding value through increased efficiency and reducing costs by providing specific tools for difficult jobs. The additional value offered distinguishes Eden Garden Tools from its rivals and enables it to charge higher prices, which are perceived as competitive in the specified target markets throughout the world. The overall strategy is based on sub-strategies of new product development, market development both at home and overseas, and combined diversified strategies where new products are targeted at new B2C and B2B user groups throughout the world. Product development will in particular be the platform for growth relating to the upgrading of the portfolio generally and specific initiatives that involve innovative offers to existing and new customer groups.

5.4 Marketing mix programme

The marketing activities to support the strategies to achieve Eden Garden Tools' objectives can be broadly categorised into: product, price, communications, channels, services and internal marketing. The mix of components utilised to achieve success requires planning and integration at a number of levels within the organisation, and in conjunction with partners and stakeholders.

5.4.1 Product

The range of products could be defined in terms of tools and equipment. The tools essentially comprise a complete range of Eden Garden Tools-branded hand tools (trowels, hand forks, spades, hoes, rakes, shears, etc.), which are ergonomically designed to maximise the benefit in terms of effectiveness and ease of use. This will be extended to the Garden Elves sub-brand, which has a full range of scaled-down tools dedicated for children's use. There will be a general push to uplift the standard of all the tools produced as well as to fill any gaps in the portfolio so that a complete range is available under the Eden Garden Tools brand banner.

Equipment is centred on the Slick Mower, which is to be upgraded and relaunched to make it more modern in its features and design and to fend off competition from potential rivals. The underlying technological advantage remains and this will be the key dimension of the drive to take the new model forward. At the same time opportunities for developing the motorised equipment range will be identified, together with the specific tree-pruning saw development.

The Eden Garden Tools brand will be an integral aspect of the company's product policy, with some redesign of the logo to be undertaken in conjunction with the launch of the Garden Elves range. The products will all be branded and contain the strap line 'Innovative garden solutions for everyone'.

Additionally, non-branded items will be produced to be sold and marketed under retailers' brand names where appropriate margins and volumes can be justified.

5.4.2 Price

The price points for all of the different products will be determined separately around an overall premium pricing strategy to support the differentiation and innovative value-added solutions that Eden Garden Tools' range offers. The mix of products within the range will be reflected in actual price points: hand tools relatively low and motorised equipment high. Nonetheless, each of these groups will be appropriately priced to reflect the brand's positioning against the competition. This will be affected by the expected value that buyers put on the purchase and this will vary between household (amateur) consumers and professional (business) buyers.

In addition, the pricing strategies for the new products will be based on a penetration policy looking to establish long-term growth and return through building the brand as the market leader. This will be the case for both the Garden Elves range and the tree-pruning machine within the Eden Garden Tools range.

Clearly, beyond the positioning element of the pricing decision there will be a need to consider competitors' products (if there are any) in the different geographical locations that the business is intending to move into. Moreover, the pricing will need to take account of the influence of the distributors used in the different market locations. In the UK, then, margins may have to be reduced to take account of the buying power of large multiple retailers and garden centres, and policies that they may have on positioning garden tools and equipment in their range. In international markets, the type of intermediaries to be used will be a key factor in determining final price points and margins, as will a range of other macro influences on overall demand such as income distribution, exchange rates and competition from local suppliers.

5.4.3 Distribution channels

The main channel strategies adopted with consumer products will be a combination of intensive and selective distribution. For mass-market product range we will need to get maximum market exposure through the main multiple retailers (including online distributors) both in the UK and in overseas markets. This will apply to the garden tools in particular, whereas there may be a more selective approach for the equipment around more specialist garden centres and garden tools suppliers. Although adding value even in the garden tools range is our key differentiator, consumers generally perceive these to be relatively low-cost items which will not invoke a major amount of shopping around. It is critical therefore to have them listed in all the top retailers. For the higher-priced equipment we can be more selective in our stockists as these items may be subject to a greater degree of decision-making time and comparison shopping, which may focus on specialist suppliers.

In overseas markets there will be a strategy put in place to support our international expansion. We plan to move away from the current use of export houses to the use of mainstream distributors (retailers and wholesalers) in countries where we are intending to develop significant business. A planned development of our distributor network will be put in place, which will be phased according to the potential of each market, starting with developed Western European countries, followed by emerging East European states, North America and the Far East. Southern Asia and Africa will be secondary targets beyond the five-year timescale of this plan. A fully integrated channel-promotion strategy will be implemented to ensure maximum push of the products through to intermediaries, which will fulfil our brand awareness targets.

Business channels will involve the use of selected distributors both at home and overseas, including agricultural and horticultural merchants. There will also be an element of direct selling, either through our own sales staff or through agents.

We are planning the launch of a website sales interface by end of 2010 and this will be suitably resourced to ensure that the targets for online sales are achieved.

5.4.4 Communications and promotion

Brand awareness is a key component of our overall marketing strategy and this will be achieved through an integrated communications plan for both the consumer and commercial target markets, which will also have a domestic UK and international dimension. The plan includes details of 'push' and 'pull' communications activities, which will revolve around communications directly to customers and trade intermediaries.

Consumer communications for the mainstream brand of Eden Garden Tools will be based on a highly targeted magazine campaign combined with consumer exhibitions and shows launching the new Eden Garden Tools range of hand tools plus the Garden Elves speciality range for children. These will also encompass the relaunch of the Slick Mower. Some radio advertising will be incorporated to stimulate interest from the target audience. There will be competitions to support the launch of the children's range (organised with a popular children's TV programme) and the relaunch of the Slick Mower (with a top-selling gardeners' magazine). Targeted publicity for the new Slick Mower will be based on demonstrating its effectiveness in extreme cases of uneven lawns, and its use by celebrity opinion leader gardeners.

Trade-push communications will encompass a concerted salesforce campaign backed by in-store point-of-sale display materials. There will be a joint initiative with retailers to support the launch of the new range and products through a promotional discount coupon-based scheme over the initial launch period for each. Trade discount and over-rider incentives will also be used to stimulate sales in the early stages, as will retailer salesforce competitions.

In commercial markets there will be an initial in-house direct-selling campaign and another through channel intermediaries in more dispersed geographical markets. In addition we will launch the pruning saw through an exhibition and trade-show campaign in strategic locations both at home and overseas. A further trade-based campaign will use incentives to maximise distribution exposure, which will be tied into the brand values of innovative practicality and the savings that are possible in the commercial sector.

A key strategic project to be undertaken by the marketing team at Eden Garden Tools will be the development and launch of a sales and information website by the end of 2010.

5.4.5 Service

The Eden Garden Tools policy on service to customers and intermediaries will be reformulated to provide the highest levels of information and support. We will provide a one-year warranty on tools and a two-year extended warranty on parts and labour on equipment. A network of local garden machinery suppliers will be registered as approved distributors and service agents for the motorised equipment. Training and support will be provided through our professionally qualified technical salesforce and a phone-line support desk as well as a web-based technical resource.

We will set up a dedicated internal sales team to support key retailer and distributor accounts, backed by an appropriate shared information database to facilitate ordering and through electronic data interchange. Further to this, our external sales team will work closely with customers in the field to plan promotional support initiatives and intelligence on new marketing opportunities.

A no-quibble returns policy will be introduced which will ensure maximum satisfaction for customers if in the unlikely event they are dissatisfied with their purchase.

6 IMPLEMENTATION AND CONTROL

6.1 Timings, responsibilities and budgets

The scheduling of activities will be set out in a detailed Gantt chart in line with the achievement of the specified objectives set out above and the sales forecasts presented in Section 5. This will provide details of the marketing programme and each element of the mix activities sequenced in an integrated manner to maximise their impact on sales. The responsibilities will be determined both within and outside the company in accordance with the priorities set out in the programme.

The marketing manager will have overall responsibility for implementing the marketing plan and the sales manager will be responsible for overall coordination of consumer- and trade-related sales activities. The structure of marketing within Eden Garden Tools will develop as the firm progresses its development based on global expansion of the brand. The intention is to work towards a geographical structure within which there will be dedicated support for consumer and trade buyers.

The projected budget for non-staff marketing has been calculated in line with the forecasted sales revenues presented below.

Year	Projected sales revenue (£m)	Non-staff marketing budget (£m)
2010	3.2	0.16
2011	9.4	0.47
2012	12.0	0.60
2013	17.3	0.865
2014	22.1	1.105

6.2 Monitoring and control

Systems will be set up to monitor financial and non-financial performance against targets, and a regular reporting system will be introduced that will feed directly to the marketing manager, the sales manager and the relevant directors of Eden Garden Tools.

The introduction of new products and movement into new markets will be carefully monitored against projected sales forecasts and mechanisms will be employed to control for market uncertainties to ensure that variances can be remedied with appropriate action through the marketing mix. In particular plans and forecasts will be revised to take account of unplanned events and these will be enacted via contingency planning procedures, with the overall plan schedules revised accordingly.

6.3 Internal marketing

It will be necessary to ensure that all staff within the organisation are fully cognisant of the mission and objectives of Eden Garden Tools, particularly its innovation platform. A programme of internal marketing communications events and other initiatives will be integrated into the detailed marketing planning schedule. These will include staff meetings, email updates, internal newsletters and magazines (also to be circulated to key external stakeholders), staff development in marketing, sales and marketing recognition and reward schemes.

7 APPENDIX

Key assumptions relate to the internal and external influences upon market and company behaviour in the future and include the following:

- Economic and political stability in targeted geographical markets.
- Sustained growth of the gardening industry through continued drive from demographic and social demand factors.
- Technological advantage stays with Eden Garden Tools through the intellectual property invested through its owners and employees.

- Competition remains at current levels in the plan based upon risk assessment of major market entry by low-cost overseas suppliers.
- Distribution structures remain predominantly consistent with anticipated relationship and power dimensions.

These will be revised where possible and the plan modified as marketing research and intelligence are made available to further understand market dynamics.

8 SUPPORTING MATERIALS

Key Note Market Report, Garden Equipment (May 2009): Thirteenth Edition (Hampton, Middlesex: Key Note Ltd).

Horticultural Trades Association website – www.the-hta.org.uk/index.php

Target Group Index, London, BMRB International Ltd, 2008.

Exercise on further development of the plan

As indicated at the outset, this is an outline of a marketing plan which has been presented by Eden Garden Tools to its potential investors within a short timescale.

1 *What limitations do you think the plan has?*
2 *How would you go about revising the plan to ensure that these limitations are overcome?*
3 *What additional sources of information would you need to acquire to develop the plan?*
4 *Critically evaluate the outline plan in terms of its core strategy and tactics.*
5 *What changes would you make to this if you were responsible for setting out the future direction of the business?*

Glossary

Ad-hoc data Information collected over a short period for a specific purpose.

Balanced scorecard A means of benchmarking company activities across a range of measures.

Barriers to entry Those factors (economic, technical, financial, legal and so forth) which limit access to a market.

Bottom-up planning An approach whereby future activities and direction are decided by reference to people working at lower levels in the organisation, and especially people who have direct contact with customers.

Business level The tactical decision-making point in the company.

Business organisation The structure of the business itself.

Business orientation The general business philosophy of the organisation.

Business scope The boundaries of the organisation's activities.

Capabilities The combination of competencies which enables an organisation to achieve useful outcomes for itself and its stakeholders.

Competencies The combination of skills, resources and knowledge which distinguishes one organisation from another.

Competitive advantage The degree to which a firm can perform better than other firms in the same industry.

Consumerism The collective power exerted by consumer groups in influencing producers.

Continuous change An innovation which clearly builds on previous solutions.

Culture The set of shared beliefs and customs which distinguishes a given group of individuals.

Customer centrality The belief that the needs of customers should be paramount in business decision making.

Customer winback The act of reinstating customers who have defected to the competition.

Data mining Analysis of large databases to generate useful marketing information.

Data warehouse An electronic storage facility which holds very large amounts of information about customers, or information on a very large number of customers.

Decision support system A computer-based information-gathering system which provides instant data on which to base decisions.

Demography The shape of a population in terms of age, gender, wealth, income, and so forth.

Discontinuous change An entirely new innovation which has little or no connection with previous solutions.

Ecology The interaction of forces within the natural environment.

Economies of scale Those savings which accrue from larger production volumes.

Empowerment The act of increasing the level of autonomy stakeholders have in deciding the tactics and strategy of the organisation.

Environmental scanning Continuous observation of factors which might impinge on the firm from outside in order to identify threats and opportunities.

Equity The difference between what the firm owes and what it owns.

Expansion by acquisition The act of buying out firms in the same or similar industry in order to increase market share.

Extranet Computer-based systems which allow firms to share some information with outside individuals and organisations, while at the same time maintaining trade secrets.

Facilitators Individuals and organisations which are external to the company, but which enable the company to carry out its aims in a more effective way than would otherwise be the case.

Flat database A computer system in which all the information about any given customer is stored, but with little or no capability for cross-analysis with other customers' data.

Functional efficiency An assessment of the efficiency of internal training systems, communications and management systems.

Functional perspective The belief that marketing exists solely to develop the use of the 7 Ps in order to achieve tactical outcomes.

Globalisation The business approach which sources raw materials from the most effective suppliers, and which markets to the most beneficial segments, without regard for national borders.

Goals-down-plans-up planning A planning approach in which the overall aims and objectives of the company are disseminated throughout the organisation, and suitable plans are drawn up at departmental level for their achievement.

Internal marketing The set of activities aimed at meeting the needs of stakeholders such as employees and suppliers.

Laid-back competitors Organisations in the same market which are slow to respond to market changes, or which do not respond at all.

Macro forces Those factors which affect every company in a given industry.

Management information system A set of procedures which creates a continuous flow of data which can be analysed in order to inform decision making.

Market challenger An organisation which seeks to increase its share of the available business, usually through the use of aggressive marketing techniques.

Market-driven A set of strategies and tactics which results from an understanding of the realities of dealing with competitors, customers and other stakeholders.

Market-driving A set of strategy and tactics which moves customers, competitors and others in new directions.

Market followers Organisations which take their lead from market leaders.

Market innovation The process of developing new approaches to customers.

Market nicher An organisation which seeks to meet the needs of very specific, small or specialised segments.

Market share The proportion of the potential customers which the company serves.

Marketing audit The comprehensive process of assessing the firm's overall approach to the market.

Marketing information system A set of techniques for collecting a continuous stream of data which can be analysed to create an overview of changes in the marketplace in order to inform marketing decisions.

Matrix organisation An organisation structure in which leadership changes according to the tasks facing the company.

Micro-environment The factors which are relevant only to the company, e.g. competitors, suppliers, employees.

Micromarketing Meeting the exact needs of small groups or individuals.

Mission The business the organisation sees itself in.

Mission statement A document which outlines the organisation's overall direction and intentions.

Objective A quantifiable aim.

Organisational level The highest decision-making point in the company.

Performance evaluation A measure of the company's effectiveness in meeting its general aims.

Planning gap The difference between what planners expect will happen as a result of new initiatives and what they expect will happen if nothing is done.

Positioning The process of creating an appropriate brand image in the customers' minds, relative to the brand images of competing products.

Primary research Data gathering from an original source, specifically for the purpose of solving the problem at hand.

Product innovation The process of developing new solutions to customer problems.

Public responsibility Consideration of the impact of the company's activities on the rest of the community.

Publics Those groups of stakeholders which the company might seek to influence through its corporate communications programmes.

Reference projection An estimate of what will happen if no action is taken by the firm.

Relational database A computer system in which data about customers can be accessed against many different criteria.

Relationship marketing A set of activities aimed at developing repeat business with existing customers and consumers, as opposed to focusing on the single transaction.

Resource-based marketing The process of creating a close fit between the needs of customers and the ability of the firm to meet those needs.

Sales turnover The gross income of a company.

Secondary (desk) research Information gathering from existing data which has been collected for another purpose but which is still relevant to the problem at hand.

Segment An identifiable portion of an overall market.

Segmentation The process of dividing the overall market into groups of customers with similar needs.

Stakeholder An individual or organisation which has a material interest in the activities of a specific organisation.

STEP analysis Social, technical, economic and political factors in the company's environment.

Stochastic competitors Organisations in the same market which regard the market as unpredictable.

Strategic intent The overall aim of the company in terms of its environment and competition.

Strategy The set of plans and decisions which is intended to ensure the organisation's survival and ultimate prosperity in the marketplace.

Switching cost The drawbacks, financial or practical, which tend to prevent a customer from changing from the use of one product to the use of another.

SWOT analysis An assessment of the organisation's strengths, weaknesses, opportunities and threats in relation to a given market.

Tactical plan The set of decisions which outlines what needs to be done to achieve the corporate strategy.

Targeting The process of deciding which segments of a market should be approached with a given set of marketing tools.

Tiger competitors Organisations in the same market which respond rapidly and strongly to market changes.

Top-down planning An approach whereby future activities and direction are decided entirely by senior managers.

Value chain analysis An examination of the ways in which the organisation increases the worth of products as they pass through the firm and its suppliers and distributors.

Value creation The act of combining resources to develop increased worth.

Vision The founder's view of what the company will become.

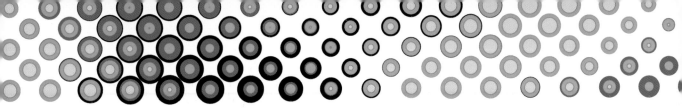

Index